CHRISTIAN THEOLOGY
IN A CONTEMPORARY WORLD

Robert H. Ayers

Studies in Religion and Society
Volume 38

The Edwin Mellen Press
Lewiston•Queenston•Lampeter

BT
75.2
.A94
1997

Library of Congress Cataloging-in-Publication Data

Ayers, Robert H. (Robert Hyman), 1918-
  Christian theology in a contemporary world / Robert H. Ayers.
    p. cm.
  Includes bibliographical references and index.
  ISBN 0-7734-8739-5 (hard)
  1. Theology, Doctrinal. I. Title.
BT75.2.A94 1997
230--dc21   96-51513
                                                                              CIP

This is volume 38 in the continuing series
Studies in Religion and Society
Volume 38 ISBN 0-7734-8739-5
SRS Series ISBN 0-88946-863-X

A CIP catalog record for this book is available from the British Library.

The Edwin Mellen Press   The Edwin Mellen Press
        Box 450   Box 67
Lewiston, New York   Queenston, Ontario
   USA 14092-0450   CANADA L0S 1L0

The Edwin Mellen Press, Ltd.
Lampeter, Dyfed, Wales
UNITED KINGDOM SA48 7DY

Printed in the United States of America

DEDICATION

To George Howard (Ph.D), a superior scholar, teacher, and department head. Throughout our many years at the University of Georgia he has been a generous, steadfast, and stimulating colleague and friend.

ACKNOWLEDGEMENTS

I doubt very much that as an Emeritus Professor I would have been able to write this book without the assistance of Professor George Howard, Head, Department of Religion, University of Georgia, who permitted me to retain my office and provided me with the use of a computer. In addition, Mrs. Zinetta McDonald, office manager, with constant good humor and cheer has rendered crucial assistance in correcting computer problems which had baffled me and in formatting the final manuscript. Not least among those who played an essential role in the production of this treatise was Mrs. Mary Frances Ayers who proofread the poorly typed original manuscript, correcting its many errors and making many helpful suggestions with respect to structure and content. Any errors which may remain are due to my failure properly to correct mistakes. Finally, I found the staff of The Edwin Mellen Press to be most cordial and helpful.

CONTENTS

PROLOGUE

To an extent what I have written in this rather small volume is a kind of testimony to my own convictional stance. It is a public avowal or profession of faith. I still recall vividly the pressure the adult teacher put on me and my peers in our Sunday School class for ten year olds to make our public profession of faith before the entire congregation of the church. Such was required if we were to escape the torments of an eternal hell (vividly described by our teachers) which was the just punishment for sinners who were not saved. Since my father was minister of the church I felt the pressure even more than my classmates. So with fear and trembling we stood in front of the congregation and repeated the words which we had memorized. It was often the case that there was only a vague understanding of the words and sentences we had memorized and repeated, and there was little perception of any relevance to our actual life situation as ten year olds.

In spite of poor teaching and of some dubious psychological manipulation and adult pressure against which we later rebelled, there were some benefits. Not least among these benefits was that one knew in general what was expected and gained a sense of belonging to the community. While the theological implications of what was memorized might not be understood, one now felt accepted by and sustained by the community. There was little question about such practical matters as what actions were appropriate in light of the values taught by the community even though one did not always act in accordance with these values.

When I search the memory of my early years I can recall making my "profession of faith" as was expected, but also I cannot recall a time in my life when I did not feel an identification with the Christian faith, however limited my understanding of the faith might have been. Perhaps this was due to the fact that I was reared in a minister's home. In spite of this environment, I recall that in my teens I experienced some rebellion against doctrinaire interpretations

ix

of the faith such as those espoused by fundamentalists. Yet I rejected only these interpretations, not a commitment to the Christian faith as shedding the brightest light on the meaning of history and the ultimate significance of every individual human life.

As I studied in college and seminary this commitment deepened and my understanding of the faith and its relation to society grew. Throughout my academic life a major personal goal has been, as Anselm put it, faith seeking understanding. To be sure, there is an irreducible mystery as well as meaning in the very substance of basic Christian claims such that the understanding will never be complete. In addition, there is my own personal intellectual limitation of which I am painfully aware. Yet the irreducible mystery and the intellectual limitation do not excuse one from engaging in the task of faith seeking understanding. So I have attempted to grow in my understanding, for I am convinced that a rational and intelligible faith sustains the human spirit much better than one which is irrational and unintelligible. Now in retirement I have sought to rethink the basic tenets of the faith, to organize my thinking in a systematic fashion, and to put in a brief written form a rational apology for these tenets.

The fact that I am attempting a rational apology for what I consider the basic tenets of the Christian faith certainly suggests that at the very least I am skeptical about the worth of current theological fads whether found among conservative or liberal groups. Just as I rebelled against an irrational fundamentalism in my youth (and still do), so now I find myself rebelling against the irrational noncognitivism found in some contemporary theologies. This will be made quite clear in the introductory chapter. Throughout this treatise I am unconcerned with whether or not I am in accord with current fads and popular trends. What I sought to do is to explicate and to defend what seems to me to be a viable theology which can legitimately be called Christian and at the same time make sense in our contemporary world.

Robert H. Ayers

CHAPTER ONE
INTRODUCTION: FAITH AND REASON

1. The Current Situation in Theology

In his 1932 *The Brave New World* Aldous Huxley had satirized all utopian expectations. Yet there were those for whom this title could have been taken as a literal description of the legitimate expectations for the future based on the scientific and technological advances in Western culture. World events since that time have made such expectations difficult, if not impossible, to maintain. Indeed, a title literally descriptive of our world today might well be, *The Confused and Dangerous World*.

If we mean by 'world' all of reality, it could be said that it has always been confused and dangerous. In spite of some dangerous, irregular and chance events, the world of nature demonstrates a certain stability in terms of regularities and casual sequences the knowledge of which can minimize the dangers to some degree. The world of human history, however, is much more complex, confusing, and dangerous. This situation has been exacerbated in modern times by the enormous growth in the power for destruction made possible by modern technology and by the erosion of confidence in the 'eternal verities' held dear by earlier generations, verities which provided some sense of human worth and dignity.

In the modern period the phenomenal success of science, the remarkable growth of technology, and the accompanying development of industry, including 'high-tech' industry, have contributed to the emergence of so-called secularism, especially in the Western world. Even though it is not a logically necessary conclusion, the success and methods of science and technology provide psychological or practical motivation for persons to conclude, either implicitly or explicitly, that we live in a one-dimensional world in which only that which can be verified horizontally by repeated experiment is true. On this basis it is not difficult to conclude that the transcendent is fiction and only the concerns of this life are worthy of consideration, that values are relative

1

or non-existent, and that the human being is nothing more than the functioning of the physical organism. This so-called secularism with its one dimensional outlook became the dominant ethos of Western culture. Traditional religion declined. Even in the 'revival' of conservative religion, among those who consciously adhere to and espouse a conservative religious ideology, secularism is often implicitly present in practical attitudes and actions. Explicitly, fundamentalists seek to turn the clock back to the outlook of pre-modern times even though their practical attitudes and actions are often as secularistic as those of the so-called atheistic humanists.

With the decline of traditional religion and the growth of secularism in the world at large, a religious vacuum was created into which have rushed all sorts of fanatical cults, many of which advocate violence and terrorism. On the one hand there are those who ignore religion, but on the other hand there are those who cloak their prejudices and ideologies with a piety which justifies the use of any means to accomplish their goals, even violence against non-believers. Hatred, violence, and confusion abound in our world. There are little or no common bonds which hold groups, societies, and nations together in relative peace, harmony, and unity. Group interest and self-interest hold sway, and power and violence rather than persuasion are employed as the means of settling disputes.

The realm of theology is affected by the world situation. To an extent theology has always reflected the 'world' in which it was situated, using all sorts of thought-forms, most notably philosophical, as the means of expressing its message. In earlier times in the West, concomitant with the dominance of the church, theology was highly prized as queen of the sciences served by the other disciplines, including philosophy. With the disintegration of the church's hold on society, due to many causes such as the breakdown of feudalism, there appeared the Protestant Reformers who, with some exceptions, insisted on a discontinuity between theology and philosophy, faith and reason. Implicitly, the Reformers made a greater use of reason and were more subject to philosophical presuppositions than perhaps they consciously realized. Explicitly, theology was confined primarily to the Word of God

2

as proclaimed and encountered in Scripture. While still enjoying an exalted status, theological formulation was to an extent isolated from the other 'sciences'.

With the advent of the modern period there were Protestant theologians who attempted to formulate theologies which made use of philosophy, albeit a philosophy different from that of Thomas Aquinas and other medieval thinkers. In 19th century Germany distinguished liberal theologians such as Friedrich Schleiermacher, Albrecht Ritschl, and Adolf Von Harnack developed theologies which were dependent to a large extent upon the philosophy of Immanuel Kant (1724-1804) and which were able to accomodate the results of science and the disciplines of culture. As the modern period progressed, Protestant liberalism was further developed and popularized. In America the champions of liberalism in the first half of the twentieth century included such teachers and preachers as William Adams Brown, Harry Emerson Fosdick, Walter Rauschenbush, and Douglas Clyde Macintosh. They did not go unopposed by conservatives. The theological situation, in America at least, was relatively simple. There were two major opposing camps, the liberals and the fundamentalists. The issues over which they fought (such as evolution, scripture, salvation, eschatology) were relatively clear cut as were their contrasting responses to these issues. Yet, however differently they responded, there was never any question in either camp that there is a God (however differently his mode of operation might be understood), that human beings have a mind or soul, that life is meaningful, and that there is a goal of some sort in this life and the next.

For a while liberalism attracted a considerable following, especially among intellectuals. It provided a way of combining faith and knowledge and of dealing with the social problems of the world. However, liberalism's optimistic estimate of human nature and possibilities and its utopian view of human history soon ran aground on the shoals of the tremendous cataclysms of recent history such as the two world wars and the great depression. Partially in response to this situation there emerged theologies variously labeled Neo-Orthodox, Neo-Reformation, Crisis Theology, and Christian Realism. The theologians representing

3

these positions concluded that liberalism in general or at least in certain important aspects was inadequate. They sought to renew essential Reformation perspectives, especially those dealing with human nature and possibilities, revelation and soteriology. In a few cases (Karl Barth and his followers) the results of science were largely ignored, and there was an effort to isolate as far as possible the truth of the gospel from the disciplines of culture. In other cases (such as Richard and Reinhold Niebuhr, Paul Tillich and Rudolf Bultmann) there was the attempt to recover the essential Reformation perspective but also to relate it in meaningful ways to the disciplines of culture and the assured results of science. Yet in both cases these great theologians provided a bulwark against the growing materialism and relativism illegitimately inferred from science.

With the passing of these theological giants a bewildering variety of theologies arose. No longer was it a choice between the relatively clear cut theologies of fundamentalism, liberalism, and neo-reformation thought. Instead a plethora of theologies arose (secularity, story, play, liberation, process, etc.) most of which acknowledged no established traditions and/or masters. It could be said that the kingdom of the queen of the sciences has been sundered into a multitude of city states each with its princeling and/or group of princelings. There is little in the way of effective communication between the princelings of the different city states. Indeed, since many theologians today find symbols everywhere but little or no realities represented by the symbols (an odd state of affairs in which symbols represent nothing or at best only other symbols), it is not surprising that they cannot agree on the meanings of the symbols and thus habitually talk past one another. Much in theology today resembles fiction and is unconcerned with truth value. 'Belief that' is regarded as both unnecessary and an illusion. In the so-called post-modernism, most of which, with the exception of process theology, is an essentially negative or deconstructive perspective, God, self, purpose, meaning, a real world, and truth are eliminated in an anti world-view. The deconstructive thinkers not only celebrate the one-dimensional world-view of secularism but also carry it forward in a kind of evangelistic affirmation of nihilism. So corresponding to the confused

4

and ambiguous situation with respect to religion in the world at large is the ambiguity and confusion in the theological 'academy.'

It is somewhat of an anomaly that given this situation there has been an increase in academic programs in religion in higher education, including state universities and colleges. Teaching about religion in a relatively objective fashion is deemed academically respectable. Programs generally give precedence to historical studies of various kinds and to the more technical linguistic and critical studies of scriptures. Studies in constructive theology in which there is an attempt to develop a systematic theology, to explicate and defend a particular faith and tradition, are generally at a minimum due in part to the largely unfounded fear that such theology cannot be explicated in a non-sectarian manner. While the quality of the work of those who do constructive theology may be excellent, their influence is not as great as that of the theological giants of the past generation. For one thing, these giants did not have to contend with what may be called 'subversion from within' the theological community itself in the form of deconstructionism. Atheists, nihilists, and ethical relativists did not teach and write in the field of religion but were openly and explicitly non-religious secularists and humanists. Since the field of 'theology' has been invaded by the deconstructionist, and since there is a multitude of 'theologies,' both non-cognitivist and constructive, there is considerable confusion and vagueness as to what the proper task of the theologian should be.

The common usage meaning of 'theology' traditionally has been taken to be rational reflection about that which is worthy of worship, namely a transcendent and loving God and his relationship with the universe. Today there are those both outside and within the theological 'academy' who dismiss this enterprise as a non-discipline unworthy of serious attention. Sometimes it is ridiculed as in the well-known aphorism that philosophy looks in a dark room for a black cat which isn't there and theology finds it. The theologian deals dogmatically with that which ultimately is no more than unreal fiction. This is surely too simple an appraisal. There may be some conservative religionists who hold to some fantasies as dogmas. But the great theologians of the past generation mentioned above demonstrated an openness, liveliness, creativity, and determination to follow where the facts and truth lead. Vitality and realism characterized the theological realm. While with the passing of the great theological masters a rampant pluralism has invaded the theological arena and confusion abounds, it does not follow that theology is dead. For some purported 'theologians' God is dead and their 'theologies' are actually atheologies. Nevertheless, a certain vitality and realism remain in the theological realm no matter how much the scope of its influence may have diminished and even though there is no one <u>dominant</u> 'school of theology' on the current scene.

What the future holds in store for theology cannot be predicted. I hope that some truly great theologians will arise and develop constructive theologies which will become dominant in the so-called 'post modern world.'

What I will attempt in this treatise is to set down some constructive theological reflections. It most certainly will not be as profound and total a constructive theology as that of such process theologians as David Griffin and John Cobb. It is more of an attempt to put my random reflections, stored up over many years, into some sort of order and completeness. Though influenced to some degree by process thinkers, I make no claim of being a process theologian. I doubt very much that I am a 'post-modern' theologian, if I have understood what this term means for those writers who use it. I know that I am not a deconstructionist type of post-modernist, however sound some of their analyses of modernity may be. I have tried to read some writings of those so-labeled (in the field of religion) and find them to be often unintelligible, generally boring, and certainly lacking any promise of meaning and hope for the human condition. Throughout the years I have been influenced by the perspectives and thought of Reinhold Niebuhr, and I think his theology is still valid today. Developed within the general context of process philosophy and James' pragmatism, Niebuhr's theology, I believe, preserves the essence of the Christian faith while relating it in meaningful and creative ways to science and the disciplines of culture. This is a constructive approach which I find sensible and satisfying.

Although I must acknowledge my theological indebtedness to Niebuhr's thought, I do not intend this treatise to be a descriptive and/or scholarly analysis of his theology. Previously I have published articles on his thought which conformed to the requirements of the 'scholarly ritual' in the sense of containing copious references documenting and justifying assertions. As already noted, in this treatise I wish to explicate my own theological perspective. Niebuhr's influence will be obvious but so will that of some other thinkers. What I am attempting here is to give in an orderly and systematic fashion a sort of testimony to my own theological reflections and arguments without enslavement to the 'scholarly ritual.' I hope to keep quotes and references to a minimum.

I intend to offer my reflections on a number of topics, the major ones of which will be: (1) methodological considerations - the nature and relation of faith and reason; (2) human nature and destiny; (3) the existence and nature of God and the problem of evil; (4) Christology; (5) soteriology; (6) Christian ethics and community; and (7) eschatology.

2. Methodological Considerations: The Nature and Relation of Faith and Reason

All theologians, indeed thinkers in whatever fields, use some sort of method in investigating and discussing the issues and subjects which are of concern to them. In some cases the methods to be used are stipulated explicitly and in some detail at the very beginning of the discussion. In other cases methodological considerations are simply implicit in the discussion of substantive issues, or they are explicitly mentioned here and there throughout the entire corpus of the thinker's writings. A full description and adequate appraisal of the methods require a gleaning of the entire body of the thinker's writings. While it is not always the case, the former approach (description of the method at the beginning of the discussion) often makes for greater clarity. It may help clarify assumptions and presuppositions. It may help interpreters to more adequately understand the thinker's positions. While those who use the latter approach may be as profound in their discussion, if not more so, as those who use the former, interpreters often will fail to glean fully and/or adequately the methodological considerations and thus make wrong and misleading statements concerning the thinker's positions on substantive issues. Given our intellectual laziness, our tendency to be unaware and thus uncritical of presuppositions, and our tendency to generalize on the basis of inadequate information, it is probably better as a practical matter to begin a theological treatise with a discussion of methodological presuppositions and guidelines.

There are all sorts of obstacles which make clarity of thought and expression difficult to achieve. These obstacles include not only unrecognized and/or uncriticized presuppositions but also the nature of language itself. While language is certainly one of the greatest human endowments enabling us to express our thoughts, dreams, and hopes to others, to learn from the past, and to anticipate the future, it also causes problems due not least to the ambiguities which infect natural languages. So semantics has an essential role to play in any meaningful and constructive human discourse.

A third obstacle which surely is as serious as the two just mentioned is the tendency to oversimplify the methodology such that it unduly restricts the substantive area to be considered or conversely to overextend the methodology such that any absurd claim is thought to be legitimate. This situation is analogous to the old means/ends issue. Method and subject matter as well as means and ends are correlative. They are bound up together. Good ends cannot be achieved through bad means. Similarly, adequacy and wholeness of subject matter cannot be achieved through an overly simple, one dimensional method or an irrational, anything goes, methodology.

For example, on the one hand, ideological naturalists and/or humanists are correct in emphasizing the importance of an empirical approach but wrong in limiting methodology to this approach alone, for this obscures human freedom and dignity and eliminates transcendent elements from human life and experience. On the other hand conservative religionists are correct in holding that this so-called 'atheistic humanism' is incompatible with the Christian faith but wrong in sometimes using unchristian means (force and compulsion) to deny freedom of thought and expression to their opponents. Also they are wrong in failing to recognize that certain ingredients in their

8

methodologies such as appeal to authority, to blind faith, disdain of reason and evidence, restrict their version of the Christian faith such that it is often absurd, inconsistent with established facts, and irrelevant to the concerns of modern life.

A case in point is that some conservatives claim that it is bound to be a fact and so true that Moses wrote the Pentateuch because God has so informed them. The use of historical criticism with all that this entails in terms of higher and lower criticism is an impious enterprise which is a waste of time. Moses wrote the Pentateuch precisely as God dictated it to him. Such an unrestricted and uncriticized methodology which rests on appeal to authority and blind faith not only leads to conclusions which are false but also to an impoverished faith, for there is the failure to appreciate the richness of the *heilsgeschichte* recorded in the Pentateuchal story.

Perhaps a clearer example is found in the claims of at least one conservative who sought to prove by the empirical methods of the natural sciences that the earth ceased its rotation for a day so that, as expressed in Joshua 10, the sun stood still. Clearly this approach (with many false moves) and conclusion is absurd. Absurdity is avoided and nothing essential is lost to the story through the use of the appropriate method of higher and lower criticism which yields the sensible conclusion that the original passage was a poetic or idiomatic way of saying the day was long enough for Joshua to accomplish his purposes. In the interest of truth and faith, method must be appropriate to the issue or subject matter in question, and this requires our very best rational efforts.

However much in the theologies of those great Fathers of the Church, Augustine and Aquinas, may be irrelevant to modern life, their conviction that a rational and intelligible faith sustains the human spirit much better than an irrational and unintelligible one is relevant in any age. It was not that they regarded reason as superior to faith. Always reason functioned as the servant of revelation but a most essential servant. Its function was to relate that which was revealed to all the disciplines of culture and facts of life such that a holistic theology was achieved. Although the disciplines of culture and conditions of life have changed radically since the time of the Fathers, it is still the case that

9

the primary criterion for judging the adequacy of a theological system is how successfully it relates the transcendent truths of the Christian faith to the facts of life and disciplines of culture so that a holistic view results.

A basic question, then, is what are the ingredients of a methodology which would allow a theology to achieve this result. Obviously, as already indicated, reason has an essential role to play, and this role involves three main functions. The first of these functions is to insure the internal consistency of the discourse and the system. Contradictions in and/or between statements (both A and not A) make literal nonsense out of the statements and so corrupt the theological discourse in which they appear.

This was the fundamental flaw in the discourse of some proponents of the "God is dead" 'theology' of a few years ago. Apparently they were not using the expression as only a metaphorical way of describing an historical or cultural condition, of saying in a striking and short hand way that contemporary human beings no longer have or need an awareness or experience of God. Had they used the expression in this sense it would have been meaningful whether empirically true or not. Instead, they denied that the expression was being used simply as symbolic rhetoric and affirmed the literal death of God. Of course, in the context of highly anthropomorphic and polytheistic conceptions of deity it would make sense to say that God died literally, but these 'theologians' were operating in the context of Western monotheism. It was in this context that they claimed that God once lived but no longer does so. But in this context the word 'God' means the one self-existent, infinite, eternal loving being. By definition an infinite, eternal being cannot not be (not both infinite and not infinite). As Kant maintained long ago, if one admits the existence of God, he cannot deny self-existence, infinity, and so on without a contradiction any more than one can admit the existence of triangles and deny three angles without a contradiction. Of course, there is no contradiction in denying the existence of a triangle together with its three angles. Similarly, there is no contradiction in denying the existence of God together with his attributes or properties. Atheists claim that God never has existed, and so their claim is logically consistent and meaningful whether it is true or not. But the claim of some "God is dead" 'theologians' that God did exist at one time but does not exist now, cannot escape contradiction and so is literally nonsense and meaningless.

It is perhaps important at this point to distinguish contradictory utterances from paradoxical and/or dialectical ones. As suggested above, contradictory utterances are those in which there is an assertion and denial of the same property to the same thing at the same time and in the same respect. By contrast, a paradoxical utterance at first glance may appear to be a contradiction. Yet if it is placed in the context of the entire passage or discourse, the apparent contradiction dissolves, and it turns out that the paradox is simply a striking and short hand way of expressing a truth. Consider, for example, a saying attributed to Jesus in the Synoptic Gospels. Following Luke (9:24) it reads, "For whoever would save his life will lose it and whoever loses his life for my sake (The Kingdom of God? Mark 8:35 adds "and the Gospel's"), he will save it." If the words "for my sake," the following verse 25, and the context of the entire passage are omitted, the utterance is a contradiction. But kept in the context of the entire passage which urges faithfulness in the face of opposition (as do the passages in the other two Gospels), which does say "For my sake" (or the kingdom's), and which in verse 25 adds "For what does it profit a man if he gain the whole world and loses or forfeits himself," the apparent contradiction dissolves, and the truth strikes home. Devotion and faithfulness to a cause greater than oneself in spite of opposition and personal difficulties such as loss of friends, etc. can result in the strengthening of character and a genuine personal fulfillment.

The terms paradoxical and dialectical are often used synonymously in designating certain types of utterances. Both have to do with polar concepts which are contraries but not contradictories. That is, the polar concepts are opposites, not an affirmation and a negation. Sometimes 'paradox' is used to designate a more vivid way of stating the contraries which easily gains the attention of listeners or readers. But both terms (as used here and by others) designate utterances which state contrary propositions, each of which is

11

incomplete and inexact in some way but both of which are needed for a fuller disclosure of the issue in question or the truth sought. There is some legitimate reason that contrary propositions taken together provide greater understanding than each alone. Obviously, this is not a Hegelian dialectic of thesis, antithesis, and unifying synthesis on a higher level, but the use of polar concepts which are not contradictory but contrary and both of which need to be kept intact although some tension between them may remain. Examples of some polar contraries are individuality-community, particularity-universality, dynamics-form (Tillich), and freedom-destiny (also Tillich). Both polarities must be given proper attention if there is to be an adequate understanding of the real world. Too often we are prey to the "all or nothing" or "great either/or" fallacy. For example, some people claim that the choice is between creationism which affirms that God created the universe in six days or evolutionism which affirms that the emergence of the universe is due entirely to natural causes. Often this either/or claim is used in an attempt to force people to take sides. But it is a false dilemma which rests on the fact of an unduly limited classification. There is a third alternative which consists in holding both to creation and evolution. God, it is held, is indeed the creator, and the evolutionary process is the means he used and is still using to bring into being the universe, including the world and its inhabitants. Thus it is possible to affirm both the creation by God and the evolutionary process for which there is so much empirical evidence.

Another example is found in the way the old debate between determinists and indeterminists is sometimes formulated as an either/or exclusive disjunction. But without some kind of relative indeterminism there could be no creative advance, progress, and freedom in the world, and without some kind of relative determinism (cause and effect) there could be no regularity, order, and dependability in the world. Understood in this way, these polarities seem to be more in accord with the facts of experience and can be accommodated in an inclusive disjunction.

It is the case, of course, that there are some states of affairs which can be stated only by use of the exclusive disjunction. We are either in this room or not in this room. At a given time we are either at point A in space or at point B but not both. Yet the states of affairs which are affirmed by the use of the inclusive disjunction are numerous indeed. For example, we may purchase item x either in store A or store B. Obviously here either/or is equivalent to both/and. Mistakes are made when exclusive and inclusive disjunctions are confused. Such confusion may arise due to incomplete specification, misunderstanding of the classification involved, and the confusion of negatives with opposites.

Experience should teach us that in human life and relationships we are most often confronted with 'both/and,' with polarities which need to be balanced as much as possible if we are to deal adequately with actual situations. We need to be on our guard against the ploys of those who for the sake of some supposed vested interest or for whatever reason seek to fool us into regarding what are actually inclusive disjunctions as though they were exclusive either/or propositions.

Since we are human beings and not computers or even gods, we are, of course, subject to error. Often we make mistakes in our attempt to be consistent, but consistency should be a goal for which we strive. Nowhere is this more important than in the attempt to develop a theology. The subject matter itself is difficult enough without our compounding it with nonsense in the form of contradictory utterances.

Some who do not wish to be bothered with the burden of struggling for consistency often quote the aphorism "consistency is the hobgoblin of little minds" as though the striving for consistency indicates a little mind. This, of course, is an example of misquoting for the sake of one's own position. What Emerson (in *Self-Reliance*) actually said is "a foolish consistency is the hobgoblin of little minds, adored by little statesmen and philosophers and divines."[1] This has nothing to do with logical consistency but with the tendency of some to stubbornly hold on to a belief even though it is shown to be wrong. The courage to change when such change is warranted by the facts does not violate the requirement of logical consistency in a system of thought, provided whatever is entailed by the change is also changed in a consistent manner. Even the clear articulation of the change requires statements which are in accord with the rules of logical consistency.

Thus far I have sought to make a case for the proposition that in theological construction method must be appropriate to subject matter and that reason has an essential role to play. This role involves three functions, the first of which is the striving for logical consistency.

Having discussed this function, I turn now to a second, namely, the conformity or coherence of the theology with truths from other levels of reality. This does not mean, of course, that the transcendent elements of the Christian faith are banished from the theology. What it does mean is that although the transcendent elements cannot be proved in terms of strict empirical proof, they are not impossible and incredible even in the light of modern science, and they can be shown to make sense of human experience and history. To ignore or deny the verified truths and assured results of science and the facts disclosed in common experience is to so isolate the theology that it is of little relevance to the real world. To argue for ghosts, for example, is incoherent with the characteristics of the natural world and of historical reality as we know it.

Perhaps a more important, though similar example, is that the belief of some in the miraculous, understood in a certain way, is incoherent with the truths of science. Generally, discussions of miracles produce more heat than light primarily because the word 'miracle' is used in so many senses. Indeed, it might be well if we called a moratorium on its use. Sometime ago a famous religious leader wrote a brief article in which he claimed that religious people should have no difficulty in believing in miracles. But he used the word 'miracle' in at least three different senses. First, he used it to designate some remarkable technological achievements (color Television.) which utilize the laws and processes of nature but the principles of which are not understood by the non-scientist. Second, he used it to refer to the providence of God such as the appearance of creative events and geniuses but which do not entail the violation of the known uniformities of nature. Third, he used it to designate interventions of the supernatural in nature which do not conform to any natural laws and which result in temporary suspensions of natural laws. Obviously, by using the word 'miracle' to designate the first and second areas, the first

14

of which depends upon the scientific utilization of the laws of nature and the second of which is not incompatible with science, this leader was attempting to justify belief in 'miracle' in the third sense as also not incompatible with science and thus reasonable. Yet, in fact, the three senses are quite different, and acceptance of the first two does not entail acceptance of the third. To insist that reality confronts us with creativity as well as regularity, with mystery as well as meaning, does not require belief in the miraculous as suspension of natural laws.

There are a whole host of problems which cluster around the assertion that there are miraculous events which do not conform to any natural laws and which result in suspension of natural laws, some of which were pointed out by David Hume (1711-1776) long ago. How can one be certain that an event which is regarded as a miracle is not some instant of an isolated operation of a yet undiscovered law? A glance at the history of science demonstrates that through the years scientists have come up with explanations of events that previously seemed to defy natural law. What about the reliability of witnesses? Also even if some events did occur which do not conform to natural law, this only confirms indeterminism rather than any activity of God. Further, there is the danger that belief in miracles in the third sense will become a kind of crutch for faith, a kind of guarantee. But if faith is trust, it endures no matter how or even in spite of the way things go in the observable order.

A theology which is coherent with the truths from other levels of reality can and will accept the providential activity of God who makes creativity possible in the world of nature and human life. It can and will accept the power of a spiritual force to work in both the human psyche and body. It can and will accept the mystery that animates all beings, the divine margin in all achievements. But it will not reject the assured results of the sciences. While it seems easy for some to deify science and technology, to ignore their limitations, and to believe that they are the saviors of the world, this unscientific and naive view on the part of a few is not sufficient reason for the theologian to reject science and technology as such. It is surely the case that science and its achievements are here to stay and must be reckoned with in any sound theology.

15

A third function of reason in theological construction is that of striving for comprehensiveness. This has been implicit already in what was said about the dialectical polarities being more in tune with reality than either/or's and about the coherence of the theology with truths from other levels of reality. Failure in these two realms will result in failure to achieve a holistic theology. They are necessary conditions for comprehensiveness. There is, however, another condition to some extent entailed by, but not limited to, the dialectical polarities and coherence with other truth which needs to be explicated further. Not only do the experiences from which the secular disciplines draw provisional criteria for distinguishing truth from falsity need to be taken into account but also common sense conceptions based on daily experience and the experience of the generations. What William James called "radical empiricism" is needed for a holistic theology. Radical empiricism accepts the experiences of daily life as an indispensable basis for meaningful assertions, perspectives, and theories which transcend the narrow scope of scientific thinking, positivistic empiricism, and rationalistic monism. A necessary condition for radical empiricism is the avoidance of rigid dogmas from whatever source and an openness to evidence and hypotheses from whatever source. No experiences and hypotheses are arbitrarily ruled out of court. Entailed also is a pluralistic and inclusive understanding of reality in which objects, occasions, possibilities, beginnings, ends, crises, evils, catastrophes, achievements, values, the moral life, love, and God are held to be real.

It is a truism, of course, that common sense is often subject to errors, ambiguity, and misuse. It cannot stand by itself but needs criteria in light of which its judgments are evaluated. These criteria include those already discussed, namely, logical consistency and coherence with other truths and established facts. In addition there is the criterion of how well the judgments fare in light of the total drift of human experience and thought. Finally, there is the norm of the compatibility of common sense with a "supernatural frame of reference"[2] (to use Reinhold Niebuhr's expression). Given these criteria, common sense can be a useful guide to sound perspectives.

We have discussed the role of reason as made up of the functions of logical consistency, coherence with other truths, and comprehensiveness or applicability to common human experience. In this role it can be useful in disclosing the inadequacies of ideologies and in arriving at certain pre-understandings (to use Bultmann's expression) which provide a point of contact with revelation. Not all natural theology is antithetical to revelation as Barth held. A modest natural theology in which the sentence "there is a God," is guaranteed to have cognitive significance is surely a necessary condition for any sound theistic theology including the Christian. It is not, however, a sufficient condition, for this requires revelation. So it is not the role of reason to attempt the construction of a "natural theology" in the sense of arriving at views of God, man, and the world on the basis of rational reflection upon only those data accessible to human beings as such. Any such attempt would result in limited perspectives and would inevitably become slanted by the unrecognized presuppositions and frame of reference of the theorist. The frame of reference or principle of interpretation needs to be made explicit so that dialogue can take place on this level in terms of possible justification for the frame of reference.

Facts and experiences as such do not come labeled as meaningful or meaningless, important or unimportant. They simply are. There must be a translation into the domain of meaning through the use of a frame of reference or principle of interpretation. Even the most basic empirical observations require a conceptual framework which transcends the particular observations. Surely, the scientist does not undertake his observations with his mind a *tabula rasa*. Already there is a wealth of knowledge and experience inclusive of hypotheses which he seeks to confirm or disconfirm. Scientific hypotheses are relevant to experience but do not arise entirely out of experience. Always there is an element in an hypothesis which transcends the immediacy of the observations because the value of an hypothesis is judged in terms of its explanatory power which entails comprehensiveness and predictive value. But universality and the presupposition that the future will resemble the past are beyond the ken of the observer. The data observed provide evidence for the probable truth of the hypothesis, but

17

they do not provide it with the apodictic certainty of a logically necessary truth. Of course, hypotheses which are wrong may be falsified through observations of data, provided the methods of observing are sound. It takes only one negative instance to falsify a purported universal law. But granted the principles of comprehensiveness and predictive value, it is impossible to completely verify empirical laws. Induction rests on the causal principle which in turn entails the principle of the uniformity of nature - that the future will be like the past - and any attempt to prove these principles inevitably falls into the fallacy of question begging. They cannot be proved, and yet without them the whole edifice of modern science would collapse. There is, then, a pragmatic justification for accepting them.

As in science so also in theology the understanding of experience requires a principle of interpretation which even though relevant to experience does not arise out of experience. It is a given which transcends experience. At this point the analogy with science does not completely fit. While it is true that the principles of science such as the casual principle and the uniformity of nature are presuppositions which transcend the empirical data presented, they do not transcend human cognition and perspective in precisely the same way that in the Christian faith the revelation of God is held to be transcendent. Not only does it occur primarily in the less predictable arena of history rather than in the more predictable arena of nature, but also while not arbitrary it is a given which comes from beyond. Accepted, it may be applied to experience and serve to provide depths of meaning not seen before. Even though revelation comes from beyond, it does not come as some bolt from the blue but through human receptors who may have rusty listening devices. Even the original faith witnesses were not magically transformed into some sort of demi-gods, freed of their cultural limitations and human frailties. Given that fact plus the human frailties of interpreters both past and present, it should be clear how important it is to give attention to the criteria for judging how adequately the conceptual framework is formulated.

The argument here is, of course, somewhat circular but not, I think, invalid. Facts and experiences to have meaning require a

18

principle of interpretation which itself cannot be deduced from the facts and experiences. It is a given. Yet it does not fully control experience. Facts and experiences along with the criteria of consistency and coherence may falsify inadequate interpretative principles or inadequate formulations of an interpretative principle or conceptual framework.

If the interpretative principle or frame of reference is a given through revelation, just how can it be communicated to human beings? Since it is from a transcendent source, it certainly cannot be expounded adequately or fully in terms of a mundane, prosaic, and literalistic discourse. It is here that myth (or story) has an indispensable role to play. In this vehicle of communication the dialectical realities of the Christian faith such as the transcendence and immanence of God, his love and justice, human possibilities and limits can be most adequately expressed. They can provide a frame of reference in which is found clues to the nature of the transcendent and the meaning of life and history without abolishing the inherent mystery of either.

In the last several years scholars in various fields have engaged in considerable discussion of mythology, much of which has been rather opaque. Undoubtedly this is due, at least in part, to the vagueness and ambiguity infecting the usage of the word 'myth' itself. Much popular opinion, including some dictionary definitions, understand the word to designate a primitive false story seeking to explain some uncontrollable and/or mysterious feature of the natural world. Taking falsity as a defining characteristic of the word 'myth' restricts too much the area of the word's denotation. Is it the case that we can call myths only those stories which are known to be false such as the earth hatching from a giant egg? What about those stories which speak of transcendent realities which are not known to be false, because these realities are not subject to empirical verification? Is it not the case that if a myth is false, it is false not by definition but for the same reason anything else is shown to be false? It seems to me that a definition of 'myth' which provides an adequate scope for the word's denotation is as follows: 'myth' is a value-charged story expressing those realities, transcendent and/or immanent, in terms of which believers find their life orientation.

19

These stories may contain all sorts of accompanying characteristics endemic to the times and cultures in which they originate. To use Reinhold Niebuhr's term, there are "pre-scientific" myths or aspects of some myths in which the known ordered course of the world, the known causal relations in nature and history, are either unknown or disregarded. These, of course, must be abandoned or radically reinterpreted in a scientific age. In dealing with myths everyone, to use Rudolf Bultmann's term, "demythologizes" in some fashion or other and to some degree or other. Yet it does not follow that all myths can or should be reinterpreted, especially in terms of an existentialist's philosophy which deals solely with human nature and existence. Even though he claimed at points that myths should be reinterpreted and not eliminated, Bultmann himself admitted at other points that some myths or features of some myths could not be reinterpreted but had to be eliminated. In my judgment Bultmann's inconsistency and subjectivism are avoided if one adopts Reinhold Niebuhr's distinction between pre-scientific and permanent myths.[3]

Permanent myths are those which deal with transcendent realities and with meanings which are beyond the capacity of science either to verify or to falsify. Scientific analysis and verified knowledge are transcended but not contradicted. It may be that some nonessential details in the story are time-bound contradicting what is known through science, but the core of the myth is not thereby falsified. The creation myths in Genesis, for example, contain features such as a six day creation or the forming of man from the dust of the ground which are incompatible with scientific knowledge. Yet the central message that there is a God who is responsible for the fact that there is something rather than nothing, that the world is good, and that human beings possess indeterminate possibilities for both good and evil transcends but does not contradict scientific knowledge.

Permanent myths do not have to be taken literally in order to be taken seriously as providing meaning in the midst of mystery. Literalism destroys both the meaning and the mystery. The mystery of the transcendent cannot be captured in some sort of literalistic discourse. This mystery is not due to ignorance which will be dispelled by the advancement of human knowledge. It is as permanent a feature of the human condition as is knowledge. There may be points of light but we are time bound earthlings and not gods and so must see in a mirror dimly. This point is exemplified in a central myth of the Christian faith as expressed by the Apostle Paul, namely, "in Christ God was reconciling the world to himself" (2 Cor. 5:19). A further discussion of Christology will be undertaken in a later chapter. Here I simply want to point out that even through a reasonable and meaningful formulation of just how God could be specially present in the life and activity of a particular individual can be developed (and many interesting ones have been developed in the history of Christian thought, not least of which in modern times is the so-called process Christology), there is still the mystery of why this particular individual, Jesus of Nazareth, rather than some other should have been the object of and receptive to God's purpose. This is a mystery which cannot be eliminated.

If there were nothing but mystery, all that would be left would be blind faith which perhaps is worse than no faith at all. If there were nothing but literalistic total intelligibility, nothing of the transcendent would remain. Mystery and meaning are contraries, both of which are required in a holistic view. Permanent myths serve as a means of expressing this and other dialectical realities.

I have suggested above that there are two essential ingredients in the construction of a theology, namely, the use of reason and the acceptance of a frame of reference. The latter entails the acceptance of some permanent myths. There may be permanent myths in other religious traditions, but our concern is with those which make up the Christian story or *mythos* and provide the frame of reference for a Christian theology.

While the basic make-up and understanding of the Christian *mythos* has a long history, the sectarian divisions within Christendom indicate variations and fluidity in the understanding of the *mythos*. Therefore we need reason not only to develop a theology based on the *mythos* as a frame of reference but also to assist us in determining which myths and/or features of myths belong in the body of myths comprising the genuine Christian story. For example, given the strong

21

monotheism in so many Old Testament myths, the criterion of consistency would require us to eliminate from the *mythos* the few henotheistic features found in some other Old Testament myths, or if a myth made Jesus of Nazareth into some sort of magician rather than a person with a unique relationship with the divine, however that might be understood, it would be eliminated as inconsistent with the long history of the Christian tradition. The role of reason here is primarily negative.

There is also a positive function of reason, namely, to demonstrate that the myths contained within the Christian story illumine experience and are in turn justified by experience. Obviously this is not proof in any strict sense but pragmatic justification. Do the myths motivate persons to do such things as seek understanding, resist forces which feed on hatred and enjoy the suffering of others, insist on the dignity and worth of each human life, and engage in common endeavors for the betterment of both human and non-human life on this planet.

Given these criteria, both negative and positive, some myths will be eliminated and others have certain elements eliminated or revised before they are incorporated in the *mythos* which provides the frame of reference for the theology. There is, then, a reciprocal relationship between *mythos* and *logos*. While the *logos* does not create the *mythos* which is a given, it does serve to purify and protect the *mythos* from prescientific, alien, and corrupting influences, and to interpret it in such a way that it is intelligible and relevant.

In conclusion, I would briefly summarize the argument I have attempted to make in this discussion. In the formulation of a theology it is important to be as clear as possible about the method used due to the fact that method and substance are correlative such that inappropriate method leads to inappropriate substantive results. An appropriate method in theological construction makes use of reason which entails consistency, coherence with other truths, and comprehensiveness or relevance to all of reality disclosed in human experience. Reason operating on only the data accessible to human beings as such may arrive at certain pre-understandings which are a necessary condition for a sound theology. Yet these pre-understandings do not constitute a sufficient condition for a sound and holistic theology. For that, revelation is required and revelation is communicated through myths. Reason has a role to play here, for there is a reciprocal relation between *mythos* and *logos*. Even though the revelation communicated through the *mythos* *is* a given which comes from beyond, *logos* *is* required in order to eliminate from the *mythos* pre-scientific elements, to interpret and understand it, and to relate it in meaningful ways to all the concerns of human life.

---

[1] *Essays, First and Second Series,* The Harvard Edition (Houghton Mifflin CO., 1929) p. 57.

[2] *The Nature and Destiny of Man,* vol. I (Charles Scribner's Sons, 1941) pp. 129-130; *Beyond Tragedy* (Charles Scribner's Sons, 1937) p. 14.

[3] *The Self and the Dramas of History* (Charles Scribners' sons, 1955) pp. 97-98.

CHAPTER TWO
HUMAN NATURE AND DESTINY

While it is not an absolute necessity, I think there is some justification for beginning a discussion of substantive issues in theology with a consideration of human nature and destiny. As indicated in chapter one, I am aware that in radical Protestantism (Karl Barth and his followers) this is to begin at the wrong end of things. In this view human beings as such possess no capacity for arriving at genuine knowledge of God and thus of themselves or even of receiving the gift of God's grace. Since sin has erased the *imago dei*, there is no "point of contact." If God's grace is accepted, it is because God creates the conditions for its acceptance. Human beings can understand themselves as persons only on the basis of a knowledge of God's personality disclosed in his word. But this, it seems to me, comes close to reducing faith to faith without understanding. Is it not the case that we can intelligibly use the concept of personality in talk about God because of our human experience with personality?

Furthermore, can the "point of contact" be denied without coming close to affirming a sort of magical faith in which salvation is due solely to the predestinating activity of God? Doesn't this tend to make human beings into pawns of God, thus depreciating the doctrine of creation, minimizing any universal natural human dignity, and ignoring for the most part the disciplines of culture? I think it simply does not follow that acceptance of a "point of contact," of a natural human capacity to receive God's revelation, corrupts the revelation and the understanding of human nature entailed by the revelation. A critical appraisal of human nature does not lead necessarily to an elimination of the need for the Transcendent. Instead, it simply provides one of the necessary conditions for making sense out of the "I-Thou" encounter. Surely, there must be good grounds for affirming the existence of an 'I' with some capacity for transcendence before the 'I' can be meaningfully said to have a relationship with the Transcendent. In this discussion I shall attempt to use the tools of rational analysis to construct a view of

24

human nature and destiny supportive of that found in the Christian faith in order to undergird faith with understanding.

It is rather singular that with all the advances in knowledge human beings rarely cease to be deeply puzzled by themselves. Long before René Descartes' (1596-1650) *cogito ergo sum*, John Scotus Erigena, the early medieval thinker, claimed that man knows that he is but does not know what he is. That we exist seems to be intuitively certain enough. Centuries before Erigena or Descartes, Augustine argued that while we can doubt all sorts of things, there is one thing we cannot doubt, namely, our own existence. To the skeptic who might assert that since in the past our knowledge claims have often been mistaken, we might also be mistaken in claiming to know that we exist, Augustine pointed out that those who would be the ones mistaken must necessarily exist in order to be mistaken. Even in the very act of rigorous doubting, including the doubting of one's own existence, one is tacitly affirming his own existence as the doubter.

What of the second half of Erigena's claim, namely, man does not know what he is? In Erigena's view not even God knows what he is since what is neuter and God is personal. This might be challenged in light of process thought. There is a what to God though he transcends the what as a who. The what of God is contained in his consequent nature in which, in a sense, the world is immanent in him. Put in another way, the world might be thought of as the 'body' of God. That is, the world is present to God as the body is present to a person. Yet he transcends his body just as a person though identified with his body nevertheless transcends it. This view is, of course, panentheism but not pantheism.

With respect to human beings, there is considerable knowledge of the what in so far as this designates physical bodies. Anatomy and Physiology have made great progress in recent years such that the store of scientific knowledge concerning the organic realm has reached proportions never thought possible in earlier times. The psychological sciences have developed also, but there is still a residue of mystery about the human psyche. It could be said, then, that on one level we know very well what we are. Yet when we shift from the neuter what to

25

the personal <u>who</u> we enter the realm of mind, personality, or spirit and thus into some degree of mystery. Surely, the <u>who</u> is not entirely caught in the <u>what</u>. In terms of our experience in the actual world, it would appear that personality, mind, or spirit depend upon a physical body and are certainly influenced to a considerable degree by the body but are much more than the body. There is here the quality of transcendence. Many essential Christian doctrines (such as the image of God in human beings, their indeterminate capacity for both good and evil, for reconciliation with God and for ultimate fellowship with him) rest on this assumption.

The claim that the self possesses the capacity of transcendence needs to be considered in more detail. What does it mean and how can it be justified? Any attempt to deal with this question must necessarily give attention to three key issues, namely, the mind-body problem, the question of freedom and determinism, and the issue of the individual-community relation. Does the self transcend nature (including its own body as suggested above)? Is there a capacity to transcend its human environment, at least to some degree? Does it transcend its own fancies and emotions, and can it in some sense transcend itself? Is it free not only to develop a governing center responsible for its actions, but also is it free to modify to a greater or lesser extent this governing center? In the discussion which follows these questions will be considered as well as the question of the ultimate destiny of human beings. Unless a case can be made that the self possesses the quality of transcendence, it is logically impossible for human beings to have a destiny which transcends this earthly life.

It is clearly evident that if we are to talk sensibly about the self, we need some understanding of what we are talking about. Probably we all have some intuitive sense of what we mean when we use the term 'self', but it may be helpful to indicate at least a provisional definition. This, of course, is not easy. Since even standard dictionaries provide so many definitions, it is difficult to prevent ambiguity from arising in discourse. While we may not be able to eliminate ambiguity altogether, we will seek to prevent it as much as possible by indicating the primary meaning of the term as found in *The Shorter Oxford English Dictionary*.

All of the defining statements offered here suffer from some degree of vagueness, but they seem to come closest to suggesting the meaning generally accepted in common usage. The 'self' is a permanent subject of successive and varying states of consciousness; it is that which a person really and intrinsically is in contradistinction to that which is contingent; it is the ego, often identified with mind or soul as opposed to the body. The first two statements are in a sense ostensive in nature. In the midst of all the contingency and change in our lives we still have the consciousness of being the same person. However, the last statement does raise some problems due to the fact that in the history of Western thought the concept of soul became imbued with such a strong metaphysical sense.

If 'soul' is understood metaphorically to refer to the sense of a permanent subject of states of consciousness, then the conceptual problems are minimized. But if 'soul' is taken in the Platonic metaphysical sense, then all sorts of problems arise with respect to meaning and truth. In the Platonic view the soul is claimed to be a substantive, unalterable, and indestructible entity which upon entering the world is imprisoned in a body made of matter which is the source of the evils and troubles in the world. The soul directs and often opposes the body, and this means that it can be independent of the body. Indissoluble, the soul exists after the death of a particular body, and having severed 'personal' ties with its past existence except for behavioral dispositions, it takes up residence in another body. The ultimate destiny of the soul, however, is reunion with the eternal. This destiny may be achieved by repeatedly renouncing the world of the senses and by finding refuge in the intelligible and timeless until at length the dross of earth has been eliminated. This dualistic anthropology which gave an exalted metaphysical status to the soul and denigrated the body greatly influenced, with some modifications (i.e. rejection of reincarnation), the thought of the early and medieval Church Fathers, the development of monasticism and the puritan ethic. Yet this dualistic view of soul and body which became rather traditional was a departure from the earlier, more realistic, biblical understanding of 'soul'.

In most cases, especially in the Old Testament, there was no question of two separate entities, soul and body. The Hebrew word translated as 'soul' designates the life principle which always appears in some form, without which it would not exist. While persons may transcend their physical bodies, they are persons only as they possess some kind of bodies. Always life is a totality which expresses itself in some sort of bodily form. Later, when the notion of a postmortem existence emerges, it envisions a resurrection 'body' given by God, a spiritual 'body.' So the body, even the physical body, is not by its very nature at war with the soul. Every living being, indeed, all of nature, is the handiwork of the Creator and as created is good. So the physical body as such is not the source of temptation and sin. It may be the vehicle of sin but is not its source or cause. Persons may sin sexually, but the sexual impulse is not the cause of sin. Sin is prideful rebellion against God and rejection of human community. It involves the total person.

It is rather unfortunate for the history of Christian thought and practice that the medieval Fathers such as Augustine and Aquinas were not consistent in their perspectives concerning all of natures' creatures, including the human. Accepting an hierarchical view of reality as structured in ordered gradations with man occupying the highest rank in the created order, they, nevertheless, insisted that all natural things are ordained by the supreme art of the Creator and are essentially good. While nature is neither divine nor an object of worship, it is the handiwork of God and thus good.

Given this view, one would think that the human body would be included in the goodness of nature, and in a sense it is but only as created. Due to many causal conditions, not least of which were Platonic and Neo-platonic notions embedded in the thought forms of the times, the early threat of Gnosticism with its hidden god and its evil creator god, the Fathers sought to account for evil in such a way that no responsibility for it could be attributed to God. This responsibility had to be laid on human beings and so the myth of the fall of Adam was used to account for the source of evil in the world. Interpreted with Platonic categories, the myth was understood in such a way that the body with

28

its impulses, including the sexual drives, becomes the culprit instead of God or some demiurge. Further, salvation was understood to depend ultimately on the subjugation of the body, the doing of good works for the sake of the immortal soul.

1. The Mind-Body Problem

Although challenged from time to time a dualistic anthropology has been generally accepted in Western thought, especially in philosophical thought, until modern times. Not only was this the received tradition in religious circles, but also it was defended in the thought of important philosophers such as Descartes, one of the molders of modern culture. Unfortunately, he extended the seventeenth century mechanical explanation adopted in Physics and Astronomy into every department of natural life, including Biology and Physiology. So animals were regarded as automata devoid of consciousness (one of the causes for the widespread disregard of animal rights in modern Western culture). Human bodies also were regarded as automata. The human body, being part of the mechanical order, is itself a mechanical apparatus, but in human beings there is also the mind with its innate truths directing the course of the body through its contact with the body in the centrally located pineal gland. This, of course, does not solve the problem of how a non-material, non-mechanical entity, the mind, could have an effect on a mechanical body since presumably the pineal gland is physical and thus mechanical (today, it is well known that this gland serves no known function). Thus Descartes was unsuccessful in explaining how mind and body interact or in finding an organic unity between mind and body, thought and nature.

After Descartes, John Locke (1632-1704) gave cogent reasons for denying that the mind possesses innate truths, and Kant (1724-1804) affirmed that the mind can know only the realm of appearances but not the real world of things-in-themselves. A twofold reaction to the problems raised by these philosophers ensued. On the one hand, extreme idealism denied that there are external physical objects to cause our sensations and insisted that nothing exists except minds and their ideas. On the other hand, in extreme materialism there was the claim that only material things possess genuine reality and that ideas

29

are at best a kind of by-product. If thoughts and sensations do exist, they are physical brain events and not mental at all. There are many variations on these extreme positions, at least among philosophers. In recent times idealism has not been advocated by many. Instead, some form of behavioristic materialism appears to have gained the largest following.

The identity theory of the body-mind relation advocated by materialists was supported strongly by some of the logical empiricists or linguistic analysts in the philosophical community. Among other things, they claimed that the meaning of the words 'mental events' was the same as the meaning of the words 'physical events'. They are simply two expressions for the same thing. Person words have no more meaning than that which can be defined ostensibly. Their meanings cannot and should not be taught by any means other than by pointing at people. They do not designate any mysterious incorporeal substance. Gilbert Ryle, a leading British empiricist, in *The Concept Of Mind*[1] advocated abandoning the Cartesian "dogma of the ghost in the machine." Along with other logical empiricists and verificationists, he insisted that mind statements have no more meaning than statements about certain observable bodily behavior.

This position is consistent with the verificationists' principle of meaning and its corollary, namely, that if two statements have precisely the same verification or confirmation, they have the same meaning. For example, verificationists claim that the cash value of the statement, "Electrons exist," is to be found in the sum total of statements which are adduced as evidence for the electron hypothesis. The cognitive meaning of the electron statement is the same as the combined meanings of the evidential statements. To think of electrons as something over and beyond the sum total of the evidential phenomena is simply to be subject to the mistake of picture thinking. Electrons are logical constructions, and this means that to say something about electrons is to say something about phenomena which are in principle observable. One can verify or confirm the existence of electrons only by verifying or confirming the occurrence of these phenomena; the verification or confirmation is the same, hence the

30

cognitive meaning is the same. Any dispute about the nature of electrons, if it is not merely verbal, is a dispute about phenomena which are observable in principle-phenomena that have occurred, now occur, will occur, or would occur under specifiable circumstances. Many of the logical empiricists' theories concerning the mind-body issue came to a similar conclusion to that concerning the electron hypothesis. Mind statements have no more meaning than statements about certain observable bodily behavior.

'Minds' are logical constructions. The use of the term 'mind' is a shorthand way of referring to certain behavioral phenomena which are in principle observable. There is no mental realm over and beyond overt behavior. The common notion that each person by means of introspection has a privileged access to the consciousness of an inner self is little more than muddle-headed nonsense.

This view of the logical empiricists was certainly a precursor of the anthropology propounded in deconstructionist theology, though the latter lacks the clarity of the former. Yet the deconstructionists agree that the notion of an inner self which to some degree transcends bodily behavior and relational properties is not only a fantasy but also harmful. Just as we should will the death of God so also we should will the death of the self. In spite of the murder of the self by both logical empiricists and deconstructionists, it is often claimed that intelligent purpose is not thereby eliminated. This claim is highly questionable. In terms of what is ordinarily meant by 'intelligent purpose,' is it not contradictory to affirm that there can be intelligent purpose without such consciousness? How can what we call 'intelligent purpose' in human life be reduced to nothing more than bodily behavior? Surely, such a position inevitably involves a mechanistic behaviorism no matter how much its proponents try to squirm out of it, and, I think, is not required in order to avoid the clutches of Cartesianism. Furthermore, its inadequacy can be demonstrated on the basis of an appeal both to our experience and to an analysis of our use of certain person words.

To imply that it is either a Cartesian dualism of mind and body substances or a behaviorism as described above is to pose a false

31

dilemma. Whatever the origins of consciousness or whatever the physical casually necessary conditions for states of consciousness, reductionism is neither logically necessary nor empirically compelling. Our own personal experience suggests that we are more than that which "meets the eye." There is that self-awareness, that sense of personal identity, that sense of being the same person although much has changed in terms of one's bodily structure and behavior, which cannot be reduced to observable behavior. Drastic changes in the body such as loss of limbs does not, at least in most situations, change the sense of being the same person. There are, of course, some psychological abnormalities in which there are multiple personalities (*The Three Faces of Eve*) where the persistence of a generic bodily form plays a larger role in providing the awareness, at least at times, of being the same person. The distress of the persons in such cases, as well as in cases of amnesia, the desire to regain the 'lost' self, the sense of personal identity, certainly suggests that on the level of experience persons desire a unified self which is more than the body and its publicly observable behavior. There are testimonies from those who have suffered from temporary amnesia as to the great relief on recovering selfhood and the sense of personal identity.

There are many examples from our personal experience that there is an inner, mental, self to which each of us has privileged access. Take the case of the experience of pain. This is an experience which is not publicly observable even in principle. It is its causes and effects which are publicly observable. When I say, "I have a pain," I am not referring to a group of diverse phenomena, the causes and effects of my pain, but to the pain itself which I know through immediate experience. I do not have to look in a mirror, feel my pulse, get a doctor's diagnosis, or visit a psychiatrist, to know that I feel a pain. Further, I cannot feel anyone else's pain. I may sympathize strongly with him but I cannot (logical 'cannot') feel his pain. While it is logically possible for me to feel pain when another's body is injured, I would in that case call it my pain. Conversely, if he felt pain when my body was injured, he would call it his pain. Whose pain it is is determined by who feels it. It is logically impossible for me to feel another's pain or for him to feel mine. It follows, then, that states of consciousness while closely correlated with the neural processes in the brain which are publicly observable in principle are not the same thing as these processes, and that these states of consciousness are not publicly observable although they are privately experienceable.

To put it in another way, it would appear on the basis of our present empirical knowledge that neural brain processes are a causally necessary condition for the occurrence of states of consciousness. But if A is a causally necessary condition for B, then A and B are not one and the same thing; A could hardly be a necessary condition for itself. If B is causally dependent on A, then it follows that there are two things, A and B. In terms of empirical possibility, it seems that consciousness is utterly dependent on brain activity, but this is by no means to say that consciousness is brain activity. Physical things and processes are locatable in space. They take place somewhere. The sensory and neural processes associated with mental events such as sensations, memories, thoughts, and images take place inside a person's head. But where are the sensations, memories, thoughts, and images? They do not take place in space nor are they publicly observable. Surely, it is a prejudice to claim that therefore they are unreal. This is to deny common human experience.

Let us consider one further example which to an extent is hypothetical but suggested by advances in medical technology such as the CAT scan. Suppose that each of us has in his possession a very sophisticated and advanced machine somewhat similar to a very small TV but which could function as an 'auto-cerebroscope.' This machine enables each one of us to observe what is going on in his own brain. Each of us could see just which nerve pathways were stimulated with each experience. That is, he could see exactly what happened in the occipital lobe of his cortex simultaneously with experiencing the deep red of the roses on the bush in front of him. There is nothing intrinsically absurd about such a possibility and it may become actual someday. But even if it did, one would hardly be tempted on that account to claim that the red he sees and whatever is going on in his brain when he sees red are identical processes or that his red sensation is unreal. If it be

33

could imagined further that there is an omnipresent physician in attendance upon each of us constantly observing what is going on in our brains by means of our auto-cerebroscopes such that he could establish a constant correlation between the peculiar wiggling of a little ganglion and our experience of red, it would not follow that he was thereby having our experience of red. His experience would be that of a certain wiggling and of whatever color a ganglion might be. Doubtless the physician also could have an experience of red by also looking at something red such as the roses. But he, no more than we, would have to appeal to the evidence of his own auto-cerebroscope to know that he was experiencing red. He, just as we, would know it as an immediate visual sensation.

Thus far I have argued that mental events are not reducible to physical or brain events, that the self is more than overt activity, that each of us has privileged access to his own self, and that this argument is supported by our own experience. Further support is to be found in the peculiar role played in our language by the first person singular pronoun. This is rather obvious when one is attentive to the following considerations as pointed out by William H. Poteat in an interesting article entitled, "God and the 'Private-I'" found in *New Essays on Religious Language*.[2]

Most of the terms in our language, with the exception of proper names, are more or less adaptable to use by persons in a variety of situations for pointing out particular features in these situation to others. Demonstrative pronouns such as 'this' and 'that' have maximum adaptability. They may be used as substitute names to refer to any kind or any individual particular in any situation. Third person pronouns have a high degree of adaptability but not as great as 'this' and 'that.' The first person singular pronoun has even less adaptability. While 'he' may be used by any number of persons on any number of occasions and may mean a different person on every single occasion, 'I' can mean only one person on every single occasion. That is, 'I' always functions reflexively; it always denotes the user. Furthermore, no matter how much others may think that what I mean by 'I' is identifiable with reports of bodily behavior or dispositions to behavior, it is impossible for me to do so. For me there is always something more which cannot be wholly incorporated into ordinary subject-object discourse. If the structures and patterns of our language are not due simply to arbitrary conventions but reflect to some extent the nature and structure of reality, then the peculiar role of 'I' in our discourse represents the fact that, however publicizable 'I' may be, there is always something more which cannot be put into public discourse but which is experiencable and real.

It is this very feature of the peculiar role of 'I' in our discourse which leads those who affirm the "no-ownership" or "no -subject" theory (that there is no self to provide experience with a unity beyond what is given to experience by being causally dependent on a single body) into the trap of a self-contradiction. In order to analyze away the self the theory must use the language of self in order even to state the theory. As the theory puts it, "All my experiences are uniquely dependent on the state of a certain body." This dependence is supposed to be causal and thus contingent. Yet it cannot be contingent unless experiences can be identified as mine independently of their causal relationship with a certain body, and this is precisely what the theory denies. The contradiction could be avoided by means of the trivial tautology, "This body's experiences are this body's experiences," but that would hardly be satisfactory. Thus, whether our appeal is to our experience, to the peculiarities of the role of the first person singular pronoun in our language, or to the incoherence of the no-ownership theory, the conclusion is the same. Mental events do transcend physical events; the self does transcend the body, and each one of us does have privileged access to his own self. Further, the self transcends not only the body but also all of nature. Although a creature and tied to nature, a person by virtue of his capacity to stand outside the world, to control nature, at least to some extent, and to describe himself in nature, transcends the nature thus described. This position does not necessarily entail a return to Cartesian dualism with all of its difficulties. Bodies and physical events need not be thought of in terms of a mechanistic model nor the 'soul' in metaphysical terms as a simple, permanent, single, spiritual substance.

35

Whiteheadian process thought with its emphasis on the organic and processive nature of all reality makes it possible to give an account of human creatureliness and transcendence consistent with the facts disclosed in experience and supportive of the biblical perspective concerning human nature. The basic constituents of this organic and processive reality are actual occasions or 'drops' of experience with 'mental' and physical poles, "prehensions," and subjective 'aims,' eternal objects, and societies which are made up of actual occasions. Each creature (human, animal, and vegetable) is a living society which may include, especially on the animal level, a dominant 'personal' society of occasions. Occasions of experience aim at enjoyment, and in those societies which are bodies this is primarily simple physical enjoyment. However, given the fact that the direction of evolution has been toward increased centralization, there emerges a dominant, coordinating, and governing society of occasions which can entertain aims that transcend the body and its needs. While to some degree affected by the body, it can direct the body in many ways, and in spite of continual changing, it gains a sense of continuity through time. Thus the self emerges, related not only to its own body but also to all of nature, and yet it is discrete and transcendent as an individual self. It is not a matter of two separate and distinct substantive entities, matter and spirit, somehow united in a single body, but of similar organic realities at different degrees or levels of complexity.

A person, then, is composed of low grade occasions (primarily bodily or physical) and of high grade, central, dominant, coordinating, and governing occasions in a living nexus or society. It is this central, dominant, and governing coordinating society which I have been calling the self. Undergirded by this analysis, explications of Christian doctrine concerning human nature and destiny can be freed of outworn metaphysical baggage and fulfill one basic necessary condition for making sense of these doctrines in the modern world. Without a self in the sense of a governing center of consciousness, talk about the self transcending nature and itself is literally nonsense.

2. The Freedom-Determinism Issue

In adddition to the existence of the 'self' as a governing center of consciousness, there is another necessary condition for making sense out of the Christian claims concerning human nature and destiny, namely, the self's possession of sufficient freedom to choose the center from which it organizes itself. Without this the Christian claim that each person is responsible not only for what he does but also for what he is would be literally nonsense. Therefore it is necessary to consider both the meaning and nature of freedom.

The subject of freedom is a notoriously difficult one to discuss because the key terms of the discussion have been loaded with such a variety of meanings. The first task, then, is that of "clearing the decks" with respect to the meanings that are to be attributed to these terms so that at least some clarity may be achieved.

First, 'freedom' itself is a loaded word in our common usage. It is often used in the negative sense in which it means absence of constraint. One is free if his acts are not compelled by external forces nor by certain internal forces such as kleptomania. It is also used in a positive sense to mean that one can do certain things. That is, one is free to do those things he can do if he chooses to do them. In this sense, one is free to lift a plate from a table if he chooses to do so but is not free to lift a building however much he may wish to do so. In these two senses, negative and positive, it is obvious that 'freedom' is a matter of degree, varying from person to person and from place to place. A third sense in which 'freedom' is sometimes used may be indicated under the rubric of "freedom of the will." That is, 'freedom' means not only absence of constraints and ability to act as one chooses to act but also some relative freedom of choice. Within limits one could have chosen otherwise than he in fact did choose.

A second slippery term which appears in discussions of freedom is 'determinism.' Sometimes 'determinism' is used in a sense in which it is absolutely incompatible with all the senses of freedom discussed above and is roughly synonymous with 'fatalism.' Perhaps no one is ever a consistent fatalist but if there were such, he would claim that whatever happens does so regardless of what we do. Surely this flies directly in the face of obvious empirical facts. In other discourse, especially

37

philosophical discourse, 'determinism' is used as a convenient way of referring to the principle of universal causality. That is, it is the assumption that for every class of events in the universe there is a class of conditions such that given an instance of each member of a particular class of conditions an instance of a particular class of events will occur. Thus the meaning of 'determinism' is to be distinguished from that of 'fatalism,' for the causal principle does not exclude human actions from the causal conditions of many events which occur .

A third loaded term which is often found in discussions of freedom is the term 'chance.' There are at least four senses in which this term is used. (1) It is used in the sense of an unintended or unplanned event such as when one unexpectedly meets an old friend on the streets of a city. (2) It is used to refer to our ignorance of the causal conditions for the occurrence of some event either because these conditions are so complex or because we do not consider it worth the trouble to find out what they are. (3) It is used to refer to probability, not of an *a priori* mathematical type but of a statistical type which considers the past record of the frequencies of each alternative. In none of these three senses is there a denial that there were causal conditions for the events which occurred. (4) 'Chance' is sometimes used to refer to a few events which, it is claimed, occur *ex nihilo*. There were no causes for their occurrence. According to 'hard' determinists this fourth sense of the term 'chance' is also the meaning of 'indeterminism.' Thus the position of the indeterminist is that while most events are determined in the sense of having causal conditions, there are a few events, especially in the field of human volition and actions, which are undetermined. That is, they are outside of any direct chain of causal conditions.

If determinism is taken to mean the principle of universal causality and indeterminism to mean that some events are without cause, then these two positions are absolutely incompatible and neither is provable. Certainly there is no empirical evidence for indeterminism in this sense. There is no class of events in the universe which is <u>known</u> <u>not</u> to be caused although there are many which are <u>not known</u> to be caused. Just what kind of evidence could be presented to establish conclusively that an event was without cause? Isn't it inconceivable that any such evidence could be provided? The determinist can always claim that the cause is simply unknown, that one has not looked long enough for the cause, or that the ignorance of the individual or of mankind makes the cause unknown, not that there isn't one.

On the other hand, determinism is also faced with difficulties. To be sure, it is in a relatively stronger position than indeterminism since we do know the causal conditions of many events, and this area of events is constantly expanding as our knowledge grows. But obviously there are many events in the world the occurrence of which have not yet been explained in terms of causal conditions. Yet the principle of universal causality states that for every class of events in the universe there are causal conditions. That is, it presupposes the uniformity of all nature, and while regularities in nature are innumerable, so also are the relations which are irregular. Any attempt to prove this universal principle from known uniformities or causal relations, since it must assume the principle as a major premise, inevitably ends in fallacies such as affirming the consequent or question-begging. Moreover, there can never be conclusive verifying evidence in support of this principle. It is logically impossible for us in the present to observe events of the past and the future, for we cannot (logical 'cannot') be here now and somewhere else at the same time and location. Unless we were God, it is even impossible in practice to observe all present events.

The situation with respect to the causal principle is very curious indeed. With any empirical generalization, there is the possibility of refuting it with empirical facts. It takes only one white crow to wreck the generalization that all crows are black. But what could possibly wreck the generalization that every event is related to a set of conditions as stated in the causal principle? Determinists, especially 'hard' determinists, affirm that the discovery of more causes confirms the principle, but that failure to find causes is due to the limitations of our powers of detection and not to the absence of causes. They are simply unknown. Thus there is no possibility of disconfirming the principle. But what kind of principle is it that can be confirmed by empirical evidence but not disconfirmed by the same means? If the possibility even in principle of disconfirming evidence is not admitted,

39

then it can hardly be an empirical principle, for a part of the very meaning of 'empirical principle' is that it is subject to the possibility of falsification.

Is it the case then that the causal principle is an *a priori* principle? This does not seem to be true for, as stated, the causal principle is obviously not an analytic statement or tautology. It does not say that every effect has a cause. Clearly this would be a necessary statement since the predicate and subject terms have correlative meanings. Rather the causal principle states that for every class of events in the universe there is a class of conditions such that given an instance of each member of class C an instance of class E occurs. 'Events' and 'conditions' are not correlative in meaning. The meaning of 'event' is simply that something occurs. It does not involve the meaning of 'conditions' or 'cause.' Thus the causal principle is not an analytic *a priori* statement.

Moreover, the causal principle does not seem to be a synthetic *a priori* statement. The facts of the history of science would appear to contradict the claim that it is a synthetic *a priori* in the Kantian sense, that is, a category of thought which the mind brings to experience. Further, it does not seem to be a synthetic *a priori* in the sense that it is a statement logically deducible from a more inclusive generalization which has relevance to the world disclosed in experience, and the statement so deduced being necessarily true granted the premises of the argument. There does not appear to be a more inclusive generalization from which the causal principle could be logically deduced. It is itself, either explicitly or implicitly, a major universal premise in all scientific explanations and in most other sorts of explanations. But if it is neither an analytic *a priori* nor a synthetic *a priori*, then it can't be an *a priori* principle since there are no other options.

If the causal principle is neither an empirical nor an *a priori* principle, then what is it? Some have answered this question by claiming that it is a leading principle of investigation, a resolve to approach nature with this as one of the key planks in the methodological platform. Of course, enormous practical consequences have ensued from such procedure so that there is strong pragmatic justification for

40

operating in terms of the principle. But pragmatic justification does not constitute proof, and a leading principle is not an assertion but a resolve, and resolves or directives are neither true nor false.

It would seem, however, that the successful application of this principle has been so impressive, particularly in the natural sciences, that some thinkers, especially 'hard determinists,' are led down the primrose path of regarding it as having the same status as any other law of nature. They regard it as a law which holds universally and tailor their view of freedom to fit this purported empirical law. Laws of nature simply <u>describe</u> regularities that occur in nature and how persons do in fact behave; they do not prescribe or compel one to behave in a certain way. Compulsion is, of course, a certain kind causality. So, the determinist affirms, while it is the case that all compelled events are caused, not all caused events are compelled, and freedom is the opposite of compulsion, not of causality. 'Freedom' means only the absence of constraint and the ability to <u>do</u> certain things if one chooses to do them. This is all the freedom there is or needs to be. Our volitions and our choices are completely determined by the causal conditions of our recent and distant past. It is only on this basis, the determinist claims, that persons can be held responsible for their actions and disciplinary punishment be justified.

Further, the determinist may assert, and rightly so, that the positions of indeterminism and fatalism, while beginning with contrasting positions, come ultimately to a similar conclusion, whether recognized or not, in that both eliminate the basis for holding persons <u>responsible</u> for their actions. Fatalism eliminates such grounds by holding that whatever happens does so regardless of what we will or do. But if our volition's and actions make no difference, then we can hardly be held responsible for whatever happens. The indeterminist, on the other hand, holds that some of our acts are without cause, that they occur *ex nihilo*. They are not affected by our characters or by our habits. In a sense they can hardly be called <u>our</u> acts. How then can we be held responsible for them? Surely sheer chance and moral responsibility are mutually exclusive. Thus in the determinist's view,

41

responsibility and freedom (as he defines it) are possible only to the extent that determinism (the principle of universal causality) is true.

Is it not the case, however, that this determinist's position is involved in a shifting ground technique as far as the common usage meaning of 'freedom' is concerned in order to avoid the more basic problem of freedom of the will? Is not freedom of the will required if there is to be any genuine responsibility for our decisions? If the determinist's position is true, then the Christian claim that persons have sufficient freedom to make decisions regarding their governing centers is meaningless. It applies the word 'free' to a realm outside the scope of its meaning, for its only meaning has to do with acts which are uncompelled. Decisions, on the other hand, are parts of causal chains. Thus on a second occasion, if all the circumstances were the same including the character of the agent, the agent would not choose differently than he did on the first occasion. But does not this mean that he could not have chosen otherwise than he in fact did choose? Another person with complete knowledge of all the conditions and circumstances could accurately predict the precise choice that would be made by the agent in a particular situation even though this omniscient person himself did not compel the agent to make this precise choice. If there is such a precise chain of causal conditions for each single decision that is made, then I do not see how the determinist can escape the clutches of compulsion with respect to choices no matter how much absence of constraint there might be with respect to acts and no matter how much the determinist proclaims that causality has to do with uniformity and not with compulsion. If we would not (or could not) have chosen otherwise, given the same situation, then surely the choice is not free. We can hardly be held responsible for our choices if there is no possibility of choosing otherwise. Therefore, I think the determinist who takes the principle of universal causality as an empirical generalization ends in a position which is only slightly different from that of fatalism.

This need not be the case if the principle of causality is taken as a leading principle. As such it is not a description of the universe at all but a demand, hope, or request which we put to the world. It says in effect: "Let us look for causal uniformities for the discovery of such are or may

42

be of great benefit to human existence in the universe. In terms of the uniformities already discovered and those yet to be discovered, the conditions of life in nature may be greatly enhanced and the possibility of freedom in the sense of increased absence of constraint greatly enlarged." But if the causal principle is a leading principle, we can hardly base a theory of freedom on its truth or falsity, for a resolve is neither true nor false. As we have indicated, there are pragmatic reasons for employing the principle in our investigation of nature including human nature, but we need not make a methodological principle into an empirical or metaphysical truth encompassing our entire concept of freedom.

The causal principle, then, is not incompatible with freedom of decision. Decisions, however, are not made in a vacuum. There are relevant causal conditions, and while these conditions make certain decisions and actions probable, they do not make them necessary. Since the 'laws' of psychology, as in other sciences, are essentially statistical in nature, it is often possible to come to fairly accurate statistical conclusions concerning some probable actions of large groups of people, but this is a quite different thing from arriving at exact statistical laws concerning the decisions and behavior of a particular person. In this realm it is often the case that no precise causal explanation can be given as to why and how a person decided to act in certain ways. This is the case due to the fact not only that the causal conditions are so numerous and varied, but also that there is not a definitive one to one constant conjunction of cause and effect as is sometimes the case in nature. The causal conditions do not necessitate one and only one outcome. Rather they limit to a greater or lesser degree what can happen. This can be illustrated by a simple example. Often superior athletes excel in more than one sport. Let us imagine that one of these athletes, due to certain childhood experiences, simply cannot play golf but does excel equally at baseball and football. Obviously, he will not waste his time trying to become a professional golfer but will decide on one or the other or both of the other two sports. Causal conditions will play a role here. Issues such as offers, income, family situation, danger of injury, enjoyment of the games, and so on will

43

be involved in the decision making, but they will not be as limiting a factor as in his decision not to strive for proficiency in professional golf. Predictions as to what particular decision this athlete will make in this situation may be quite wrong, for that decision is not necessitated by the conditions. Rather they make the decision possible, whatever it may be.

Moreover, if process thinkers (i.e. Whitehead, Hartshorne, and the earlier Peirce) are correct and becoming is the fundamental aspect of reality as evolutionary development suggests, then this surely entails some degree of creativity. This means that it is not just our ignorance of causes which prevents us from seeing the effect in advance. If becoming is real, then the causal relation is not totally the mere repeating over and over again of identical effects from identical causes. Becoming creates some new quality and quantity or else it creates nothing, and nothing ever genuinely becomes. The latter would entail the conclusion contradicted by overwhelming empirical evidence that there never has been any evolutionary development. In the process view the highest level of creativity is found in man's moral life in which the creative leap inherent in all process is influenced by consciousness of ethical principles. This creative leap involves causal conditions which make it possible, but the causal conditions do not require the <u>particular act</u> which takes place for they make other acts possible as well. Choices then are real, and decisions are not fated by virtue of pre-existing conditions.

If choices are real and not merely a fantasy, then there is no compelling reason to rule out the possibility that one may make decisions regarding the governing center of his or her person, as to what he or she as a person will be. To be sure, such decisions are not easy. But history and our present experience seem to provide us with evidence that some persons do change. Christian theology generally has recognized that it is extremely difficult to change the governing center of one's person and has emphasized the need for divine assistance or grace. Yet except for extreme predestinarians, it has also maintained that one must decide to accept divine assistance in further decisions for and actualization of the change. This assistance comes in the form of God's *agape* or love, and, by virtue of its meaning, existence in *agape* is

44

radically self-transcending existence. For this to be possible it is necessary for there to be both determinism (presence of causal conditions) and freedom of decision. Our common human experience makes it evident that the situation with respect to human volitions is dialectical. It is not an either/or, either freedom or determinism, but a both/and situation.

If the arguments presented thus far are sound, it follows that (1) each person, whatever else he is, is also a self which is more than overt activity and to which he has privileged access, and (2) that each person has sufficient freedom of choice such that he may choose, however difficult it may be, the center from which the self organizes itself. It is precisely this freedom, this capacity for transcending nature, which is the basis for human greatness and weakness. Although tied to nature, human beings can use nature in constructive or destructive ways, and they can be aware of themselves as mortal beings in nature. Aware of their finitude, human beings seek to escape, to make themselves into invulnerable gods and thus inevitably yield to sin. As St. Augustine and the Protestant Reformers insisted, sin is more than immoral acts. Such arise from a more basic condition, namely the egocentric attempt to become invulnerable gods. This condition finds expression in many forms not least of which, as Reinhold Niebuhr clearly saw, is pride of power, pride of knowledge, and pride of virtue. So it is a condition not just of 'sinners' in the popular sense (thieves, adulterers, murderers, etc.) but also of the 'high', the 'mighty', and the 'virtuous.' Similarly, salvation is more than checking off a laundry list of righteous acts, for this leads to self-righteousness, the pride of virtue. Rather, salvation comes from humble acceptance of God's forgiving *agape* (love) which brings awareness of one's true condition and thus the desire for change with the assistance of the divine energizing persuasive power. None of this would be possible, of course, if human beings did not possess selves with relative freedom of will. Obviously, the relatively free self is a necessary condition for the meaningfulness of Christian claims with respect to sin and salvation.

3. Individual And Community

While the discussion in the previous sections has centered on establishing reasonable grounds for affirming the existence of a centered self with some degree of freedom, this discussion has relevance to the issue of the nature of the relation between the individual and the community. It is surely a truism to say that the existence of community as a source of cultural achievements and social organizations such as governments requires the existence of individuals to enter into relationships and to contribute to cultural achievements. Human beings live in a 'world' in which they are related to individual persons, groups of persons, institutions, animals, and material objects used by persons. The relationship between the individual and the community is a very complex one due not only to the multitude of relations in this 'world' and the diversity in evaluations of these relations, but also to the fact that it is a dialectical relationship in which for persons there is both individualization and participation in varying degrees for various people at various times. In a stable society this dialectical relation between individualization and participation, individual self-realization and community interests and sanctions, is kept in a relative, if uneasy, harmony. Such relative harmony of polar opposites is often forced to yield before the assaults of extremists devoted to one pole or the other.

In early primitive tribal societies the group or the community was the dominant reality. The community's survival, goals, rites, and traditions took precedence over any individual interests and needs. Indeed, it would have been inconceivable for individuals to have interests that were not those that were shared by at least sub-groups and sanctioned by the entire tribe. While it may be difficult for the modern mind to conceive, it is the case that in early societies the individual and the community were fused in a psychic unity. In a sense, the individual as such (i.e. the modern sense of 'individual') hardly existed at all. Persons 'existed' only as integral parts of and participants in the community. Existence apart from the community was inconceivable. To be banished from the community was to lose one's existence, often in the very realistic sense of one's life.

46

Instances of this perspective concerning the solidarity of the community are found in some Old Testament narratives concerning early tribal Israel. A prime example is the story (Joshua 7) concerning Achan who stole spoil from Jericho which had been devoted to God and thus was forbidden. This act was taken as the reason for the defeat of the forces of Israel by the men of Ai. That is, it was believed that the entire community was tainted by this act of one of its members. Only after Achan and his family, property, and the 'devoted' things were destroyed would the community be cleansed and assault on Ai be successful. Here is vivid evidence of the unquestioned sense of social solidarity among early peoples, including early Israel. Scholars often designate this sense of solidarity with the expression "corporate personality," and it is most certainly a basic assumption of early Israel's covenant faith. While toward the end of the Old Testament period and in the early Christian era there appear hints of individualism, this was not perceived in the modern sense of the term. Groups were still dominant, and in the Christian era the church soon became the dominant group, controlling individuals and other institutions such that individual life became subservient to this community. This subservience was not broken until the Renaissance and Reformation.

In modern times communist and fascist collectivism, though different from one another, were similar in that both were a reversion to primitive tribalism. Only the man of destiny, endowed with special power like the tribal chief or shaman, had the vision and authority to determine the goals of the community and to direct its activities. A major presupposition, either consciously held or simply assumed, was that the community, even though it could be largely controlled by the 'shaman,' had its own independent existence as an entity, irreducible to the lives of its members. Individuals were simply "grist for its mill," and could be sacrificed with impunity for the supposed good of this entity. The 'shaman' was thought of as embodying the community and the community the 'shaman' such that they were fused into a psychic identity having a supposed existence separate from the lives of the individuals making up the community.

47

It is rather an anomaly that in an age when collectivisms are disintegrating, some social theorists and 'theologians' in the West make much of communal personhood, denying that individuals have any existence as private selves. Human beings are essentially social, and it is totally in social process that the self emerges. Self-realization is determined by the conditioning and role images of the dominant groups. Everything is on a horizontal plane, and there is no vertical dimension to the self. It exists only as a 'social' self. An even more radical view is found in deconstructionism which, as indicated in section 1, celebrates not only the death of God but also of the self. A human being is made up of properties, relations, information exchanges, and nothing more. The notion of a centered self which includes but is more than these properties, relations, and information exchanges is a fantasy. Just as the earlier positivists had claimed that 'self' simply refers to a construct or shorthand way of designating behavioral phenomena which are observable, at least in principle, deconstructionists by one avenue or another come to the conclusion that 'self' is a construct of more elementary processes which, except for the basic physical properties of the body, are social in character. 'Self' is simply a shorthand way of referring to an intersection of relations, properties, and information exchanges.

Both radical social theorists and deconstructionists have much to say about freedom and creativity. Obviously, the only kind of freedom which they can consistently defend is freedom from constraint, not freedom of the will. In the one case, the self and its volition's are completely determined by society. In the other, there is no centered self to make decisions but only an intersection blown this way and that by the pressures of relations and information. All has collapsed into the horizontal, and it is difficult to see how on this basis there can be any creative advance for individuals or society.

At the opposite extreme from the view of the social theorists and deconstructionists is the 'rugged' individualism presupposed or explicitly enunciated in popular Protestantism and American capitalism. Behind this, of course, was the undermining of the authority of the all inclusive church, due to the rise of several movements such as nominalism and

Renaissance humanism in which the reality, status, self-sufficiency, and liberty of individuals were emphasized. Not least among these movements was the Protestant Reformation in which, as in mysticism, there was an insistence on the individual's capacity for an <u>immediate</u> individual relationship with God. This religious individualism, at least in later Calvinism, was not confined just to the sphere of evangelical piety, but, assisted by the doctrine of election, became one of the causal conditions for the rise of modern capitalism with its doctrine of a *laissez faire* individualism in both the economic and political realms. In America, this doctrine received reinforcement from the frontier experience in which some individuals apart from the constraints of settled communities braved the rigors of the wilderness to make homes for themselves and to live fairly independent and private lives. Religious reinforcement for this doctrine has come from the religious evangelical 'right' with its emphasis upon individual salvation and its tendency to ignore the social evils which plague society.

These extreme positions present us with a false dilemma. The first ignores the creativity, vitality, and freedom of the individual over all forms of social cohesion. How can one account for the message and actions of the great prophets of Israel simply on the basis of social conditioning? Almost without exception, they took issue with the popular attitudes, perspectives, and mores of their times and often suffered because of their attacks on the community. Of course, it was due to their loyalty to the covenant faith with its God who required the loyalty of the community that they attacked the actual community for its disloyalty to the ideal community. But why did they not simply accept the popular view of priests, rulers, and landed gentry that Israel was a favored nation which could do no wrong? Was it not due to their freedom as individuals, their capacity to transcend their actual community and to answer the call of Yahweh to be a critic of this community from the perspective of the ideal community? Without some degree of individual freedom and thus transcendence of the actual community, they hardly would have arrived at their message and remained loyal to this message in spite of opposition and persecution. Surely it is the creativity, vitality, and freedom of individuals over all

49

forms of social cohesion which makes history possible with its indeterminate possibilities both for new creative forms (Who would have thought that in our day Communist states in Eastern Europe would collapse into new forms of political arrangements?) and, unfortunately, for new destructive forces which result in the suffering and death of whole communities and millions of persons.

At the other extreme pole is the absolute individualism which ignores the importance of the social dimension of life and exalts individual self-sufficiency as the proper goal of life. There is, of course, no absolute freedom in history. We are all to a large extent conditioned by the communities in which we were reared and now live. As indicated above, the human community was a reality in primordial times. There was never a time when human beings were not social. The social character of human existence is a natural fact, and the individual is so related to the community that the actualization of his own individuality and fulfillment of his own life arises to a large extent out of the community. It was claimed above that the great prophets of Israel are an example of the capacity of the individual to transcend the community. Yet they did not emerge in a social vacuum. They were well aware of the beginnings of Israel under Moses, the periods of relative loyalty to the covenant, and the numerous lapses of the community from the purity of the covenant faith. The rise of such prophets in another community is simply inconceivable. It was from their understanding of the commitments made by the community in accepting the covenant with Yahweh, and from their understanding of what constituted faithfulness to the covenant, that they gained the vision which led them to attack the social evils in the actual community of their own times. Though Yahweh might speak to them directly, the social dimension of their messages had a grounding in the social dimension of the covenant.

Process thought has made us vividly aware of the organic and interrelated character of all reality, and, of course, this includes the individual's social relationships. Individuals are organically related to the community. They grow to be responsible persons capable of good and evil choices only in a social context, in interaction with others.

50

Social sanctions may provide for a certain stability and equity in society. However, given the fact that all human beings are both saints and sinners, every human community is infected with some degree of moral ambiguity, and thus, unfortunately, there are also sanctions which place a premium on conformity to customs and traditions which perpetuate gross social evils such as war, racial discrimination, economic injustices, and materialistic standards of sensuous self-indulgence. Often it seems to take modern day 'prophets,' persons of great moral insight and courage, grounded in deep religious commitment to a God of love and justice (Dr. Martin Luther King, for example), to motivate society to break out of the shackles of such conformity. Not only interrelatedness but also process is a characteristic of reality. On the human level, this means that individuals have some degree of freedom such that there is a measure of transcendence over the community and the total historical process without which progress would be impossible.

The dialectic of individualization and participation is then a characteristic feature of human life. There is a constant tension between these two poles. For both individual and community there is as it were a pendulum which tilts toward one pole or the other in varying degrees at varying times, but except in very extreme cases the opposite pole is never entirely obliterated. A healthy individual and a healthy community will seek to reduce the tension between these polar opposites and to establish as much harmony as possible between them. A healthy dialectical tension but also a relative harmony between individual and community is preserved best in that type of religious community in which there is a commitment to a transcendent God of love and justice who acts in history and who requires the practice of love and justice on the part of both individuals and community. Both individual transcendence over community and the social character of human existence are preserved in such a way that neither individual nor community becomes an idol, but rather both seek to become servants of God and humanity.

In the Christian view genuine understanding of self comes from beyond, from the vertical rather than the horizontal dimension. The

51

revelation of a transcendent but loving God awakens human beings to their capacity for freedom, for the transcendence of nature, history, society, and even self, and thus for indeterminate possibilities for good and for evil. This revelation (Word of God) witnessed to in the entire biblical testimony culminated conclusively in the life and teachings of Jesus of Nazareth in whom was disclosed the perfect *agape* (love) of God. In his life is found a model of what God intended human life to be. Here persons may see vividly displayed the indeterminate possibility for good in human life, but at the same time become vividly aware of how far short their own lives fall from measuring up to this model - that they are both saints and sinners (Christology and soteriology will be discussed more fully in later chapters).

It is in light of the incarnation that the doctrine of God creating human beings in his own image is most meaningful. Yet, even in light of the incarnation, the doctrine of the image of God in persons is meaningless if there is no human capacity for freedom of choice, for transcendence, for the uneasy conscience which accompanies the awareness that one could have chosen and acted better than one did in fact choose and act, and for the indeterminate possibility for good.

So understood, the doctrine has profound implications for individual life and for society. It can mean no less than that all individuals possess inalienable worth. If all human beings are ultimately related to God (by virtue of creation, if nothing else) who transcends human value and at the same time supports human value, then their worth is transcendent and inviolable. It is the widespread lack of the conviction that this is the case which has so greatly contributed to the gross inhumanity of our times as illustrated in so many ways not least of which were the Nazi gas chambers. If a person is considered to belong wholly to the nation, the party, the community, or whatever social group, then his worth is only that which he contributes to these entities. His worth and rights are easily sacrificed to the supposed good of these entities, and it becomes not unreasonable to use him, in Dostoevski's words, "to manure the soil for the future harmony."[3]

Whenever the transcendent element is eliminated and human beings are regarded only as unusually clever social animals, there are hardly any limits to restrict the oppression of individuals by socially organized groups, especially nations, and the violence of group against group. It must be admitted, of course, that the practice in so-called 'Christian' communities throughout history has often violated the implications of the doctrine of persons made in the image of God with even the church sometimes being the source of an oppression of individuals. Yet this doctrine has served as a leaven in society, motivating and supporting those movements seeking an increase in human rights, a greater degree of human freedom, and a greater sense of individual and social responsibility.

On the other hand, a genuine understanding of the full implications of the doctrine of *imago dei* would lead to a rejection of that rampant sort of individualism which today so often ends in what might be called a moral solipsism. In philosophical epistemology, solipsism is the view that there can be no knowledge of other minds (and in some extreme views, of any external reality) but only of one's own sensations and thoughts. What I am attempting to designate by using the term in the context of morals is extreme ethical relativity. Often people express this moral solipsism by saying, "Oh, if he or she thinks it right, then it's right for him or her, although I do not think it is right for me." The implication of such a view is that anything and everything is acceptable. Whatever the individual wants to do is justified simply because he wants to do it. There are no objective moral standards but only subjective wants and preferences. Again, if the individual is the measure of all things, then anything is acceptable, and there are no limits beyond the individual's ability to get what he wants. Other persons' legitimate needs, wants, and rights will be readily sacrificed if they stand in the way, or appear to stand in the way, of securing an aspired goal. Ironically, this solipsistic individualism and collectivisms often follow paths which merge in some sort of dictatorial absolutism of some sort of group in which individual desires and rights are ignored and gross social evils perpetrated.

It is the doctrine of the *imago dei*, especially when understood from the standpoint of the incarnation, which can keep individual and community in proper perspective and help to maintain that relative balance between individualization and participation so necessary for the health of individual and community.

4. Human Destiny

In the three sections above I have sought to establish the reasonableness and truth of the claim that there is a self, a 'private I', which is more than observable behavioral activity, and that the nature of this self, while determined by many causal conditions including the social and cultural, nevertheless possesses some degree of freedom of will. It is not that such freedom is absolute, for human beings are historical and social beings as well as private selves, and thus exist in a dialectical relationship of individualization and participation. In history, individuals and communities are morally ambiguous because human beings are both saints and sinners. Yet, in spite of horrendous evils, there has been some progress in history, and this would suggest that human beings have indeterminate possibility for good and for evil. From this it follows that persons have the capacity to transcend nature, community, history, and even the self as thus far formed. If this is the case, then it has profound implications with respect to the question of ultimate human destiny.

I will deal with the issue of eschatology more fully in a later chapter. However, I think it is appropriate here to indicate briefly what follows from the view of human nature discussed above for the question of human destiny. I think this may be made clear by giving attention to the stark contrast of the implications for human destiny which follow from positivism and deconstructionism with those which follow from the view of the self defended above.

If positivism and deconstructionism are correct, and there is no such thing as a centered self transcending physical characteristics, behavioral activity, and social programming, then everything ceases at physical death. The only sort of 'survival' which is logically possible on this view is a rather temporary type of what is often called "objective immortality," namely, the memory of the deceased in other minds, including the mind of God if the existence of God is accepted. But since for positivists and deconstructionists "God is dead," the only memory of the deceased is in the minds of a relatively few mortal human beings

54

(family and friends), and thus the 'survival' of the deceased is of short duration indeed. Soon the deceased is 'out of mind' and there is nothing. Obviously, on this view all has collapsed into the horizontal, and there is no transcendent or ultimate meaning to human life.

If there is no concept of an inalienable and transcendent human dignity, then it is easy for sensuous pleasure and materialistic success to become regarded as the sole value and goal of life. That this is the case in society today is amply illustrated in television advertising. But as some of the ancient Greek cynics and pessimists pointed out, for the mass of people the pain of unsatisfied desires predominates. Genuine pleasure is rarely attained, and even if it is, there is one certain thing about it, namely, that it will soon pass away. This causes pain, and given the other pains of life, life is hardly worth living. Indeed, it was claimed that the best thing that could happen would be never to be born at all and, next to that, to die as soon as possible after birth. Human life then is the ceaseless round of birth, struggle, pleasure, pain, and death; " a tale told by an idiot, full of sound and fury, signifying nothing." The only escape is to 'nothingness' by departing from the world either by severing all ties in some form of total meditation or by suicide.

To draw out the deleterious effects entailed by the positivists' and deconstructionists' view does not, of course, prove the contradictory belief that in each person there is a self, and that this self has the capacity to transcend nature, community, history, and death itself. Such beliefs can never receive the kind of corroboration by empirical evidence as do the laws of science. But what it does do is provide a pragmatic justification for accepting the latter belief rather than the former. If contradictory beliefs can be supported by rational arguments in which one side is somewhat stronger than the other or the two are roughly equal and one has harmful consequences and the other good results in terms of practical human morality and dignity, it would certainly be reasonable to accept the one producing good practical results. As William James argued, a world in which God and immortality are believed to be a part is a more livable and workable world than one from which they are excluded.

55

The argument was made in section one that linguistic and experiential considerations provide a more reasonable and stronger basis for the belief that there is a self than for the belief that there is not. While the definite description of the self given does not prove that this self is immortal in the subjective sense, it does make 'life' after death logically possible so that it is not absurd to believe it. Along with the pragmatic considerations just mentioned, it provides a rational basis for the belief in the self and immortality.

Sometimes as with Charles Hartshorne, a contemporary philosopher, the argument is advanced that even though there is a self with relative freedom it is still mortal in a subjective sense. This is the case because there could be no awareness of self identity without temporal limitations and immortal life is by definition without any such limitations. On this view there is only an objective immortality. There are no postmortem experiences, no postmortem self, for death is the last word of the last line on the last page in one's book of life. However, the entire story (experiences and thoughts) of one's life is stored up in the mind of a loving God. In this sense nothing is ever lost. While this may be true, and objective immortality is fine as far as it goes, there is no logical necessity to stop with it and reject the possibility of subjective immortality.

If there is a self with mental events which are not reducible to observable behavior and which transcend physical events, there is no logical impossibility for this self to survive the death of the body. It could (logical could) exist in a mind dependent realm in which it retained memories and similar mental propensities and personality it had in this life. Even though existence in a postmortem 'world' is unending, given the memories of existence in this physical world, of having grown up in a certain environment in which there was birth and death, there would hardly be an unawareness of that once one did not exist and thus was subject to temporal limitation. Would this not be sufficient for a sense of personal identity?

In a personal conversation, I once put this question to Professor Hartshorne, and he agreed that subjective immortality is not logically impossible. It would be logically possible for there to be memories which

56

made one aware of a temporal beginning and of limited knowledge sufficient for a sense of personal identity. However, he maintained that in light of what is known empirically about the mind's dependence on bodily functions, subjective immortality seems unlikely to be an actuality, and a stronger case can be made for objective immortality alone. Since in his consequent nature God experiences all events in the world both evil and good, the evil as lack and the good as a source of enjoyment, this experience includes the totality of everyone's life. So it is that everyone contributes to the divine pain and/or enjoyment. This certainly is an exalted view which lends further support to the notion of human dignity, that human beings may actually contribute to the enrichment of God's experience. Nothing good is ever lost for it is stored up as memory in the mind of God. It follows, then, that this view provides for a certain sense of permanency in the face of change and decay.

Yet if views of immortality (objective and subjective) are logically possible and there is some sort of pragmatic justification for both, it could be that a combination of elements from both would yield a stronger and more satisfying conception of immortality than either one alone.

Objective immortality alone leaves each person at death in precisely the stage of growth reached by that time. What one has become, one will always be as a memory in the experience of God. Obviously there is no possibility of rectifying any failings of this life, for there is no longer a self to have experiences or to change. Subjective immortality, as often presented in the history of Christian thought, views the postmortem state as one of ultimate degradation or perfection in which there is no more growth. If I remember correctly, Augustine claimed that at death the righteous miraculously become thirty years of age with full physical powers and spiritual fullness which they enjoy forever. In both cases the postmortem state is viewed as static, although in the latter there is some sort of experience. But does this represent any advance over the former? Surely in a state of <u>absolute perfection</u> there could not be an awareness or memory of any sort of limitation and thus no sense of self identity. There would be no sense of continuity with oneself in the pre-mortem state and no possibility of growth. Existence under such conditions would be dull indeed.

The most viable view of immortality both in terms of logical possibility and pragmatic justification would accommodate from the objective position the notion that the world is permanently enriched by the past, that God himself is enriched by the goodness of each person, and that goodness is never lost. At the same time, with the subjective view it would maintain that the experience which endures throughout life, namely the experience of being in the present, remembering the past, and anticipating the future, of continuity with oneself, can continue in a postmortem 'world.' Only the environment would have changed. In this 'world' many of the failings and difficulties of this life would be left behind due to the changed environment. Others would be overcome under the persuasive tutelage of a loving God. Growth in knowledge, fellowship, and enrichment of life could take place, and even if one attained the goal of an agapeistic spirit and fellowship, there still could be the progressive enrichment of experience as in the case with God's consequent nature.

Of course, we do not know empirically whether there is an immortal life or not or what it is like if there is such, but if it is the case, when we die we will know it by experiencing it. At that time we will be able to verify it. However, if it is not the case, we will never know it for it is logically impossible to experience ourselves having no experiences. Usually there is a symmetry between verification and falsification, but that is not the case here. On logical grounds the belief in an immortal life is somewhat stronger than its denial, for if is true, it is capable of verification, while the denial is not.

Granted that the arguments above are sound, it follows that the canons of reason do not prevent us from accepting a view of the afterlife in which there is continued growth of knowledge and love in fellowship with God and others, and that such a view is reinforced by a strong pragmatic justification.

5. Summary

In this chapter I have attempted to delineate arguments which would provide a rational basis in support of essential Christian claims

58

concerning human nature and destiny. I argued, against positivists and deconstructionists, that there is a self, that this self which has ties to nature and community nevertheless has sufficient freedom to transcend nature and all forms of social cohesion such that history is possible. The either/or of rugged individualism or social personality is a false dilemma which should be rejected in favor of keeping both individualization and participation in as much harmony as possible. Further, given the nature of the self, continued existence of the subject self after physical death is logically possible and pragmatically warranted.

In addition, it was argued that a genuine understanding of human nature and destiny requires an awareness of the Transcendent, of a loving and creator God, in light of whom human beings see themselves truly as saints and sinners, possessed of indeterminate possibilities for good and evil, and in partnership with whom they may augment the good and diminish the evil, thereby contributing to the enrichment of even God's experience as well as that of other human beings. This growth in grace in fellowship with God and others is unending.

Further, it was claimed that history provides stronger pragmatic justification for this view of human nature and destiny than for that of positivists, deconstructionists, and certain social theorists. Human dignity and rights cannot be provided with any lasting sanctions on the basis of these horizontal positions. The doctrines of *Imago Dei* (transcendence of self and relation to the Transcendent) and of immortality do entail such sanctions. A world in which self, freedom, immortality, and a loving God are accepted as at least leading principles does tend to be one in which there is a greater degree of individual moral excellence and of social justice and harmony, to be a more livable and workable world, than one in which these principles are lacking or minimized.

The Christian understanding of human nature and destiny may be supported then by giving attention to experiential, logical, and pragmatic considerations. Such considerations provide a rational warrant of confidence in the actuality of that which is claimed to be the case.

Several times in the preceding discussion claims have been made to the effect that the conviction that there is a loving God who is both transcendent and immanent is a necessary ingredient for a genuine understanding of the self, its existence, nature, and destiny. However, the existence, loving nature, and activity of God were simply assumed. Can this assumption be supported rationally? Probably no one ever comes to a theistic faith by way of rational arguments alone, and probably there is always a leap of faith (trust). But does it follow that faith must be simply blind? Is it possible, as Anselm believed, for faith to gain understanding? This issue will be dealt with in the next chapter on God.

---

[1] London: Hutchinson, 1949 pp. 15-16.

[2] Dallas M. High, editor (Oxford University Press, 1969), pages 127-37.

[3] *The Brothers Karamazov*, Random House, Modern Library, p.300.

CHAPTER THREE
GOD

It is with considerable hesitation and humility that I approach the subject of God. Certainly there is neither a more difficult nor a more fundamental issue with which a theologian must deal. Others have dealt with this topic much more profoundly than I am capable of doing, but since this treatise is an attempt to put my theological reflections into some kind of comprehensive order, I cannot avoid this topic no matter how difficult it may be. Furthermore, I argued in the previous discussion on human nature that a thorough understanding of the self was dependent on being understood from beyond, that is, by God. The issue of God, then, is not an isolated topic, but is closely correlated with the issue of the nature and destiny of the self and also for this reason may not be avoided. In this discussion I shall attempt to deal with issues such as the terminological; the existence, nature, and revelation of God; his providential activity and the problem of evil

1. The Terminological Issue

I suspect that there is no word which throughout the ages has been so misused and abused as the word 'God.' Throughout the ages, and even today, we humans have drawn wretched caricatures and labeled them with the word 'God.' We have slaughtered and are still slaughtering each other and saying, "In God's Name." We perpetrate hatred and injustice and are convinced that we have divine authorization for such hatred and injustice. God, of course, is on our side whatever it may be and however much suffering it may cause in the world. We seek to learn of his 'will' only for the purpose of his preserving us and our group. Even when misfortune strikes we believe that this 'will of God' will bring us some unexpected good in the future.

A few years ago in a very conservative religious community after several days of rain a dam burst and several people living in homes below the dam were killed. A statement heard from some survivors was, "We don't understand it now, but we must accept God's will." Several things can be said about this statement and the attitude it represents.

61

For one thing, it suggests a rather primitive notion of God as a sort of ancient potentate who dispenses his favors or his punishments rather arbitrarily according to his own pleasure as he is appeased or displeased. Any failure to learn and to practice the 'right' belief system and/or ceremonies can bring harsh punishments of various kinds. Secondly, it could imply a kind of predestinarianism which can only be identified as a divine fatalism. That is, whatever happens God directly wills it. While those conservatives who take such a stance do not recognize or at least acknowledge it, this entails that God is as responsible for evil in the world as he is for good. These conservatives do talk much about the devil but the logic of their position makes the devil superfluous since God performs the devil's functions or has the devil as a kind of subordinate agent.

A third possible implication of the statement is based on a rather common human tendency to separate the sheep from the goats. Those who died in the flood had committed some sort of sin, perhaps covertly, which had incurred the wrath of God. This reflects the old retribution dogma. Indeed, it is as old as the biblical book of Job in which the 'friends' of Job, in spite of his protestations of innocence, insist that his suffering is a result of sin. There are two fallacies here. One is known as *post hoc ergo propter hoc* and is the assumption that if one thing follows another in time, there must be a causal relation between the two; and the other is the fallacy of <u>affirming the consequent.</u> Sin causes suffering. There is suffering. Therefore there is sin. This fallacy can be made obvious by the following example: Whenever it has rained the streets are wet. The streets are wet. Therefore it has been raining. But the streets may be wet from a number of other causes such as a broken water main. So suffering does not necessarily imply sin. It may be the result of mere chance events or the sinful deeds of other people, and there are all too many examples of this in history (the holocaust in Nazi Germany; the bombing of innocence civilians in modern warfare, to mention but two examples). In a certain sense, of course, we are all sinners, and there are some sins which <u>obviously</u> cause suffering for ourselves and often for others, but just because one is suffering it does not follow that one necessarily has sinned, at least not to such an extent

62

as to <u>deserve</u> the suffering. Thus, Job insisted on his innocence and rejected the retribution dogma. It is rather strange that today it is often the so-called Bible believing Christians who espouse the retribution dogma in very much the same terms as the friends of Job. They fail to identify with the main character of the book who insisted that often the wicked prosper and the righteous suffer. In the end Job does not arrive at a rationalized solution for the problem of evil but does come to the conclusion that though one suffers, he may still have God as a friend.

A fourth implication of the statement assigning the flood to the will of God was that those who affirmed this were seeking to avoid assigning any human responsibility for this event. According to news reports, officials in the community had been warned that the dam was in need of repair but had failed to have the necessary work done such that the dam would hold up when there was a large amount of rain. It is so often the case that we "pass the buck" to God. It is well known that the late President Harry Truman had a sign on his desk which read, "the buck stops here." For many the "buck" stops with God. Human responsibility is rationalized away by being placed on the 'shoulders' of God.

Some years ago, Dietrich Bonhoeffer, the young German theologian martyred by the Nazis, in his *Letters And Papers From Prison*[1] wondered how it would be possible to speak of God in meaningful ways in the modern world and insisted that the view just described was totally inadequate for the task. This God is a *Deus ex Machina*, a kind of glorified 'bell hop' who is called in to do for us what we want done; that is, to defend us, to solve the problems which we will not or cannot solve for ourselves, and who is then blamed if they are not solved.

At the other end of the spectrum are those anti-religious people who tend to treat the caricature of God, explicitly stated or at least implied, in the theologies of some radically fundamentalists groups as if it were truly descriptive of the divine reality. They take this as a more than sufficient reason for viewing the notion of God as nonsensical and belief in his existence as irrational. In this way they set up a 'straw man' who is easy to knock over. It is a kind of shifting ground technique in which one avoids the difficult task of dealing with the many profound and rational expositions concerning the being and nature of God which have appeared in both philosophy and theology. Furthermore, it tends to reinforce in the popular understanding the notion that the only possible conception of God is the wretched caricature and abuse of the divine name held by some radical fundamentalists. Such a caricature should be rejected, not on the basis that there is not a divine reality but on the grounds that his nature is quite different. I must admit that were I forced to choose (which I am not) between the caricature of the extreme religious right and the type of 'atheism' propounded by someone like Ludwig Feuerbach, the nineteenth century German philosopher, I would prefer the latter. Even though there is no transcendent ontological reality in his understanding of God who is simply a personification and at large projection of the highest human ideals, at least his God is totally good and loving. However, I am convinced that we are not limited to these alternative views, but that it is possible to provide rational grounds justifying the belief that God both actually exists as a definite and distinct being and is totally good and loving.

Just as with some of the more recent deconstructionists, it appears that Feuerbach wished to retain the word 'God' because of its symbolic value and emotional appeal even though it had no referent other than the highest human ideals. Some deconstructionists tend to be less clear than Feuerbach in their claims that 'God' is symbolic of a symbolic construct or useful fiction[2] (although it is not all that clear just what this symbolic construct or useful fiction is). In any case, it is created by human beings and has no other referential meaning than the fictional. Of course, this is one way to respond to the earlier logical empiricist philosophers who claimed that the sentence "There is a God" has no cognitive meaning because it is logically impossible to verify or falsify this claim. Obviously, one can verify or falsify that there is or is not a symbolic construct or highest human ideals which some thinkers call 'God.' But in this case cognitive meaning for 'God' is preserved at the high cost of a radical departure from the common usage meaning of the term.

It is quite clear that both designations for 'God' (symbolic construct and highest human ideals) are "out of whole cloth," a total

64

departure from the common usage in Western culture and thus arbitrary stipulative definitions. They actually make mortal human beings the measure of all things. History and our own experience provide abundant evidence that this represents a too optimistic view of human nature precisely because it is insufficiently dialectical. Humanity has formulated high ideals and symbolic constructs but the way in which persons perceive these ideals and constructs is always tainted with self-interest. Furthermore, whenever human beings act, even if they claim it is in terms of noble ideals, that act is tainted with sin. If nothing else, there is the awareness that it is their act, and thus the pride of virtue raises its ugly head. If 'God' is only man spoken of with a loud voice (Barth), then this God is caught in mortality and in the dialectic of being both saint and sinner. This was a major problem in the popular understanding in early Greek religion of the gods on Mt. Olympus. They were all too human and so failed to survive as objects of worship.

Just as the extreme fundamentalist view of God's nature seems to me to be a caricature, so also I think the stipulative definitions of 'God' offered by Feuerbach and the deconstructionists entail a caricature in that they eliminate from the <u>designation</u> of the word certain defining characteristics which the word has in common usage such as infinity, necessity, supernatural, supremely worthy of worship, etc. In their view, then, 'God' as generally understood in Western culture turns out to be a fiction, a fantasy. Even though we are free to stipulate as long as we indicate what we are doing, it is <u>generally</u> preferable in our discussions of issues (theistic as well as others) to follow common usage as much as possible. Sometimes, of course, we may need to stipulate because the word in question is employed in common usage in such a vague and indefinite way that we wish to indicate a more precise meaning. Sometimes words in common usage such as class words which designate more than one class of things may be used ambiguously, such that it is impossible to tell from the context which one of the several classes of things is being talked about. Then we need to stipulate the precise designation we are employing. It is to be noted, however, that in these cases we have not stipulated an *ad hoc* meaning

65

ex nihilo as did Feuerbach and the deconstructionists. We have not come up with some entirely new meaning but actually are dependent on a common usage base. That is, the stipulation simply delimits and/or modifies common usage in order to make more precise the sense of the term being employed.

The word 'God,' and its equivalents in other languages, has through the ages been assigned a plethora of meanings. In very early times there was an abundance of departmental gods in the various polytheistic pantheons. In some cases, however, a tribe or ethnic group became henotheists in that the tribe or ethnic group settled on one god to be exclusively worshipped by the group even though the reality of the gods of other peoples was recognized. In Greek philosophical thought there emerged the notion of the ultimate as one and beyond contingency and change (Plato and Aristotle) and the pantheistic monism of the Stoics in which everything in the world and its sum total is god. All these views contrast sharply with the ethical monotheism which emerged in the early Hebraic perspective.

Polytheism entails a pluralistic view of reality in which everything in nature and every aspect of life is sacred to some god or other. In Pantheism, too, every single thing is sacred, not because it is sacred to some deity or other but because it is permeated by the One, the divine. That is, everything is God. God alone is genuine reality. Differences and multiplicity are only appearances, not reality. This is a strictly monistic view in contrast to the pluralism of Polytheism. In Hinduism there was some attempt to combine the two by viewing the gods of popular religion as expressing various aspects of the ultimate one neuter spirit which permeates everything. In the dualisms of Plato and Aristotle the ultimate is understood, very much as in Hinduism, to be the eternal One, but unlike Hinduism the world to some extent exists in its own right since it is made up of uncreated matter which has had forms imposed upon it by the demiurge or lured into forms by the perfection of the unmoved mover so that the actual world comes into being. But matter can resist the forms through inertia or opposition and this resistance is the source of evil in the world.

The ethical monotheism of the Judeo-Christian tradition stands in contrast to all of the above. With some exceptions it seeks to affirm the reality of everything in the external order, not as sacred or permeated by the divine or as containing the source of evil in matter, but as the creative 'handiwork' of the one all loving, all good, all powerful personal deity. There is at least a certain epistemic 'distance' between God and the world. In a sense and to an extent the world exists in its own right. But since it is God's creation, it is good. It may be misused and abused by human beings, but in itself it is good and should be treated with respect. Moreover, unlike the unmoved mover of Aristotle or the absentee deity of the deists in the early modern period, this creator God is not absent but remains active in the world in ways which do not destroy the freedoms of his creatures.

It should be obvious by now that in spite of its abuse and misuse I intend with some modifications to use the term 'God' in our discussion to designate that which traditionally in Western culture it has been used to designate. That is, I take 'God' to refer to that supreme personal necessary Being - distinct from and creator of the world - who is supremely worthy of worship and who possesses the attributes of omnibenevolence, omniscience, and omnipotence. Some modification of the traditional meanings assigned the last two attributes will be necessary but not such as to totally change their meanings.

Sometimes confusion arises in theological discourse due to the failure to make the simple distinction between designation and denotation. The former has to do with meaning; the latter with the actual things included in the designation. For some 'God' is an empty class, having a designation but no denotation. So an atheist may use the term such that it has the same meaning as when used by a theist, but he will deny that it has a referent. When that happens the atheist and theist are talking about the same thing, though they differ as to its existence.

On the other hand, there are those who claim that 'God' functions only as a proper name and proper names denote but do not designate (have definitions). So 'God' denotes an individual for whom a definite description can be given just as a definite description can be given of

Robert Ayers. The difficulty with this approach is that the definite descriptions of persons and objects in this world having proper names can be or have been checked by actual empirical observation so that two persons using the name Robert Ayers can be assured that they are talking about the same person. This process is not possible with God since, as the Fourth Evangelist (Gospel of John) proclaims, "No one has ever seen God." In the interest of clarity, it seems preferable to determine the meaning of the term before proceeding to a discussion of existence, for we want to know just what it is the existence of which we are seeking to establish.

I have been attempting to specify certain defining characteristics included in the designation of 'God' as generally used in Western culture. Defining characteristics have to do with the meaning of the word in question in contrast with accompanying characteristics which are descriptive of _facts_ about whatever is named by the word. It may be said that the _specific_ acts of God in revelation are accompanying characteristics, but that necessity, transcendence, supreme worth, creator, and personal are defining characteristics. These, I think, are generally included in the meaning of the word 'God' in Western culture.

Some support for this claim might be found in an analysis of the five ways of St. Thomas Aquinas. My former colleague, the late Anthony Nemetz, in his graduate seminar on Aquinas used to insist that Aquinas' ending of each of the ways with some such expression as "to which everyone gives the name God" or "this all men speak of as God" has not been taken seriously enough by interpreters. In Nemetz's judgment these closing statements were not simply a matter of convention but indicated that a major purpose of Thomas in the five ways was to locate 'God' "on the map of signification." In other words, Thomas was more concerned with meaning than with proof. Whatever may have been Thomas' major intention, and whether or not the ways are successful as proofs, it is nevertheless the case that they do indicate essential defining characteristics for the word 'God.' The first two ways actually constitute an argument from the nature of causality and the fifth from the evidence of design in the world. Both entail God as creator. The third argues that contingent things could not exist without an

68

ultimate <u>necessary being</u> who is not subject to the process of contingency. And the fourth argues from degrees of perfection to perfection. In these five ways, then, we have explicitly stated or implied the defining characteristics of creator which entails supreme knowledge and power, of necessary being which entails transcendence, and of perfection which entails supreme goodness and love which in turn entails personal being.

2. The Existence, Nature, and Revelation of God

More difficult than the issue of the meaning of the term 'God' is the question of whether or not 'God' as defined has a referent or is instantiated. I have put the question this way in order to avoid the temptation of treating existence as though it were a predicate. In terms of strict logic it is an impropriety to ask, "Does God exist?" However, in popular discourse it is common to talk about the existence of God, and I will continue to use this expression as a shorthand way of saying, "There is an x such that x is God."

It is well known that the late Paul Tillich claimed it to be theologically improper to raise the question of God's existence. In his view it is as atheistic to affirm the existence of God as it is to deny it.[3] This is because as "ground of being" or "being-itself" God is above existence (and essence) and the term 'existence' can be applied only to things within the created realm. God is not <u>a</u> being alongside of other beings in the universe. But Tillich's designation of God as ground of being or being-itself is fraught with difficulties not least of which is that it actually sets up a limiting point about which nothing can be said. As such God is ineffable and this entails that the fundamental statements in theology signify nothing. Furthermore, while we may grant that God is not a being alongside of others in the universe, we still want to know whether <u>there is</u> or <u>is not</u> an ultimate personal reality which (who) is not a <u>part</u> of the universe, is its creator, and is one in whom we may trust. Given this, I find no compelling reason to abandon the more popular expression. In using the expression, "the existence of God," I am not making existence into a predicate or talking about a being alongside of others in the universe. But I am raising the question as to whether God as defined is actual or not.

69

Protestant fundamentalists and the Neo-Orthodox disciples of Karl Barth also deem it theologically improper to rationally consider the question of God's existence but on grounds quite different from those of Tillich. Both hold that sinful man is incapable on his own of arriving at any genuine knowledge of God. For the fundamentalist it is totally a matter of faith based on the inerrancy of Scripture. If one is asked if he believes there is a God, the answer might well be, "I just do" and "The Bible tells me so." Expressed here is the dubious notion that faith, belief in or trust, is sufficient to warrant the belief that the object of the faith exists. But this simply won't do. Very small children believe in fairy godmothers and believe that they exist because they have not as yet come to distinguish fantasy from actuality. But for an adult it is surely a necessary condition that a person, Jones, exists before one can sensibly say, "I believe in Jones." Similarly with respect to belief in God. It is reasonable to trust him if he exists, but it makes no sense to claim that he exists because one trusts him. Instead, we need reasons for thinking that he does in fact exist.

For Barth the revelation of God in his word, Jesus Christ, provides knowledge (belief that) and grounds for trust (belief in). There can be no other reason for thinking that God exists, because man as such has no capacity to know God. The knowledge of God's existence, life, and action comes totally from above, by revelation. Any attempt to give reasons for the existence of God (other than revelation) or to seek for proofs is at best fruitless and at worst almost an impious and atheistic enterprise. God can be known only through himself, in his own revelation. So Barth ruled out any natural theology because he felt that this elevated sinful human reason above the 'Word of God' and tended to distort it.[4] He sought to isolate the Christian message from the disciplines of culture and coherences of life, ignoring the results of science as though they did not exist.

Yet, if God is actively present in the whole of human life and in all persons, as Barth's theology of the Word affirms, then surely persons, apart from the acceptance of the Word, have some capacity to gain some knowledge of God. Then, too, if God is the creator of our universe, surely there are some hints or indications of him in the created order. I find no compelling reason to conclude that the insights gained from the whole of human life and from the created order must of necessity distort or be in competition with the conclusive revelation of God in Jesus Christ. Indeed, these insights can provide us with a preunderstanding (Bultmann) or preparatory relation to, and in part confirmation of, that revelation. A natural theology <u>may</u> provide good arguments for affirming the existence of God without in any way being inconsistent with or detracting from the fullness of God's revelation. Surely, faith is strengthened if <u>good reasons</u> can be given for believing that the object of the faith does in fact exist.

A fundamental question, then, is can we give good reasons for the belief that the word 'God' has a referent, that God does in fact exist. In the history of Western thought several cogent arguments have been formulated both for and against the claim that God exists. None of the so-called proofs have been granted universally the apodictic certainty of a mathematical formula or the practical certainty of laws of nature such as the law of gravity. Undoubtedly, after we have done all we are capable of intellectually with respect to this question, there will remain a residue of mystery. What else should we expect, given God as a transcendent, infinite, creator being? The otherness of God is surely not as absolute as in Barthian Neo-Orthodoxy, yet it is true that the finite and fallible human mind cannot on its own grasp the <u>fullness</u> of God's being, of his evaluations of the world. But mystery is not the whole story, for there is meaning as well. What else should we expect, given God as creator? There is order and meaning in nature and human life. Human reason is not so corrupt and blind as not to be able to construct rational arguments which even though they do not provide knowledge of God's intentions and evaluations and are not all equally convincing, nevertheless support the claim that God exists. These arguments may never convince the skeptical unbeliever, but at least they provide the believer with a rational and intelligible <u>basis</u> for his faith. As I pointed out above, "belief in" makes no sense, is indeed absurd, unless there are good grounds, reasons, for "belief that."

I have indicated that some have viewed Aquinas' five ways as dealing primarily with the signification of the word 'God.' Here I am

71

concerned with appraising them in terms of their cogency as arguments. The first three - from motion to first mover, from efficient cause to uncaused cause, from contingency to necessity - are generally designated the cosmological argument. These, along with the argument from degrees of perfection to perfection and the teleological or design argument, begin with what is experienced in the world - causes, motion (or change), contingency, relative goodness, and order or design - and move from these types of experiences to God. The five ways as stated in the *Summa Theologica*, especially the first three, appear to require the premise of the impossibility of an infinite regress in time, that the world could not have always existed. As is well known, Immanuel Kant demonstrated that equally valid arguments could be given in support of the claim that the world is eternal and the claim that it is not eternal. Thus they cancel out each other. Also he argued that from contingent effects only contingent causes can be legitimately inferred, but that the cosmological arguments commit the fallacy of a transcendental leap. With respect to the design argument, Kant claimed that from the presence of disorder as well as order in the world, the only inference that could be drawn was that the designer was a rather poor architect.

While Aquinas' first three ways (the cosmological argument) seem to depend on the impossibility of a temporal infinite regress, in the larger context of Aquinas' thought this is not the case. As the later Kant, Aquinas admitted that <u>philosophically</u> sound arguments could be formulated in support of the claim that the world exists eternally (although he accepts creation as a revealed dogma). The cosmological ways do not depend on the impossibility of an 'horizontal' infinite regress but of a 'vertical' one. That is, they do not seek to prove the existence of a being who is first in the temporal series but of one who is first in the order of being, which is to say first ontologically. Without such the universe would have no ground, conditions, or reason for being, no ultimate meaning or explanation.

I think the strongest defense of the cosmological argument rests on this approach. It is not unlike the way in which explanation is understood in the sciences. In science an event or process is said to be explained when it is brought under a law. That is, the statement of the thing to be explained is logically deducible from the statements giving the explanation, at least one of which must be a universal descriptive law. For example, if we ask why the water in a pot is boiling, that event can be explained with the following syllogism:

All water boils at 212 degrees Fahrenheit at sea level pressure. This pot of water has been heated to above 212 degrees Fahrenheit. Therefore this pot of water is boiling.

This example, of course, is rather simple and limited. The scientist seeks to bring the largest range of events possible under one law with the largest possible predictive value. Further, he seeks to bring not only events and processes under laws but also laws of lesser generality under laws of greater generality such that laws, too, are explained. That is, a law is explained in terms of another law or laws, and this in terms of others, and so on. At some point the stage is reached when the laws providing the explanation cannot themselves be explained by others. They appear to be ultimate. In the development of science through the ages, laws thought to be ultimate were later found to be explained in terms of laws of greater generality. So Newton's law of gravity with its enormous explanatory power was thought for ages to be ultimate, but now it is thought that it in turn can be explained in terms of a space-time curvature formed by all the matter in the universe (whatever that means). Yet just as we cannot go on forever deducing one statement from another but must at some point arrive at fundamental laws of logic which cannot be deduced from other laws, so in scientific explanation there cannot be an infinite regress of explanations, a forever explaining of laws by bringing them under other laws. At some point we will get to rock bottom, to laws which are ultimate and in light of which the world of nature is seen to be basically intelligible.

So whether intended by Aquinas or not, the cosmological argument can be formulated in terms of explanation, namely, that if the universe is to make sense, explanations cannot go on to infinity. There must be an ultimate and self-existent being whose existence constitutes the ultimate explanation of the whole. Without this the universe is

73

unintelligible brute fact. There is no logical <u>necessity</u> to accept either horn of this dilemma. Neither the claim that there is an ultimate explanation of the whole in a self-existing God nor the claim that the universe is unintelligible brute fact is an irrational claim. However, there is a stronger pragmatic justification for accepting the former rather than the latter. Surely the latter entails the very real possibility of license in the treatment of the natural environment, of an extreme ethical relativism, and of a nihilistic attitude toward life in which it is regarded as "a tale told by an idiot, full of sound and fury, signifying nothing."

While the cosmological argument does not make the conclusion that there is a God a logically necessary one, it does provide us with a rational support for the belief <u>that</u> God exists. It does not, of course, stand alone. It can be reinforced by other arguments such as the other two of Aquinas' ways, the teleological and axiological, and the famous ontological argument, first proposed by St. Anselm and revived by some thinkers in our own times.

It is well known that Immanuel Kant, even though he pointed out the flaws of the teleological argument as a strict proof, nevertheless proclaimed that it should always be treated with respect. I think that modern knowledge concerning the long sweep of evolutionary development simply adds to the feeling of respect for this argument. Some formulations, most notably that of William Paley, the 18th century Anglican divine, are too weak to be taken seriously. Paley argued that since from the design and working of a watch one could infer the existence of a watch maker, from the intricate designs found in nature (such as the eye) one can infer the existence of a designer of the universe. But this is an argument from analogy, and such arguments, however compelling the imagery may be, are logically invalid. Empirically, arguments from analogy carry some force if the items compared are very similar. But surely this is not the case with respect to a watch and the universe. The universe is not especially like a machine. It can as easily be compared to an organism. Furthermore, we know that watches are made by watch makers from common human experience. But no one has ever observed a God designing a universe.

74

We can observe watch makers making watches and do not need to infer from the intricate design to a maker. While the universe does display some order and pattern, we have not observed God making it as we have observed watch makers making watches.

Fortunately, we are not limited to the Paley type of formulation. The fact of evolutionary development, as indicated above, can provide the basis for a much stronger argument. Today, explications of evolutionary development in the universe are not limited to Darwinian formulations. It is held that cooperation as well as competition in the struggle for survival is important in the evolutionary process. Furthermore, 'design' may be applied to the whole evolutionary process such that the over-all history of nature may be understood in purposeful terms, the end result of which is the emergence of mind and personality. New creative forces occur both in nature and in human history. As argued in chapter two, this requires both order and freedom. If everything were totally determined by prior events, there simply would be the continual succession of the same events, and nothing new could occur. If everything were totally indeterminate random events, nothing could be sustained, not even new events. Some degree of freedom in order or order in freedom at all levels of nature (non-human as well as human) is a necessary condition for change and for the emergence of mind and personality. Yet from both order and freedom, difficulties, struggles, and evils arise as by-products (evil and theodicy will be discussed more fully later). But the point here is that both freedom and order in our world is what one would expect from a God who works by persuasion rather than compulsion to lead creatures to ever higher levels of existence.

If the universe is unintelligible brute fact, and only random natural selection the final word on evolution, how can one account for the emergence of those human artistic, musical, and ethical capacities which contribute little or nothing to survival? It surely strains one's credulity that all of this could have arisen out of brute fact or by random selection. In view of the fact that there is an immense range of possible universes, it does not seem plausible that brute fact and random selection can adequately account for the circumscribed range conducive to the rise of life and conscious intelligent beings capable of artistic, moral, and spiritual achievements and of entering into moral relations with others. It would seem more reasonable to conclude that an ultimate intelligent being patiently directed and persuaded the development of complex structures and functions in the environment such that the emergence of physical life in its developing forms and of human intellectual, artistic, and moral capabilities became possible. This does not prove conclusively that there is a God, but it does add further support to the rational grounds for the belief that he does in fact exist.

Among Aquinas' five ways, the fourth is an axiological argument. It rests on the gradation to be found in things and on the fact that we make comparative judgments with respect to goodness and truth. In order for us to make judgments concerning <u>degrees</u> of truth or goodness in the things in the natural order, we need some concept, however vague, of a maximum standard of perfection. We say that x is more probably true than y and that sunset x is more beautiful than sunset y in terms of some prior standards, and in the latter case, at least, this implies an ultimate standard of perfection.

There are those who argue that the claim concerning comparative moral judgments entailing a prior ultimate standard which in turn entails God is simply begging-the-question. The prior standards could very well be some sort of naturalistic features. In the first place, there are those who claim that values arise only out of human needs and interests, individual or communal, and are solely relative and subjective. There are no such things as objective values within the structure of reality and grounded in a transcendent being. But to deny the existence of objective values has some rather strange consequences. If the claim that x is good means no more than that I have positive feelings about x, it is impossible for me ever to be mistaken in making moral judgments (which is most certainly not the case as I know very well from personal experience). Further, since my feelings fluctuate, I would have little or no consistency in my value judgments and moral actions. That is, x would be considered good on one occasion and bad on another, depending on how I felt about x at the time. Finally, no two people could be sure that they meant the same thing by an identical value statement since the subjective feelings of people vary greatly. Ethical discourse would become confusing and break down which, to a very large extent, it has done today.

There are some who attempt to base the standard for value judgments in the community, arguing that the mores of ethnic, cultural, and national groupings serve to determine morals and values. The consequences of such a position is that there are no international standards of morals which all groupings and/or nations are obliged to accept, and decisions of the International Court of Justice often carry little weight. Recent history provides numerous examples of the brutal and atrocious acts committed by groups and/or nations which regarded themselves and their communal ambitions as of ultimate value and subject to no higher authority.

In the second place, critics of the moral argument claim that even if there are objective values which transcend individual and communal needs and interests, they do not necessarily entail a source in a divine being. It could be (logical could) that this is simply the way reality is; that cooperation and the values entailed thereby has played as large, if not larger, a role in evolutionary development as has the competition for survival. In response it might be pointed out that even though there is some cooperation in the animal kingdom and a kinship between human beings and animals such that the difference between them is more a matter of degree than of kind, it is still the case that animals have not reached the heights of artistic, moral, and intellectual capacity of human beings. But if evolutionary development is a purposeless naturalistic process, why have not animals developed the same capacities as human beings? Is this something to come in the far distant future if the world survives so long? Perhaps this would be a better world if dolphins emerged from the oceans and ruled the world! In any case, animals have not as yet developed the same capacities as humans. Of course, such capacity makes greater the potential for evil as well as for good. Yet it seems reasonable to suppose that the greater potential for good, for making moral judgments, cannot be adequately

77

accounted for on a purely naturalistic basis, but requires a purpose directed process.

Just as with the other arguments, we do not have here an incontrovertible proof of God's existence. Yet it does seem reasonable, as Immanuel Kant argued, to postulate the existence of God as one of the three necessary assumptions (freedom and immortality are the other two) of the moral life. It is a presupposition of anyone who accepts duty (the categorical imperative of treating others as ends, never as means) as an unconditional moral obligation. Surely an unconditional moral obligation cannot have its source in contingent and conditional beings, objects, and worlds. It requires an unconditional and thus transcendent source and as Aquinas put it, "and this we call God."

I think that these arguments, cosmological, teleological, and axiological, are not incompatible, but reinforce one another. Furthermore, as I will attempt to show, I think they are compatible with and are reinforced by the ontological argument, at least as it is formulated by some modern exponents. Even some opponents of the arguments have acknowledged that the cosmological, teleological, and axiological presuppose the so-called ontological argument for God as a necessary and perfect being. Kant claimed that what he called the physico-theological (design or teleological) argument must fall back on the cosmological and that the latter is only a disguised ontological argument. Here he probably had in mind one of Aquinas' versions of the cosmological argument in which he concluded that for contingent things to exist there must be a non-contingent or necessary being as the source and sustainer of this contingent world and its contingent things which come into existence and pass out of existence. But in Kant's view this is to make an illicit transcendental leap. In the world effects and causes are commensurate, and an unconditional, non-contingent, necessary cause cannot be deduced from contingent effects. The ontological argument avoids this problem, but Kant thought that it, at least in its Descartes' version, did not work either, and that it multiplied the difficulties contained in the cosmological and teleological.

It is rather obvious that the axiological argument can be reinforced by a valid ontological argument for God as an unconditional

78

being. It does not seem plausible that unconditional moral obligations (granted that there are such) find their source in the contingent and conditional. Instead, they require an unconditional source. As we have seen, even Kant argued that practical reason is justified in postulating the existence of God as one of the necessary bases of the categorical imperative on which the moral life rests. But is it possible for the existence of God to be something more than an assumption necessary for a particular proof? Is it possible for it to be a reasonable conclusion? Those who support the ontological argument seek to analyze it carefully and to justify what is claimed to be its strongest version as a sound argument for the existence of God.

Although there may have been some forerunners (Augustine's definition of God), the ontological argument was first explicitly formulated in the eleventh century by St. Anselm in his *Proslogion*, chapters two and three. In the preface, Anselm clearly indicates that in his contemplation of God, he is seeking to understand what he believes; that is, he is involved in a process of faith seeking understanding. In this musing he is seeking a rational exfoliation of the faith, and central in this task is the issue of God's existence. Since this is a musing, a process of deep thinking, it is not surprising that there is a development in the argument with chapter two representing a kind of first step which is superseded by a stronger case made in chapter three.

In chapter two Anselm begins by affirming his belief that God is to be understood as something than which nothing greater can be conceived and by claiming that even a fool can understand such a statement. But something than which nothing greater can be conceived cannot be a matter of understanding only, for it could be understood as existing in reality as well, and this would be greater. Thus this would result in a contradiction and be impossible.

This version of Anselm's argument fails as has been pointed out by so many, including Gaunilo (Anselm's contemporary), Aquinas, Kant, and others. It simply does not follow that a definition, however proper, is sufficient to demonstrate existence in reality as well as in idea. If it were, we could find referents for centaurs, perfect islands, and so on. In Kant's well-known expression, existence is not a predicate. We can attribute many predicates to centaurs such as a man's head, trunk, and arms, and a horse's body and legs, but surely existence is not included in these predicates. We can even draw pictures of centaurs, but certainly there are no referents for these pictures in the actual world.

But Anselm could say (and did say in chapter three and to Gaunilo) that the conception of God, unlike perfect islands and centaurs, represents a special case, namely, that it is impossible to conceive of God as not existing and that this is greater than something which can be conceived not to exist. In other words, a being who is unsurpassable, one than which a greater cannot be conceived, necessarily exists. It would be contradictory to affirm that there is any possibility that such a being not exist. At least two philosophers (Charles Hartshorne and Norman Malcolm) have argued that while normally existence is a not predicate, necessary existence is.[5] In existence claims concerning contingently existing things, existence is not a predicate, but here is a special case since it is necessary existence which is affirmed. In Hartshorne's *Anselm's Discovery* (Open Court, 1965) it is the modalities of existence (contingent, impossible, necessary) rather than existence which are taken to be predicates. Since the modality of necessity is defining of God, non-existence and contingent existence cannot be affirmed of him without a contradiction. Only his existence is conceivable; non-existence and contingent existence cannot be affirmed.

This position has sometimes been attacked on the grounds that the necessity involved does not have to do with the logical necessity of 'God exists' but with the logical necessity of his always remaining in existence if he exists. That is, by definition God is eternal and so if he exists, he has always and will always exist. It is in this context that it makes sense to speak of God's necessary existence. But does not the conditional contradict Anselm's notion that it is impossible to conceive of God as not existing? Is not the claim that if God exists (surely the conditional includes the Possibility that he may not), then he exists necessarily a contradictory claim? In effect this is to say that the existence of God is both contingent and necessary and these are contradictory terms. If God's existence is necessary, then it is logically impossible for him not to exist. He cannot not be!

Another assault on this position was broached by the so-called logical positivists of a few years ago when they claimed that necessity had to do only with statements, with the equivalence of symbols, and so were devoid of factual content. They provide information only about our human linguistic conventions and tell us nothing about the external world. Everyone would agree that necessary statements are those concerning which no particular occurrences or events would be considered relevant to the determination of their truth or falsity because the logical rules and definitions are sufficient in determining their truth values. But does it follow from this that necessary statements assert something only about terms rather than about extralinguistic entities, that the meanings of the conclusions of inferences are contained already in their premises?

In light of the following considerations, such claims appear rather dubious. Some of the inferences we make are intransitive, some are non-transitive, and some are transitive. In the first case, if a relation holds between A and B and between B and C, it cannot (logically impossible) hold between A and C. Thus if A is the father of B and B is the father of C, it is logically impossible for A to be the father of C. In the second case, if a relation holds between A and B and between B and C, it may or may not hold between A and C. Thus team A may win over team B and B may win over team C, but A may or may not win over C. In the third case, if a relation holds between A and B and between B and C, it necessarily holds between A and C. Thus in the spatial relation if A is north of B and B is north of C, the conclusion that A is north of C is necessarily true given the premises. But surely this statement is about a spatial <u>reality</u>. Are not statements about the intransitive and the transitive relation logically false and logically true and also assertions about <u>reality</u> rather than simply a matter of linguistic conventions? No one would question the claim that a logically indeterminate statement (the second example above) asserts a contingent state of affairs and a logically false (the first example above) or contradictory statement asserts an impossible state of affairs. Similarly, it seems intelligible to say that with the exception of statements about statements a logically true statement asserts a necessary state of affairs.

81

On this point, I tend to agree with St. Augustine. In *De doctrina Christiana,* where he displayed his skill in rhetoric which in ancient times included both the Aristotelian logic of classes and the Stoic propositional logic of inference schemas, Augustine claimed that valid inferences had not been <u>invented</u> by men but <u>discovered</u> by them. They are ordained by God and are <u>perpetual in the reasonable order of things</u>. If necessarily true statements are perpetual in the order of things, then there is no justification for attacking the ontological argument on the basis that the necessity involved merely reflects our linguistic conventions and cannot have anything to do with reality.

It seems to me that there is no question about the <u>validity</u> of the modern formulations of the ontological argument and, for that matter, of Anselm's second formulation. All the arguments presented above can be structured in such a way as to be shown to be valid. A much greater puzzle with respect to so many arguments has to do with the issue as to whether or not they are <u>sound</u>. Arguments are unsound for one or both of two reasons. They may be unsound because they are invalid. That is, there is some logical fallacy such as an undistributed middle term or a contradiction in terms or a denial of the antecedent and an affirmation of the consequent. A second reason is that even though the argument is valid, one (or more) of the premises is not true, and thus the conclusion is not necessarily true. No contradiction results from denying the truth of the conclusion. It may just happen to be true but it is not because it follows from the premises. Strange as it may seem, the following ridiculous argument illustrates a valid but obviously unsound argument:

> All dogs are green reptiles.
>
> My pet is a dog.
>
> Therefore, my pet is a green reptile.

At the opposite extreme is the following well-worn example in which the conditions of validity and truth are met so that the argument is sound:

> All men are mortal.
>
> Socrates is a man.
>
> Therefore, Socrates is mortal.

In many cases, however, we may not be able to establish with certainty the truth or falsity of the premises because the evidence is impossible to obtain or at present unavailable due to our lack of knowledge. But if they are possible (not absurd factually or logically) and especially if there is some evidence in support of their probable truth and the possibility that further knowledge will demonstrate beyond doubt their truth, then the argument, if valid, has merit. Of course, with arguments of this type, reasonable people may disagree as to their soundness. But if one does accept them as sound, he is not being irrational.

This is not the case with respect to arguments which are unsound because they are invalid. If an argument is invalid because of a contradiction or of some other error in the logic of the reasoning, it can never be shown to be sound. The conclusion of the argument is necessarily false. As indicated earlier in the Introduction, at least some of the God is Dead 'theologians' were guilty of an invalid and thus unsound argument because of a basic contradiction. It is contradictory to claim that God was once infinite and eternal but that this is no longer the case since he is dead. But this is to say that God is eternal and that he is not eternal, and this is logically false. It cannot be the case. So logical validity is a necessary though not a sufficient condition for the soundness of an argument. Without this condition all other issues are simply irrelevant.

As already indicated, the question of the truth of the premises may indeed pose problems, especially when there is not much in the way of empirical evidence. With respect to an issue such as the existence of God, the premises of the argument are more likely to be true if they can be grounded in a metaphysical schema which is consistent, coherent, comprehensive, and applicable to the common world disclosed to us in experience.

Anselm's formulation of the ontological argument presupposed a kind of Platonic metaphysics mediated by way of Neo-Platonisn and Augustine. The lack of a strong empirical relevance in this system weakens the base upon which the premises of the argument rest. So Anselm did not feel the need of providing us with a definite description of an individual who both necessarily exists and has relevance to the common world disclosed to us in experience.

It seems to me that, in general, process metaphysics provides a good context for the argument. In light of this metaphysics it can be concluded that if anything exists, God, as the sum total of all possibility, necessarily exists. Without the reality of possibility, not anything at all could exist. But something does exist and so possibility is real. Surely also the sum total of all possibility or positive predicates is a reality. In Whiteheadean terms this may be designated the primordial aspect of God. He is the totality of all possibilities and of all values. This primordial pole is the abstract aspect of God. But the common world disclosed to us in experience displays not only possibility but also actuality. The gap between pure possibilities and their availability to the ongoing process in the actual world is bridged by the creative activity of the unsurpassable one. He is ever seeking, given the previous actualities, to lure the best possible into actuality. He is the sum total of all value or positive predicates, both possible and actual, and ever luring reality on to newer and greater things. On the human level, as knowledge grows all sorts of possibilities for the future are opened up and the range of choices expands. The "greater things" may be used for good or misused such that a greater degree of evil and suffering result. But God seeks through the power of persuasion to bring as much good as possible out of the actualities. It is clear that becoming instead of being is fundamental in this metaphysics and this accords well with evolutionary development and creative advance encountered in the common world disclosed to us in experience.

I am well aware of the fact that the brief description above is quite inadequate for a proper explication and defense of process metaphysics in its totality. My attempt here has been simply to show that the existence of God is an integral and essential aspect of the process system. It requires the unsurpassable as the sum total of all positive predicates and the creative lure of possibility into actuality. The ontological argument is grounded in a metaphysics which is consistent, coherent, comprehensive, and applicable to experience. Of course, different metaphysics make for different conclusions, but

84

arguments about the existence of God would be more fruitful if they were debates about the metaphysical presuppositions instead of about the theistic arguments in isolation. Granted that process metaphysics is consistent, coherent, comprehensive, and applicable to experience, it provides a strong context on the basis of which the ontological argument may be judged to be sound. It follows from this that there are good reasons for affirming that the sentence, "There is a God," has a referent, is descriptive of an actual state of affairs, and that acceptance of it as true is not irrational. It follows also that if God necessarily exists and is unsurpassable, then the explication of the meaning of 'God' described earlier which included the defining characteristics of necessity, transcendence, supreme worth, creator, and personal, and the cosmological, teleological, and axiological arguments as descriptive of God find instantiation.

With the ontological argument grounded in process metaphysics, the description of God retains what is essential in the traditional attributes of omnipotence, omniscience, and omnibenevolence but without the contradictions of the traditional explications of these attributes, especially the first two. Omnipotence means that God possesses the power to do anything which is not logically impossible. Even Aquinas recognized that the logically impossible does not fall under the scope of the divine omnipotence. That is, contradictories (men are mules or there is a round square) can not be the case anywhere and at any time, for such is not even a word and does not have the aspect of possibility. It is unfortunate that he did not also apply the test of logical impossibility to the question of God's omniscience.

Aquinas' view of omniscience is inconsistent with his view of time and freedom. For him, time is a succession of before and after; things become actual successively. Yet God sees all things together and knows all things simultaneously. But if this is what omniscience means, then God knows all events as actual; everything is predetermined, and time and freedom are unreal. Further, it means that events can be known as actual before they are actual. But this is an obvious contradiction and so logically impossible. If the meaning of God's omnipotence is preserved by saying that God can do everything that is logically possible to do, why can't the meaning of God's omniscience be preserved by saying that God can know everything it is logically possible to know? That is, God can know all past and present actualities and all future possibilities. If time is not an illusion, then, at any given moment, this is all there is to know. Not even God can know the unknowable. To know all past and present actualities and to know future contingents as indetermined and future, relative to some past and determined actuality, is the proper meaning of 'omniscience.'

Influenced by Greek philosophical thought, classical theism in Western Christendom (including Aquinas), in the effort to preserve what was taken to be essential characteristics of the divine nature, namely, immutability, impassibility,and eternality, divorced God entirely from time and contingency. But the view adopted here does not place God in time such that he is a contingent being. Rather it places time 'inside' God so that succession, before and after, is as real in God's experience as it is in ours. At this point the distinction of Whitehead[6] between the primordial and consequent aspects of God is helpful. As pointed out above, God in his primordial nature is the sum total of all possibility. As such he is eternal, impassible, and unchanging. Such is the necessary condition for the existence of any entity whatsoever and is conditioned by none. His consequent nature, on the other hand, contains the particular concrete states of his knowledge, is conditioned by the particular contingent facts in the temporal process, and changes as new facts are added to the divine knowledge. Nothing is ever ultimately lost, but time and freedom are real and consistent with the divine omniscience.

I think little needs to be said about the divine attribute of omnibenevolence. Obviously this attribute may be extrapolated from what has been said earlier about God as the sum total of all positive predicates and of supreme and unsurpassable worth.

In the discussion so far, I have tried to present strong arguments that there are good reasons for concluding that God does in fact exist. From these arguments certain general characteristics and attributes of the divine nature (such as omnipotence, omniscience, and omnibenevolence) may be extrapolated. This is surely a necessary though not sufficient condition for belief in God. As Aquinas understood, we must go beyond 'natural theology.' We wish to know more than that God exists and has certain general attributes. We also want to know what in particular his evaluations of the world are and how we should live our lives. It is at this point that revelation becomes relevant, for it is the means whereby we come to see God as uniquely manifested in events involving particular people and particular communities. Unlike the abstractions and generalities of natural theology and the idiosyncratic flights of mystical imagination, God's disclosures are concrete and particular, of the very stuff of history.

In our Judeo-Christian tradition, the history which is of primary significance is the history of Israel and of the earliest Christian community witnessed to in the Bible. Both Jewish and Christian religions claim that they are what they are because God himself took the initiative and revealed himself rather than that man discovered his will. In the biblical understanding God's revelation is encountered not primarily in nature or in propositions about God but in the events of history. For both those who experienced them and for those who transmitted narratives concerning them, they were not perceived as bare happenings. They were regarded as events which had meaning for their own existence and for their understanding of God's will for mankind and his entire creation. History in this sense transcends history in the sense of a scientific, critical, process of inquiry. It is history in the sense of the past (or at least certain crucial past events) impinging upon the present, giving meaning and significance to the present. Even though no longer actual, past events are not unreal as far as the present is concerned but 'live on' in the present.

The dominant theme of the Old Testament is that God is an active and dynamic God, capable of feeling and change. He is involved and influenced by what happens in the world (not unlike the consequent nature of God in Whitehead). He takes the initiative and freely offers his covenant to Israel. Acceptance involves a continuing commitment, trust, and responsibility to God and fellowman. Disloyalty brings God's disciplinary judgment and call for covenant renewal. So, for the great prophets (forthtellers), Yahweh's covenant with Israel was not just

87

something which took place long ago in the time of Moses, but it was a living reality in their own times. In their view, the compassionate covenant God was continually active in history requiring faithfulness of his covenant partner and disciplining the community whenever it was unfaithful. But he is a compassionate God yearning for the community to renew covenant faithfulness, to turn and be healed. A redeemed Israel would then become a light to the nations such that all humanity would be in fellowship with God.

It is into covenant community that Jesus Christ comes. The covenant God of the community, Christians believe, now discloses himself conclusively in the person of this actual human being (the problem of Christology will be dealt with in the next chapter). Again it is God who takes the initiative, and in the whole of this man's life, teaching, death, and resurrection uniquely discloses himself as a loving, gracious, and forgiving God. While human beings have the capacity to receive this revelation, they cannot initiate it anymore than they can know another person unless that person discloses himself or herself to them. So it is that God is not fully known to us except as specific revelations of his character supplement what can be known of him in general. Even here reason can play an important role as a servant of revelation. Since it occurred in historical events, the use of critical methods of inquiry and formulation (including biblical criticism) can render a service to faith and theology by making vivid the concreteness, wholeness, and historical character of the revelatory events which become conclusive though not concluded in the whole drama of Jesus's life, death, and resurrection.

In spite of the fact that some skeptical critics and even some theologians think we can know very little about the Jesus of history, I think that the application of the historical critical method to the study of the Synoptic Gospels still enables us to recover a considerable knowledge about Jesus. Although some material in the Synoptics was clearly added later by the early church, I think we can recover enough reliable information about Jesus to know that in him there was a remarkable harmony and consistency of teaching, purpose, and act. In his life in the world for others, in his faithfulness to his vision of the kingdom of God, and in his very powerlessness with respect to the

88

rivalries of history was disclosed the divine *agape* . Here is made vivid the self-giving, sacrificial love of God which stoops to conquer. Now it can be clearly seen that *agape* is the fundamental attribute of the divine character, and that divine justice, omnipotence, and omniscience are properly understood only in the context of the divine love. If God is love (*agape*) and is omnipotent, how can we account for the fact of evil in the world? It is to this problem we must now turn.

3. God's Providence and the Problem of Evil

One attempt to deal with the problem of evil is simply to deny that there is a problem. Whatever happens is the result of the will of God (as in the earlier example of the view expressed by those religious people when the dam burst and drowned many of the people in the community). That which seems to be evil now, in God's providence, will turn out to be good. In its extreme form, this is the view that evil is an illusion. But is this not a self-defeating argument? If it is admitted that there is the illusion of evil, then there is at least this illusion, and that is evil. Even if all our pains and suffering are simply illusory, would not we prefer not to have these illusions? Under any definition of evil, these are certainly evil. So there is no argument whereby we can rid the world of evil. It is a fact both in our experience and in the world at large. Any physical pain and /or mental anguish experienced by a sentient being is included in the scope of that which is defined as evil. The evil may be the result of the action of human beings ('moral' evil) or of some natural catastrophe ('natural' evil).

Granted that evil is a fact in our world, is it the case as many philosophers, including Epicurus and Hume, have argued that the theist's position is inherently contradictory? The problem is generally put in the following syllogism: If God is omnipotent, he can prevent evil. If he is omnibenevolent, he wants to prevent evil. Evil exists. Therefore, God is either not omnipotent or he is not omnibenevolent. But the theist holds that God is omniscient, omnipotent, and omnibenevolent. Thus, in light of the fact of evil, his position is contradictory and semantically meaningless.

Is it possible to answer this argument? I think that even though we may not be able to remove all the mystery as to why there should be evil in the world, we can arrive at a definite description of God which retains the essential meanings of his attributes as discussed above and which is not in contradiction with the fact of evil in the world.

Surely the God who disclosed himself in the history of Israel and the life of Jesus desires all human beings to live in fellowship with himself and others. Since he is *agape,* his goal for creation is the kingdom of God or a universal fellowship of all beings living together with him in perfect freedom and faithfulness. Such a goal can be realized only if human beings are sufficiently free to choose or to reject the divine fellowship. In the discussion of human nature in chapter two, a case was made that human beings possess such freedom and that this freedom is a necessary condition for the development of moral virtue as well as for the acceptance of God's acceptance and love.

It appears to be an obvious truth then that it is a logically necessary condition for any world in which there is moral virtue that there be free agents in this world. From this it follows that it is contradictory to say that God could create a world in which there is moral value without creating free agents, and that it is contradictory to say that God could create free agents who are guaranteed always to do good. This would be to say that God created free agents who are not free, and this is meaningless. It could not be the case anywhere or in any universe. As we have seen in the discussion above, the omniscience and omnipotence of God do not extend to knowing and doing that which is logically impossible to know and to do.

The question now becomes, is it worth having moral agents in the world at the cost of moral evil, or would it be better for human beings to always remain morally innocent and unable to develop any moral strength of character? There is so much hatred, oppression, destruction, and killing in the world that sometimes one is tempted to wonder if it would not be better if everyone were fated to be good at all times. But if God predetermined every choice, not only would the evils be removed from the world but also the exalted decisions and acts of moral goodness and courage. If human beings were mere puppets of the divine puppeteer, or patients of the divine hypnotist acting out a series of posthypnotic suggestions, would the concept of moral value ever have

90

arisen? If we accept the conclusion that a world in which there is moral virtue is better than a world in which it is lacking, and that a relative but genuine human freedom is a necessary condition for moral virtue, then the moral evils which arise as by-products of this freedom are justified in light of the greater good of moral virtue. That is, the prevention of those evils which arise as a result of the exercise of human freedom would also prevent moral virtue in the world which is of greater value than the nonexistence of moral evils.

A similar kind of argument may be used to justify the presence of natural evil in our world. Certaintly it is open to the theist to hold that some kind of determinate order is a necessary condition for moral virtue. Moral virtue entails responsibility for one's decisions and actions. But if our world were some sort of hedonistic paradise in which no evil acts could have consequences, how could moral responsibility ever arise? The murderer's gun would never fire or the bullets would turn to jelly. All of the weapons of all the armies in the world would simply not function (certaintly this would be a wonderful thing which perhaps would not upset the determinate order too much, but it would play havoc with human freedom). There could be no suicides and no accidents, and all sorts of bad things would not happen. But moral responsibility would be eliminated. If nature operated solely in terms of 'special providences,' how could human beings develop an intellectual life, and how could ethical concepts have any meaning? Enormous advantages accrue to mankind due to the fact that there is a determinate order in our world, that there are consistent regularities in nature which can be depended upon. It is open to the theist to designate this order as the general providence of God. That is, while there is a certain openness in our world which makes creative change and progress possible, there is also a stable order upon which we may rely with confidence. In his wisdom, God created, creates, and sustains both the openness and the stable order.

A crucial question now arises, is it possible to have the advantages of a determinate order without its logically and causally necessary disadvantages as inevitable by-products. That is, any conceivable set of natural laws could not operate jointly together

91

without producing some natural evils so that even God finds that in whichever way they are framed there always will be some evils arising as inevitable by-products. If this is the case, then it is <u>logically impossible</u> for God to fashion a world in which there is a determinate order and to prevent natural evils from arising. For him to prevent the evils would mean also the prevention of the determinate order which, as we have argued above, is of greater value than the nonexistence of the evils.

Of course, it is impossible for us to <u>know</u> that every specific case of natural evil is a necessary by-product of a determinate order. We could do that only if we could view the world with an omniscient perspective. Yet we can demonstrate that many natural evils are the necessary by-products of a lawful world. For example, we cannot have all the advantages from that regularity in nature which we call gravity without the disadvantages of someone being injured by falling from the top of a tall building or people killed in plane crashes. Given this, it is not irrational to hold that from an omniscient perspective all natural evils probably are seen to be the necessary by-products of our determinate order, and that the order is of greater value than the nonexistence of the evils.

Granted the soundness of the arguments above, it follows that the fact of evil in the world does not entail the lack of omnipotence or omnibenevolence on the part of God. Moral virtue, maturity, and responsibility, and an ultimate universal fellowship of perfect freedom and perfect faithfulness necessarily require human freedom and a determinate order from which evils arise which God permits but does not will. God's omnipotence is his power to do everything which is logically possible to do consistent with his purposes. These purposes plus the revelation of himself as *agape* guarantee his total goodness. As *agape,* God is constantly seeking to persuade human beings to make out of past decisions and events the very best that is possible, to lure humanity and all reality to higher levels of goodness and creativity. The inevitable evils which arise as the by-products of freedom and order he experiences as lack or privation. To use Whitehead's marvelous statement near the end of *Process and Reality*, "God is the great companion-the fellow

92

sufferer who understands."[7] Surely this is consistent with the revelation of God in the life, suffering, crucifixion, and death of Jesus. But beyond suffering and death is the resurrection, and this suggests the goal beyond history in an ultimate universal fellowship of perfect freedom and faithfulness.

Several times in this chapter reference has been made to the revelation of God as *agape* in Jesus Christ. It has been claimed that this revelation was conclusive though not concluded. But how is it possible for an actual human being to disclose in himself the ultimate nature of God? It is this problem which will be of concern to us in the next chapter on Christology.

---

[1] (New York: The Macmillan Co., 1953).

[2] cf. Lonnie D. Kliever, "Fictive Religion: Rhetoric and Play," *The Journal of the American Academy of Religion* 49:4 (Dec. 1981) pp. 657-659; Thomas J.J. Altizer, et. al., *Deconstruction and Theology* (New York: Corssroad Publishing Co., 1982); David Ray Griffin, et. al., *Varieties of Postmodern Theology* (SUNY Press, 1989).

[3] *Systematic Theology*, Vol. 1 (The University of Chicago Press, 1951) p. 237, cf. pp. 65, 74, 204-210.

[4] Karl Barth, *Chruch Dogmatics, A Selectin*, G.W. Bromily, ed. (Harper Torchbook, 1962) pp. 29-64.

[5] cf. *The Many-Faced Argument*, John Hick and Arthur C. McGill, eds., (The Macmillan Co., 1967) pp. 301-333.

[6] A.N. Whitehead, *Process and Reality*, (The Macmillan Co., 1929) pp.521-533.

[7] *Ibid.*, p. 532.

CHAPTER FOUR
CHRISTOLOGY

It is almost a truism to say that Christology is central to the Christian faith. As stated in chapter three, for the Christian the final norm for the conclusive revelation of God, the disclosure of his evaluations of the world, is found in Jesus Christ. But is it not strange that the God with the attributes described in chapter three (especially those of eternal necessary being and universal creator) would, or even could, become incarnate in a particular human being in a particular point in history? Is it not the case that this is a difficult problem about which the majority of Christians gives little thought as to why and how this could be? Either they give it no thought, accepting it as something to be blindly believed, or they simply accept and repeat certain creedal formulas without any analysis of their meanings. While one may excuse the average lay person for failing to develop a full rationale for his faith that Jesus Christ was the conclusive disclosure of God, the theologian has no excuse for failing to deal as best he can with the problem of Christology.

I am well aware, as I was with the problem of the existence of God, that others have dealt with this problem much more profoundly than I am capable of doing. But since I am attempting to set down my own theology, and since I do accept the Christian faith, I must seek to construct a Christology that will make sense in the modern world. Such a construction cannot be done in a vacuum. Attention must be given to the life, teachings, and passion of the historical and human Jesus, and to the emergence of the Christ of faith and the creedal controversies in the early church. In light of this background I will attempt to develop a Christology which will preserve the essence of the ancient faith but in the language and thought forms of the modern world.

1. The Historical Jesus

In view of the fact that innumerable scholarly works on the Gospels and Jesus have been produced during the last century or so

94

and are still appearing, it is difficult for one who is not a specialist in the field to feel confident that he has a reliable knowledge of the historical Jesus. Although most specialists agree that Jesus was a real human and historical person, they differ widely as to how much information about him in the Gospels is reliable. The historical critical study of the Gospels has spawned a number of methods such as form criticism which emphasized the church's role in fashioning the pericopes, or units of tradition, and which was generally skeptical about finding much reliable knowledge of Jesus in the Gospels. There is also redaction criticism which emphasizes the role of the Gospel writer in selecting and arranging the material available to him and in coloring what he wrote with his own purposes. The earlier so-called source criticism has not been abandoned but is still seen as a valuable tool which is helpful in gaining a more reliable knowledge of the Gospels, especially of the Synoptics (Matthew, Mark, Luke). Many New Testament scholars still accept the source critic's conclusion that Mark was the earliest Gospel, and that the writers of Matthew and Luke used Mark as one of their common sources, the other being a collection of sayings which the scholars designate Q. In addition, the writers of Matthew and Luke each had a special source unique to his Gospel. A good Gospel Parallels makes very clear both the similarities and differences between the Synoptics and tends to support the source critic's conclusions.

Internal evidence in the Gospels (including the Gospel of John which is obviously a theological treatise of great insight but with little of historical value concerning Jesus) indicates that they were probably written during the latter third of the first century. In a sense, the authors of the Synoptics were almost like editors, putting together available materials which had come to them. Some of these materials were in written form and some were oral. Form criticism demonstrates that behind the written Gospels and their written sources there were units of oral tradition in the earliest church. Redaction criticism calls attention to the specific organizational structure of each Gospel and the differences with which sometimes the same narrative, parable, or saying is reported in different Gospels, and this provides highly probable conclusions concerning the perspectives and purposes of each writer. So the writers were not historians or biographers. There had been no one analogous to a modern newspaper or television reporter following Jesus around and recording everything he said and did for future generations. Furthermore, given the widespread conviction in the first century church that the end was near, the concern was for the immediate future and not for posterity. The major purpose of the Gospel writers was not to record history for a far distant posterity but to communicate the good news of salvation. Of course, since this good news is rooted in history, some historical facts can be gleaned from the *kergmatic* (Greek for proclamation or message) narratives.

The application of the historical critical approach to the study of the Gospels does not lead necessarily to the skeptical conclusion of some radical form critics that almost nothing can be known about Jesus because the records are simply subjective interpretations and not 'scientific' history. In some cases these critics seem almost to operate on the premise that reliable historical reports must be as certain as necessarily true statements, or if not that certain, at least the reports must be made by disinterested eyewitnesses who are without any taint of subjectivity. This, of course, would make the writing of history practically impossible. Unlike the natural sciences where subjectivity may be kept to a very low level because there can be repeated experiments performed by any number of experimenters, historical narratives are based on probable and inferred judgments about the unrepeatable events of the past. A greater degree of probability is attained if the historian by skillfully using the critical tools available is able to remove the rose colored glasses of modernity and become thoroughly familiar with the world view prevailing in the culture of the time and region he is studying.

It is possible to do this to a large extent with respect to gaining a good deal of reliable knowledge concerning Jesus. A great deal is known about his historical heritage in Judaism and about the religious, social and political environment of his times. So an important criterion for at least a core of historical reliability in a narrative concerning an action or saying of Jesus is coherence with the

96

heritage, practices, thought forms, and life style in first century Palestine. To the extent that there is inconsistency with this environment (a Hellenistic rather than a Palestinian setting, for example), to this extent the historical reliability may be doubted.

Another criterion for historical reliability is that the narrative was obviously an embarrassment to the early church such that the later sources seek to remove the embarrassment by some extreme rationalizations. Examples of such are the references to Jesus' parents and his brothers and sisters which are inconsistent with the virgin birth narratives, Jesus' baptism by John the Baptist which seems to imply that Jesus was a disciple of and inferior to John, and the crucifixion by order of the Gentile (Roman) authority which was an obstacle to the Gentile mission of the church.

A third criterion is internal coherence in and between the narratives. That is, a glaring inconsistency probably indicates additions from later tradition or writers. For example, in a few cases parables end with generalized conclusions which are inconsistent with or miss the point of the parable (as in Matt. 20:16). Such conclusions come either from a later time or were uttered by Jesus in a different context unknown to the Gospel writer or his source. Moreover, there should be a general, even if not strict, consistency between different narratives concerning what is obviously the same purported event. For example, this is not the case in the birth narratives of Matthew and Luke which contain many inconsistencies with each other. And finally, a narrative is of dubious historical worth if its content is out of character with the general portrayal of Jesus in the Gospels, such as Jesus cursing the fig tree because it is barren even though it is not the time for bearing (Matt.28:19; Mark11:14; omitted by Luke who has a parable of the barren fig tree, Lk.13:6-9). This criterion must be used with care since the church produced the Gospels rather than vice versa. But it is certainly of some significance even for the historian that the Gospels along with the Epistles are in general agreement in claiming that Jesus was a man of love, or as Dietrich Bonhoeffer put it, the man in the world totally for others.

97

A balanced and careful use of the historical and critical methods of research in the study of the Gospels enables us to place the Jesus of history in his actual life situation and to arrive at a core of reliable information about him. While it is not possible to write a full and precise biography, or to construct a detailed chronological account of his ministry, it is possible to gain from the Gospels a reliable 'portrait' of the man, his mission, and his message.

Using the tools of historical criticism, we may glean a very general sketch or outline of Jesus' ministry from the Gospel of Mark (generally followed by the other Synoptic writers). It begins with an account of the mission and message of John the Baptist and of the baptism of Jesus by John. After John is put in prison by Herod Antipas, Jesus calls some disciples and sets out on a preaching and teaching mission in Galilee. The burden of his message as summarized by Mark (1:15) was:

> The time is fulfilled, and the kingdom of God
> is at hand: repent, and believe in the gospel.

Attracted by the man and his message, rather large crowds flock to hear him. Undoubtedly, this attracted the attention of Tetrarch Herod Antipas who, according to Josephus (*Antiquities*, XVIII, 5,2.), had put John the Baptist in prison for fear that his popularity with the people and his radical eschatological message might spark a rebellion. It is probable that Herod had the same suspicion about Jesus since Luke (13:31) at least records a statement attributed to some Pharisees that Herod wanted to kill Jesus. Quite possibly because of the threat of Herod, and to escape from the pressure of the crowds in order to be able to quietly reflect on the future course of his ministry, Jesus with his disciples leaves Galilee and spends some time in the regions of Tyre and Sidon and Caesarea Philippi. Having decided that the good news of the kingdom must be proclaimed in Jerusalem, the Holy City, Jesus and his disciples travel to Jerusalem, arriving there a few days before the Passover. In view of the centrality of the crucifixion and resurrection in the theology which emerged in the early church, it is not surprising that the most detailed of all the narratives in the Synoptics is of the Passion Week. Jesus' message arouses the

98

opposition of the religious and civil authorities. He eats a last meal with his disciples, is arrested, charged with treason, and executed by order of Pilate, the Roman Procurator.

All of the Gospels, of course, end with narratives concerning the resurrection and the ascension of the risen Lord. These are phrased in terms of the pre-scientific myths (see chapter one) of the first century (such as a three layer universe) but may contain a core of a permanent myth which, along with others, constitute the Christian *mythos* which provides the frame of reference or principle of interpretation for our understanding of experience and reality.

From the very brief sketch of Jesus' ministry presented in the Synoptics, it may be inferred that his mission took place during a period of time of about one year. The truly amazing thing about this is that in such a short period of time Jesus could have had such a profound impact upon his disciples and unnamed others of his fellow countrymen that the seeds were planted which resulted finally in the emergence of a new religion having similarities with the parent religion, Judaism, but also differences. Surely this profound impact of Jesus was due to many factors including his closeness to God, the depth of his personality, his love of persons and all of God's creatures, and the simplicity, concreteness, and yet profundity of his teachings about God and his kingdom.

When we glean Jesus' authentic sayings and teachings from the Synoptics, it is evident that the central theme of his teaching was the kingdom of God, a new order of life on earth which was now dawning and which would be fulfilled in the future. This concept, if not the precise terminology, was already present in Jesus' religious heritage. In the Old Testament the covenant between Yahweh and Israel was a suzerainty covenant, and later Rabbinical prayers addressed God as king of the universe. That is, whether recognized as such or not, God is really king of the universe, and to the extent that this is acknowledged and accepted, his kingdom (God's reign) is a present reality on earth. But beyond this, the Rabbis, as had the earlier Prophets, looked forward to a future universal consummation when the kingdom would have come in fulfillment. Even allowing for some modifications by the early church, it seems fairly certain that Jesus also viewed the kingdom as both a present and a future reality (Mark14:25; Luke17:21).

Nowhere in the authentic sayings and parables of Jesus in the Synoptics do we find a formal definition of the kingdom of God. Yet they do present Jesus' perspective with respect to the nature of the kingdom and the life style of those who accept it. All of his authentic teachings deal either explicitly or implicitly with this theme and can be fully comprehended only as they are kept in the context of the kingdom theme. The early church often failed to do this and modified Jesus sayings with a moralistic and legalistic hue as in the Sermon on the Mount (Matt. 5-7). There was the tendency to allegorize the parables and thus to obscure or eliminate the very point Jesus was illustrating with the parable.

If we eliminate whatever embellishments and modifications that were made by the church and do a careful analysis of the parables, we will find that they illustrate a few basic concepts of Jesus concerning the kingdom. Often several parables will illustrate the same theme. Some of the most basic of these themes, with an example of each, are as follows:

1. The kingdom is a gift of God. It cannot be earned but only accepted or rejected, a point which is strikingly made in the parable of the Laborers in the Vineyard (Matt.20:1-16).

2. The kingdom of God is inclusive. God lovingly accepts everyone, even those who are outcasts and sinners, if they accept his acceptance. This is obviously the point of the beautiful Prodigal Son parable (Luke.15:11-32).

3. As illustrated by the parable of the Good Samaritan (Luke.10:29-37), those who accept the gift of the kingdom seek to demonstrate in the concrete affairs of everyday life a loving concern for others.

4. The dawning kingdom stands in opposition to the customary power structures of the world based on position, prestige, ruthless oppression of people, and violent conflicts arising out of hatreds, both old and new. Indeed, the *agapeistic* life style of those who accept the kingdom will ultimately rupture the framework of those structures (the nonviolent

campaigns of Martin Luther King, for example), and this is certainly the point of the twin parables of the New Cloth and the New Wine (Mark2: 21-22).

5. The kingdom is the supreme value of life, for it breaks the power of estrangement which sin had brought into human life and restores that kind of community for which God had created human beings. The twin parables of the Hidden Treasure and the Pearl of Great Price (Matt.13: 44-46) illustrate this point.

Not only the parables but also the sayings of Jesus must be kept in the context of the kingdom of God theme if we are to gain some reliable knowledge as to what Jesus did, in fact, teach. This is especially true with respect to those sayings the author of Matthew compiled as the Sermon on the Mount (chapters 5-7). Through the centuries there have been numerous interpretations of the Sermon such as the new law view, the double standard view, the two-realm view, and the dispensationalist view in which the sayings apply only in the final dispensation. These interpretations miss entirely the point of these sayings because they do not recognize the modifications which the author of the Gospel or his source made in the interest of life in the church at a time much later than that of Jesus, and because they fail to keep the sayings in the context of the kingdom theme

When we carefully analyze the authentic sayings contained in the Sermon in light of the kingdom theme, we find that they are not rules the obeying of which will earn one the kingdom, for that is a gift as we have seen in the parable of the Laborers in the Vineyard. In this parable as well as in the parable of the Prodigal Son it is obvious that, in the view of Jesus, the very nature of God is *agape* or self-giving, gratuitous, love. Thus the kind of morality by which the kingdom members seek to live is based precisely on their experience of God's gracious acceptance, his gift of the kingdom. It is most unlikely that on the one hand Jesus would speak of the kingdom as God's gracious gift which cannot be earned, and then on the other hand proclaim a set of prescriptions or laws by which it could be earned. The authentic sayings in the Sermon, then, are not prescriptive but descriptive. They are descriptive of the features in the creative life-transformation

101

aspired to by those who accept the gift of the kingdom. They aspire to this life style not for prudential reasons but out of gratitude for the gift.

The Beatitudes describe the characteristics of the life style of those who accept the gift of the kingdom. They recognize their need of God, are sensitive to the plight of the world and together are strengthened to bear the sorrows of the world, are meek to God, yearn for personal and social righteousness, are merciful to others, sincere in motives, and act for peace in human relations. In a world governed by power, greed, hatred, and estrangement, such a way of life inevitably arouses opposition and persecution, and yet the kingdom members are happy because of their community with God and with others. While the world may not recognize it, the kingdom life is the very thing which can bring light to its darkness and preserve it.

The good news of the kingdom does not abolish the old religious order or covenant but fulfills it. Those who accept the gift of the kingdom seek to go beyond simply refraining from murder, adultery, swearing, and retaliation and to develop those inner *agapeistic* (loving) attitudes which make such external moral prohibitions superfluous. Further, their worship is simple and sincere, and their ultimate trust and devotion are centered on God. Given this, it follows that their love (*agape*) is directed to all, even enemies. Finally, they do not just make a 'profession of faith' but actually engage in the practice of the kingdom life.

As perceived by the early faith witnesses, and as presented in the Gospels, the vision of reality and life proclaimed by Jesus in parables and sayings was fully actualized in his own actions, life, and person. They found in him a disclosure of God's mercy and love, and in the attempt to communicate the significance of his person used many of the honorific titles of the day with which to designate him. In the development of the Christian tradition, the original meanings of the titles were obscured as the human and historical Jesus was replaced more and more by the transcendental Lord. I suspect that Jesus of Nazareth would have been very surprised and perhaps dismayed by much of this, such as the so-called Infancy Gospels of about the third century in which the child Jesus is portrayed as exercising all sorts of miraculous powers. That Jesus was a real human being who incorporated his teachings fully in his own life must not be lost sight of, and a consideration of the original meanings of the titles may be of help to us at this point.

Some of these titles and their original meanings are as follows:

1. Messiah (anointed one, Christ in Greek) which was an adjective applied to many figures such as priests, kings, prophets, the nation, and even Cyrus, a king of Persia.

2. Son of Man which could be used as a generic term for humanity, a single individual, a group of human beings, or to designate a mysterious figure to come at the end of time.

3. Son of God which had no supernatural connotation but was used to designate the nation, a righteous group in the nation, or the king as adopted by God.

4. Servant of the Lord which was associated with the suffering servant of the Second Isaiah (Isaiah, chapters40-55) in some passages of which the designation clearly is Israel as a 'corporate personality' and in others may be a prophet or the prophets as a whole.

5. Prophet which means one who is so captured by the spirit of God that he must speak for God to the current situation in spite of opposition and persecution.

It is to be noted that in all these cases the emphasis is on function and not on the nature, supernatural or otherwise, of the one designated.

From my study of the Synoptics, I find it difficult to conclude that Jesus understood his role as that of Messiah. Typically, the Messiah is not one who suffers. Also throughout the Gospels Jesus is called Messiah by others and does not make Messianic claims for himself. Jesus' response to the Messianic 'confession' of Peter (Mark8: 27-33) in which Peter is rebuked may mean that Jesus rejected the designation, that he did not want to be known as Messiah, for that would obscure his message. Among the many Messianic views of Jesus' time a very popular one held that the Messiah to come would be a charismatic leader, a king of David's line who would sweep away the tyranny of Rome and establish a free Jewish state of freedom and prosperity. Members of the Zealot movement held this view, and probably some of their leaders made Messianic claims. Obviously Jesus did not see his role as that of leading a rebellion against Rome, and his understanding of the kingdom of God was quite different.

Another Messianic and highly eschatological group were the Essenes of the Dead Sea scrolls fame. It is highly unlikely that Jesus was ever a member of this group. He did not withdraw from society, practice strict asceticism, or hold to a nationalistic eschatology looking forward to the coming of both a priestly and a Davidic Messiah, with the latter instituting a 'holy' war in which the 'children of light' would be victorious over the children of darkness. Certainly such Messianic notions are foreign to Jesus' perspective.

The other two 'parties' in Jesus' day were the Sadducees and the Pharisees. The former were conservative literalists who accepted only the written Torah (the first five books of the Old Testament) and centered their piety in the temple. The latter, in spite of the fact that they are presented in the Synoptics as legalists, were actually the liberals of their day, accepting the oral as well as the written Torah. Thus they did accept the notion of a resurrection life and of a Messianic age, even though the latter became increasingly peripheral in the literature of Rabbinical Pharisaism. They were more concerned with bringing every aspect of life into accord with the will of God in the here and now, and thus centered their activity in the academies and synagogues for study and teaching. While Jesus was, on occasion, called Rabbi, it is unlikely that he was a member of the Pharisee 'party.' However, the perspective expressed in his authentic sayings has a greater similarity with that expressed in the literature of the Rabbinical Pharisees than with that of any of the other 'parties.' For example, in Matthew's Sermon on the Mount alone there are at least ten sayings which have parallels in Rabbinical literature. So even if Jesus did engage in some criticism of some Pharisees (similar criticism can be found in Rabbinical literature), he did seem to have some affinity for Pharisaism at its best (both he and Rabbi Hillel advocated the golden rule) and, like the Pharisees, probably viewed Messianism as a peripheral issue.

While Jesus himself may have made little of Messianism, it was the conviction of the early faith witnesses that Jesus had a special relationship with God, that he was 'anointed' by God, which led them to designate Jesus with this title, and after the resurrection experience to read more eschatological meaning into it. Later, as the church spread into the Gentile world, Christians ceased to use the term as a title to denote function and, instead, made it a part of his name, Jesus Christ.

We have seen above that the Son of Man title was used in two senses, as a substitute term for man and as a designation for a mysterious supernatural figure. In what appears to be an authentic saying of Jesus (Matt.8:20, Luke9:58 and thus from Q: "Foxes have holes, and birds of the air have nests; but the Son of Man has nowhere to lay his head."), Son of Man is clearly used of himself in a generic sense as a substitute for the first person singular pronoun, I. In those sayings where the title is used of some sort of supernatural figure who is to come in the future, there is never an explicit identification with this figure on the part of Jesus. Given its high eschatological expectations, the early church did make such an identification but it is unlikely that Jesus did.

Many of the suffering Son of Man passages (Mark8:31, 9:31, 10:33-34) are clearly 'predictions after the event' by the early faith witnesses or by the Gospel writers since they are so stylized and give so many details of Jesus' death. But the passage from Q quoted above, as well as Luke17:25 and Mark9:12, does not speak of death or give any details of the passion. Yet they do suggest hardship and suffering, with the latter two explicitly stating that the Son of Man must suffer many things, be rejected and treated with contempt. Some scholars have claimed that in the Jewish thinking of the time the Son of Man was never associated with a vicarious suffering for the redemption of others. In these sayings, which seem to be authentic sayings of Jesus, it would appear that he is using Son of Man as a self designation and interpreting his role in light of Isaiah's Suffering Servant. Jesus would have learned Scripture at home and in the synagogue and surely was quite familiar with the suffering servant passages in Isaiah (Luke

105

represents him as reading from Isaiah in the synagogue). Aware that his mission and message had aroused powerful opponents, that in the words of Reinhold Niebuhr it comforted the afflicted but also afflicted the comfortable, Jesus undoubtedly recognized that continuing the kingdom of God mission and message would quite likely bring persecution and suffering. But as with the suffering servant of Isaiah, this vicarious suffering could be redemptive.

As we have seen, the title Son of God did not in the Jewish view of the time have a supernatural connotation as it did in Greek culture. It did stress the moral relationship of love and filial obedience. In the Synoptics other people do not hesitate to use the term to designate Jesus, but the evidence is meager that Jesus ever used the term of himself. Interestingly enough there is a passage in Mark (13:32) where Jesus uses Son [of God] to refer to himself, but in it he disclaims any knowledge on the part of the Son with respect to the date of the End. Certainly this is to acknowledge the lack of omniscience. The evidence that Jesus' relationship with God was one of love and filial obedience is not at all meager. Time and again he speaks of God as father, and his whole life is a demonstration of love for God and human beings.

A discussion of the titles designating Jesus would be incomplete without a consideration of the title,"prophet." As we have seen, this title means one who speaks for God to the contemporary situation, a forthteller and not a foreteller. And yet the prophet is one who feels captured by the word of God, compelled by God to confront in word and deed the coalition of callousness, indifference, injustice, and authority of his time on behalf of the dispossessed and oppressed. There is not only the stirring word of God's judgment on the oppressors, but also his deep concern and love for the oppressed and his anguished yearning for the oppressors to turn and be healed.

All the Gospels report that Jesus referred to himself as a prophet (Matt. 13:57; Mark 6:4; Luke 4:24, "a prophet not without honor save in his own country etc.). Also they indicate that the crowds called him a prophet. A careful analysis of the Synoptics reveals that there are many prophetic characteristics in the content and style of

Jesus' message and deeds. Undoubtedly it is reasonable to suppose that Jesus was thoroughly familiar with the prophetic tradition in his own religious heritage. Given the fact that it is in the prophetic book of Isaiah that the suffering servant appears, and that in some instances this title may designate a prophet or prophets, and given Jesus' sense of filial relationship with God, it is very likely that a combination of the ideal meanings of the titles prophet, suffering servant, and son was most influential in defining Jesus' understanding of his life, mission, and death.

We cannot know with certainty, of course, what Jesus thought of himself. The early church and the Gospel writers viewed Jesus' life and death from a post-resurrection perspective and, as might be expected, infused the titles with a higher degree of transcendental meanings. It was their wish to clothe their faith in the risen Lord with an appropriate language which would make sense in both a Jewish and Gentile environment. The human and historical Jesus, however, was more concerned with doing the will of God, with leading persons to accept the reign or kingdom of God, than he was with any glory for himself. The general picture of Jesus we glean from the Synoptics is of one who, though he had a unique sense of vocation and prophetic authority in the kingdom of God mission and message, nevertheless did not make exalted claims about himself. He did not seek glory and power of any kind, but in lowliness (nowhere to lay his head) proclaimed the accepting love of God in deed and word. It is not surprising, then, that the earliest faith-witnesses came to regard him as having a unique relationship with God and that in light of the resurrection experience (whatever that may have been literally) and the spread of Christianity into the Greco-Roman world, came to invest the person of Jesus more and more with divine attributes. So even in the New Testament the exaltation of Jesus is already present. In the first chapter of the Gospel of John (about 90 A. D.) he is called the *logos* (word) of God. While never saying that Jesus is God, Paul does claim that he is the image of the invisible God, the first born of all creation, and that in him the fullness of God was pleased to dwell (1Col. 1: 15-19).

2. The Christ of Faith and The Creedal Controversies

The conviction of Paul, the author of the Fourth Gospel, and other New Testament writers, that Jesus had a special relationship with God which made him unique in his person was simply expressed in the context of what was regarded as necessary for human salvation or reconciliation with God. There was no exposition as to how the *Logos* or fullness of God could dwell in him without compromising monotheism, and how exactly there could be in any realistic sense both a human and a divine nature in one person. Two extreme positions emerged in the late first and early second centuries A. D., namely, Ebionism and Gnosticism. They are not mentioned by name in the later writings of the New Testament although the Letter of James may reflect some influence from the Ebionites (literally, "the poor") with respect to the 'law,' and there is an obvious attack on the Gnostics in I John 4:2 when the author insists that the genuine Christian must "confess that Jesus Christ has come in the flesh."

Ebionism appears to have had its major source among Jewish converts to Christianity and may even have had some beginning with those in Jerusalem who opposed Paul. Whatever the case may be with respect to the origin of this sect, there is information about it from both some opponents of the second century and a few extant writings of Ebionites. In this system of thought, salvation is primarily a matter of obedience to the 'law' (i.e., Jewish or Old Testament law) except for the laws governing animal sacrifices, and Jesus is only a man whom God had chosen to fulfill the law and proclaim his will. It was at his baptism that he was "adopted" by God and endowed with the power to fulfill his mission. This mission was the calling of mankind to obedience to the law which included circumcision of males, Sabbath observance, and following the moral laws of the Old Testament. For the Ebionites, then, Jesus was not "the only begotten Son of God," the savior of mankind, but a great moral teacher who was only a human being in his person. While Ebionism as such died out as the church became increasingly Gentile, a similar Christology (Jesus as a great human teacher of morality) has arisen from time to time in the history of the church and is held by some today. It does have the advantage of being without contradiction and relatively easy to understand.

At the opposite extreme from Ebionism was Gnosticism (from the Greek gnosis which means knowledge or wisdom). The Ebionites had insisted that Jesus Christ was only a human being, but the Gnostics insisted that he was not human in any realistic sense. While there were some variations in viewpoints among the Gnostics, probably most were influenced to some extent by the dualism of Greek philosophy, and held to the dualistic view that matter and flesh were evil and only spirit was good. Thus it follows that the Christ, the Son of God, could not have had a human fleshly body. He was entirely a spiritual being, a kind of ghostly apparition, who masqueraded as a human being and only appeared to suffer and die in order to fool the evil powers of the material world into thinking that they had defeated him when all the while he was bringing the mystic knowledge of salvation to those 'spiritual' human beings who could understand it. Gnosticism enjoyed some popularity in the early church, especially in the second century, but its main tenets, its view that creation was evil and its docetism (Jesus only appeared to be human), were abhorrent to the main body of the early church.

It is certainly the case that the picture of Jesus we find in the Synoptic Gospels is of one who, though he was unique in his relationship with God, was also fully human. He grows in wisdom and statue (Luke 2:52). He is tempted in all points as we are. His powers are limited (Mark 6:5). And he experiences not only physical pain but also the deep agony of betrayal and desertion by friends and the silence of God (Matt. 27:46). It was the case also that Gnosticism was strongly opposed by many of the early fathers such as Irenaeus who insisted that Jesus Christ became what we are in order that we might become what he is. The acknowledgment of Jesus' humanity soon became the official position of the church as is evident in the early creeds (Apostles, Nicene, and Chalcedonian) which, though they confess belief in his divinity (only begotten Son of God), insist on his humanity in such expressions as complete in manhood, like us in all respects, was made flesh, became man, and suffered and died.

Like Ebionism, Gnosticism as such died out, but similarities with some Gnostic views found expression among some from time to time in the history of Christian thought. For example, Arianism which was attacked in the Trinitarian creed of Nicea (325) had claimed that the *logos* (i.e. Son of God), though created by God out of nothing, was nevertheless divine or at least semi-divine, and this *logos* replaced the human soul of Jesus while his body was human. This entails, of course, that Jesus was not fully human. This is true also of a view expressed by some supporters of the Nicene creed just prior to the Council of Chalcedon (451). They agreed with the creed that the *logos* was of the same essence or substance as God, but claimed that this pre-existent *logos* replaced the human mind of Jesus. It was their contention that spirit and body comprise human nature as such, while mind is the location of an individual's personality. So Jesus' mind or personality was divine, but his spirit and body were human. In this way, it was thought, Jesus could be both divine and human. However, the objection was soon raised that the mind was as essential an attribute of human nature as were spirit and body, and if it were not a human mind assumed by the *logos,* then that attribute of human nature had not been redeemed. Others, such as the Monophysites, claimed that after the incarnation there was only one nature in Jesus Christ, the divine or *logos* nature, and thus the human nature is completely eliminated.

In the history of the church whenever there have appeared individuals or groups who emphasized the deity of Jesus Christ to the exclusion of part or all of his humanity, there is found at least a semi-Gnosticism. In the modern period some Protestant fundamentalists and some conservative Catholics fall into this category by their continual emphasis on Jesus' deity. In popular fundamentalism it is sometimes claimed that Jesus is God. It is admitted that Jesus had a human body, but it is emphasized that it was God who was walking around and teaching in a man's body. William Jennings Bryan asserted that the virgin birth narratives of Matthew and Luke are literally true, and thus Jesus must be taken out of the man class and put in the God class. This is precisely what the ancient Gnostic heresy did.

The ancient church Fathers who came up with the Trinitarian and Christological definitions of Nicea (325) and Chalcedon (451) were not just engaged in abstract speculations but were seeking to preserve what they regarded as essential for salvation. In their view, influenced by the Greek philosophical notion of forms or ultimate essences as that which is genuinely real, it was the whole of essential human nature which had been infected by sin with the fall of Adam. Only as the whole of essential human nature is healed would it be possible for actual human beings to accept the gift of salvation. But human nature cannot heal itself. It must come from beyond, from God. So it was necessary for the Son of God, the *logos*, to assume the whole of human nature in order that it be healed.

While the Council of Nicea proclaimed that Jesus Christ was of the same substance or essence (*homoousios*) of God, it also insisted that for our salvation he became man. The later Council of Chalcedon was even more emphatic about the manhood. According to the creed of this council it is to be confessed that Jesus Christ was at once complete in Godhead and complete in manhood, of one substance (*homoousios*) with God and at the same time of one substance with us, like us in all respects except for sin. Two natures are recognized, and it is claimed that the distinction of the natures is not annulled by their union in one person, Jesus Christ. Whatever the serious logical problems involved in the statements of this creed, it has held an honored position in the history of Christian thought, and undoubtedly this is due to its attempt to provide a conception of the incarnation which would protect and preserve the doctrine of salvation. As Irenaeus put it, he (Jesus Christ) became what we are that we might become what he is.

3. A Contemporary Christology

As indicated earlier, it is my conviction that it is important to preserve that which the councils of Nicea and Chalcedon sought to preserve. However this cannot be done in terms of the literal signification of the language in the creeds they produced. Given their culture, it is not surprising that they used Greek metaphysical concepts and declared that Jesus Christ was of one and the same substance as God and of one and the same substance as man. In the thought of the philosophers, substance is that which makes a thing what it is. It is, so to speak, the base for a thing's accidental properties, providing it with an identity no matter how varied the accidental properties may be or how much they may change. On this view, for example, there is such a reality as table substance ('tableness'?), and even though actual tables may be made of wood or stone or plastic, may be large or small, painted red or green, may have their finishes polished or blemished, they remain tables so long as there is still a certain form or substance present. Even though different things may share some accidental properties as, for example, a table and a chair being constructed of wood, they cannot share substances, for this would mean the loss of the identity of each. It is the nature of substance to be itself. Two qualitatively distinct substances can never be organically joined. Any attempt to bridge the gulf between them results in a contradiction and thus is as logically impossible as a round square.

On this point the Arian heresy was correct. As a student of Greek philosophy, Arius was convinced that the <u>substance</u> of God is his own and cannot be merged with human substance into one person. Like the philosophers he believed that substantively God is self-existent, eternal, indivisible, immutable, and impassible. But if this substantive nature of God was in the Son, how could the Son grow, suffer, and die? One cannot avoid a contradiction in affirming, on the one hand, that God is immutable and impassible, and on the other hand that the Son imbued with the divine substance suffers and dies. Given the metaphysical thought forms of the times, some sought to preserve the immutability and impassibility by affirming that the divine substance departed from Jesus at the crucifixion. But this destroys the union of the natures into one person and endangers the doctrine of salvation, for certainly a God who can forgive is not impassible. Arius sought to escape the contradiction in a different theory, but in one which is even more absurd. In his theory the substance of the preexistent Son, or personal *logos* , who was created

112

by God out of nothing, was identical neither with that of God nor of man. He was a *tertium quid*, a third something, who became incarnate as the soul of the historical Jesus. It is easy to see how unsatisfactory such a view is, for it reduces the Son to the status of the semi-divine heroes of Mount Olympus and undercuts the doctrine of salvation.

It should be clear by now that we cannot construct a Christology using the metaphysical substance concept of the ancient creeds. While, as noted above, we can appreciate the importance of what the council Fathers of Nicea and Chalcedon were seeking to do in their insistence on the dialectic of the divine and human in Jesus Christ for the sake of salvation, nevertheless it is the case that in terms of the concepts available to them they could not avoid a logical contradiction in their Christological definitions. Surely it is a contradictory claim and thus a logically impossible state-of-affairs for one to be both finite and historically conditioned, and infinite and unconditioned. Yet attempts to use the same conceptualization but to avoid the logical absurdity always seems to result in some sort of heresy in which the dialectic of human and divine is dissolved such that only the humanity or the deity remains, or in which there is a ludicrous absurdity similar to that in Arianism. Furthermore, in all these cases the necessary foundation for the doctrines of revelation and salvation are endangered. I do not see any way out of this dilemma except that of abandoning the substance concept in favor of some kind of a different conceptual schema. To a large extent, modern and contemporary theologians have sought to use different concepts which allow for consistency in Christological construction. Whether they all preserve what the framers of the ancient creeds were seeking to preserve is, of course, another question.

In what we might designate classical Protestant liberalism of the nineteenth and early twentieth centuries, human nature was thought to contain religion or a divine quality as an irreducible natural factor. Of course, such could be undeveloped and thus lie dormant, and it could be suppressed in the various corruptions of life, but it could not be destroyed entirely. It was designated in various ways such as the sense of absolute dependence or God consciousness

(Schleiermacher), human valuing activity (Ritschl), or divine quality (Macintosh). It was this which Jesus possessed to a supreme degree. There was no qualitative difference between him and other human beings but only, so to speak, a quantitative difference. In his character he expressed a unique degree of divine quality, but this was not something alien to human reason and experience. Rather it was continuous with the very best in human reason and experience. The personality of the historical Jesus was an achievement on his part. He was a superb master in the art of living (Harnack) which was not an effortless inheritance. As the superb master in the art of living he is for mankind the true moral example, the true example of right religious adjustment and thus the true revelation of God.

There is much of value in this liberal position. It most certainly does not take Jesus out of the man class, but preserves his genuine humanity as a real historical human being. It rightly emphasized that Jesus was one who was possessed of a relative freedom and used his freedom to make hard decisions. Thus in this view his achievements and his character are enhanced. Here is a real human being who experienced the physical necessities of life, the joys of companionship, the struggle with temptation, the loneliness of estrangement, the bitter disappointment of betrayal, and the agony of physical and mental suffering. Yet he was not defeated by all the difficulties he experienced but, in spite of them, became a superb master in the art of living and thus can serve as a model for us. Surely the liberal emphasis upon following the example of Jesus in terms of the moral and spiritual quality of his life, his concern for the poor, the dispossessed, and the oppressed, and for a kingdom life style individually and communally is of very great value and should be shared by all Christians whatever their theological orientations.

Even though values may be found in the liberal position, it does not fully preserve the essence of what the early fathers of the church sought to preserve through the creeds. With its overly optimistic view of the human condition, it tended to overemphasize Jesus' continuity with humanity, to view him simply as a superior moral hero. But if Jesus' quality of life, his God consciousness, is different from other

114

human beings only in terms of <u>degree</u>, certainly it is problematic that the divine quality in his life could be unique or without equal. It is at least logically possible that someone else could achieve such a degree of God consciousness or such mastery in the art of living. If such is the case, then revelation is a matter of human achievement, arising from below rather than coming from above as a special initiative of God. Logically, the notion of a special historical revelation which is unique is no longer tenable. Revelation is solely a matter of general revelation, in principle available to everyone even though a few persons achieve a greater awareness of and harmony with it.

In the chapter on God the claim was made that the revelation of God in Jesus Christ was <u>conclusive</u> though not concluded. This means that God's disclosure in Jesus was decisive, the model in terms of which the genuineness of other revelatory claims may be judged. Is it possible to make sense of this claim while at the same time preserving the genuine humanity of Jesus and the values in the liberal position?

We have seen in the previous chapter that it is reasonable to conclude that God is the sum total of all positive predicates. From this follow the divine attributes, including, of course, the divine benevolence. But benevolence cannot be simply an abstract idea or a vapid and passive sentiment. It can be genuinely real only as it is active, and it can be genuinely known only through active disclosure. In the biblical witness to the revelation of God this is precisely the case, for he discloses his nature and intentions through acting in history. So the major theme of the Old Testament, as was pointed out in chapter three, is that God takes the initiative, and out of his love and compassion freely offers his covenant to Israel. In the judgment which results from Israel's covenant faithlessness, God suffers too and yearns to forgive and renew the covenant community. Also in the New Testament the central theme is of God's taking the initiative and disclosing himself as a loving and compassionate God supremely in the life, teachings, and actions of Jesus Christ. Thus it is that the knowledge of God derived from revelation transcends but does not contradict what can be known of God from 'natural' theology (i. e. that the attribute of benevolence follows from the ontological argument).

115

The latter provides a rational basis for the former and thus reinforces the revelatory claim that God is love.

It might be possible for us to make some sense out of the claim that Jesus Christ is fully human and yet a conclusive revelation of God through an analysis of love and the self in light of some perspectives in process philosophy or theology.

It is probably the case that there is no word in common usage in the English language that is used more ambiguously or is more corrupted in meaning than the word love. If it were possible, it would be well to call a moratorium on its use. Since this is not likely to happen, we must seek to be as clear as possible about the meaning of the word, especially in terms of its use in our Christian heritage. It may be of some help in this endeavor to note that in the ancient Greek language there were three words which are often translated into English with the one word love. There was *Eros* from which we derive our English word erotic and which designated sexual love and sometimes the self-fulfilling of intellectual achievement as in the writings of the philosophers. Another word for love in Greek was *philia* which designates friendship and involves reciprocity. It is one of the root Greek words of our English word philosophy (love of wisdom). Finally, there is the word *agape* which was introduced in chapters two and three, indicating that this is the fundamental attribute of the divine character in light of which the divine justice must be understood, and that it is a self-giving, gratuitous, love.

With one exception (*philia* in Jas.4:4, "friendship with the world"), the New Testament writers use *agape* exclusively. It is descriptive of God's love for the world and all its creatures and of the responding love that human beings should have for God and all his creatures. It is an active benevolence which will go to any length for the sake of the beloved and its well-being. It is unmotivated by anything other than the necessity to be itself, spontaneous and redemptive. No better word can be found to designate the fundamental nature of the divine and his relationships than the word *agape*. It carries a much stronger connotation than other words such

116

as charity, benevolence, and friendship, for it entails sacrificial self-giving.

Daniel Day Williams expressed it well when he claimed that *agape* is not just an idea which may be added to a belief system. Understanding 'spirit' to mean the concrete personal expression of living, creative beings, it can be said that *agape* is what God's spirit is in his action in history.[1] The majesty of God is not impassibility but sacrificial love, and the truth of *agape,* of sacrificial love, can be fully disclosed only through life, the personal life of an actual human being. The picture of Jesus Christ which we find in the New Testament is of one whose life was a demonstration of *agape.* Reinhold Niebuhr was correct in his view that such a demonstration could occur only in the life on one who refused to engage in the rivalries of history, in the struggle of ego interest against ego interest. In a rather striking statement, Niebuhr claims that "the divine love can have a counterpart in history only in a life which ends tragically, because it refuses to participate in the claims and counterclaims of historical existence."[2] The cross is surely the supreme demonstration of this love.

If, as we have claimed above and the first letter of John (I John 4: 8) tells us, God is *agape,* then we are dealing with a concept which connotes attitudes, volitions, and the concrete personal expression of spirit, and we are no longer tied to the notion of metaphysical 'substance.' All the conundrums which plagued the early Fathers of the Church, such as how the impassible God could be passible in Jesus Christ, how a fallible finite human substance could contain an omnipotent, omniscient, and eternal substance, are simply irrelevant. Given *agape* as the concrete personal expression of spirit, and given the explication of the self in chapter two, it follows that it is logically possible for a person to be fully human and to express fully this love in his or her personal life.

The analysis of the self in chapter two made use of process thought in support of the conclusion concerning its transcendence and relative freedom. Consistent with the direction of evolution toward increased centralization, high grade occasions of experience develop a dominant, coordinating set which can entertain aims that transcend

117

the body. So the self emerges, not only related to its own body and to all of nature, but also discrete and transcendent as an individual self. The relation to nature and participation in community provide the relevant causal conditions which make probable certain choices and actions, but they do not make for a one to one constant conjunction as is sometimes the case in nature. They limit to a greater or lesser degree what can happen but do not <u>necessitate</u> one and only one outcome. If this were not the case to some extent even in nature, there could hardly be any creative advance or evolutionary development. The self, then, experiences the dialectic of individualization and participation, with the latter the source of most of the relevant causal conditions and the former of creative and/or relatively free choices.

Like all of us, Jesus experienced the dialectic of individualization and participation. His total life situation, including his religious heritage and the events of his day, constituted a causally necessary but not sufficient condition for his point of view. It is inconceivable that someone with the outlook of Jesus could have emerged in a Greek or Roman culture. Jesus' life and teachings could not have been what they were outside the context of Judaism in its historical development. As the Apostle Paul put it, "But when the time had fully come, God sent forth his Son, born of woman, born under the law." (Galatians 4: 4) Yet this context is not sufficient to explain the whole of his life and teaching, of why he made certain choices and engaged in certain actions and not in others. Surely this was due both to the prompting of God and to his freely chosen response to that prompting.

The dialectic of mystery and meaning confronts us at this point. Whiteheadean process thought can provide a basis for a meaningful interpretation of the incarnation such that it does not collapse totally into mystery. If, as we have argued, God is love, then it follows that he is continually seeking to lure all creatures to fulfill their potentialities. That is, God has an initial aim for each actual occasion or society of occasions. Just what this aim is depends on the status and environment of the occasion, the causal factors which led to it, and just what sort of responses to God's initial aim arise from the subjective

118

aims of the occasion. The aim for a society of low level occasions will differ from that for a society of high grade occasions. Even on the level of a high grade society of occasions, that of human selves, the initial aim of God may be different for different persons. For example, it seems obvious that an initial aim of God for an Australian aborigine would differ considerably from that of someone like the scholar and philosopher, Alfred North Whitehead. So the initial aim of God for Jesus could be and, I believe, was distinctive. Jesus was called by God to incorporate in his own life and to demonstrate fully the divine *agape*. Without this, Jesus would not have been what he was. The mystery remains as to why God called this particular person in the Jewish culture of the time.

While God took the initiative in calling Jesus, the response of Jesus was not compelled. *Agape* by its very nature does not compel; it persuades and lures. Jesus responded freely and fully to the divine persuasion. In Whiteheadan terms, he freely brought his subjective aims into complete harmony with God's initial aim for him. It may be that at least part of the mystery of the incarnation is why Jesus freely responded to God's call as he did, especially in view of the suffering it entailed. Others may have been issued distinctive calls by God and simply failed to respond as did Jesus. Of course, we can never know whether or not this was the case. What we do know is that the theme of the gospel story in the New Testament affirms that Jesus of Nazareth incorporated the reality of God as *agape* in his life and perception of the world. It was the center of his existence and constituted his uniqueness.

It is not possible to verify this in any scientific or literalistic way. In the introductory chapter on method, I argued that the basic New Testament conviction that "God was in Christ reconciling the world to himself" (2Cor. 5: 19) is a permanent myth central to the Christian *mythos*. It transcends the possibility of verification and falsification but is not absurd. For those who accept it, it provides a frame of reference which makes sense out of the experiences of life and history, and thus receives a kind of pragmatic justification. Further, while it cannot be verified (how could one even begin to do that?), it is

119

possible, as argued above, with process categories to make sense out of the incarnation such that the contradictions of the ancient creeds, the absurdities of literalism, and the bland humanism of the radical liberals are avoided. The dialectic of mystery and meaning is retained and not eliminated as in those positions. *Mythos* and *logos* are kept in a reciprocal relationship. The *mythos* provides a frame of reference, or principle of interpretation (God was in Christ reconciling the world to himself), and the *logos* demonstrates how the *mythos* can make sense on the basis of a metaphysics different from that presupposed in the ancient creeds. In his own subjective aims the completely human and historical Jesus freely responded fully to God's agapeistic initial aim for him so that, as *agape,* God was in him.

If we believe that God as *agape* was in Jesus and that the divine revelation in him was conclusive, does it follow that we are caught in that kind of Christocentric exclusivism which denies the availability of God's acceptance and love to those outside the Christian confession? On the one hand, there are some Christians who do not hesitate to answer this question in the affirmative. On the other, there are those who think that the only way to avoid such blatant restriction on the scope of God's love and the resulting intolerance for those outside the faith is to deny the uniqueness of Jesus Christ and to consider him as simply one religious leader among others. In both cases there is a failure to appreciate that the very meaning of *agape* requires the dialectic of the particular and the universal, of genuine commitment and genuine tolerance. As argued above, God's *agape* can be fully disclosed only in the life of a particular, actual human and historical being, and yet the concern for humanity of the divine love is universal in scope. That God's revelation was conclusive in Jesus Christ does not mean that it was necessarily exclusive or concluded. If God is love, he surely desires fulfillment of life for each of his creatures, that each creature attain the maximum possible satisfaction at each stage of his existence. It follows, then, that he is most certainly not inactive among the adherents of other religions.

The belief that God conclusively disclosed himself as *agape* in Jesus Christ is a non-negotiable tenet for the Christian. *Agape* is the norm in light of which all claims concerning revelation and the will of God are to be judged whether these claims come from Scripture, other Christian sources, or other religions. However, the Christian should also keep in mind that, as Reinhold Niebuhr put it, there is a "hidden Christ" operative in history such that those who do not know the revelation in Jesus Christ often act with more humility and love than those who do.[3] This view is certainly coherent with the outlook of the historical Jesus as presented in the Gospels. He did not restrict his teaching and service to the 'orthodox,' but lovingly accepted the dispossessed, the outcasts, and those who were not of his own religion. He found more faith in a Roman Centurion, a member of a foreign religion, than in Israel, and proclaimed that "many will come from East and West to sit at table with Abraham, Issac, and Jacob in the kingdom of heaven." (Matt. 8: 12 ff.) It is clear that Jesus demonstrated in his own life an agapeistic God whose love is unconditionally directed toward each individual and yet is universal in scope, concerned with the whole human family and the lower orders on creation as well.

If God is *agape* and thus concerned with each and every creature in the world, this certainly has important implications with respect to the meaning of salvation. The test to determine the adequacy of a soteriology will be its coherence with a Christology which emphasizes the agapeistic nature of the God disclosed in the life and teachings of Jesus Christ. As suggested above, any sort of unloving exclusivism must be rejected, but it is equally important that the soteriology take into account a realistic view of human nature and the dialectic of human beings as saints and sinners (discussed in chapter two). This will entail the issue of the nature of sin, of how sin is overcome by the grace of God, and of the goal of salvation. It is to these and other issues of soteriology that we turn in the next chapter.

---

[1] *The Spirit and Forms of Love*, (Harper and Row,1968), pp.11,16.

[2] *The Nature and Destiny of Man*, vol.2, (Charles Scribner's sons, 1943), p.72.

[3] Ibid., pp. 109-110, footnote 6.

CHAPTER FIVE
SOTERIOLOGY

As suggested at the end of the last chapter, views concerning the meaning and method of salvation are closely correlated with the understanding of human nature, the nature of God, and of the nature and function of Jesus Christ. Indeed, different views of human nature, God, and Jesus Christ result in different soteriological theories. This is clearly evident in the history of Christian thought. A full discussion of this topic could fill a separate volume or more. The attempt here will be simply to sketch briefly the basic views and compare them with modern and contemporary views in order to provide a foundation for a soteriological construction of my own.

1. Soteriologies of the Past

Two contrasting views of human nature and sin, and thus of what constitutes salvation, have a long history in Christian thought. With respect to human nature and sin, there is on the one hand what might be designated the optimistic and moralistic view, and on the other hand what might be designated the realistic and theologicopsychological view. Some examples of thinkers in which the latter view finds expression are the Apostle Paul, Augustine, and the Protestant Reformers, Luther and Calvin. In the Pauline writings human nature is viewed as a generic whole such that Adam's fall into the situation of estrangement under the conditions of existence infects everyone. So sin is viewed as not just an act or series of acts but as the universal predicament of human beings in the state of willful estrangement from God, others, and their own genuine selves. Sinful acts which are performed as a result of this condition are symptoms of this basic state of sin or estrangement which may be explicated in three closely related characterizations. It may be characterized as the self's insensitivity to the graciousness of God, the separation of the will from God's will. The second is, in a sense, the negative of the first, namely, hubris or excessive pride. That is, sin has to do with egocentricity, the pretension of self, the attempt to make ourselves into

123

gods. The third certainly follows from the first two and is the unlimited desire to draw the whole of reality into one's self, to take the 'sponge' approach to life and to value the world and other creatures only as they serve one's perceived self interest.

In view of these characterizations it follows that sin involves the whole person, volition, intellect, and emotions. No one was more explicit about this than was John Calvin in his explication of what generally is called the doctrine of total depravity, a doctrine which today often is misunderstood. It does not mean that fallen human beings cannot do some good deeds. Rather, it means that sin involves the total person. Even good deeds can be infected with sin. It is not so much what is done but why and how it is done. A deed which is clearly good viewed from a purely objective standpoint may be done out of calculatingly selfish, prideful, and egocentric motives. Pure egocentricism may be rare. Human motivation is a notoriously complex matter, and motives are most often mixed. There is such a thing as altruistic motivation, but this is always mixed with some degree of egocentricism. So the doing of good deeds, although better than not doing them, cannot win release form the predicament of sin. Since it is the motives and the volitions which are infected with egocentricism, no one can will himself or herself out of this predicament. An egocentric will willing is still an egocentric will willing. The cure must come from beyond.

Echoes of what I have called the optimistic and moralistic view is found as early as in the Letter of James in the New Testament and in the Apostolic Fathers. It finds expression to a greater or lesser extent in such later Fathers as Cyprian, Ireneaus, and Athanasius and in the Catholic Church as it became more and more a dominant institution in the world concerned with the morality of individuals and society. Its outstanding representative, of course, was Augustine's opponent, Pelagius, and even though Pelagius was condemned by two early church councils, what might be called a semi-Pelagianism gained a foothold in the Western Church and remains to this day in the Catholic Church.

While there may be some differences in their formulations among the representives of the moralistic view, there generally tends to be an optimistic stance with respect to the possibilities of human life under the conditions of historical existence. Sin is understood primarily as sins, acts of immorality and disobedience which may be overcome by other acts of morality and obedience. Even those who held to a generic view of human nature such that the original sin of Adam had an effect on all persons, bringing them under the sway of the devil and death, nevertheless, somewhat inconsistently, viewed the human will as essentially free. In some cases (Ireneaus, Athanasius, and even the later Aquinas) human beings are regarded as having been created in both the image and likeness of God. This idea arose from a literalistic reading of Genesis 1: 26 which failed to recognize the poetic parallelism of the original Hebrew. The image was understood as Adam's capacity for reason and freedom, and the likeness was a certain divine quality of life and the capacity for immortality. It was the latter which had been lost in the fall, while the former, though perhaps in a somewhat weakened condition, was retained. On this basis, sin is understood as certain acts of immorality due to the absence of the divine likeness.

The optimistic and moralistic view finds its most extreme expression in Pelagius. His view of human nature was atomistic. That is, each person creates his own character and determines his own destiny. Rejecting the doctrine of original sin, Pelagius maintained that Adam's fall had an effect only upon himself and not upon his descendants. While the sin of Adam did provide a bad example for his descendants, and persons do choose to follow this bad example, they still retain their freedom not to sin. At any moment they may put away their sins, turn to God, and obey.

Such an extreme view was certainly inconsistent with experience and the traditional teachings of the church as well as reducing the significance and function of Jesus Christ to that of a moral teacher. The traditional theology of the church held to the notion of original sin. Yet given the understanding of it as the loss of the likeness of God but not of the image, it is not surprising that sin is

125

understood moralistically and that the sacramental and merit system of the Catholic Church emerges. It is appropriate, I think, to designate this as a semi-Pelagianism.

For this view the soteriological problem is how can fallen human beings regain the lost likeness of God. First of all, essential human nature needs to be remade, and this was accomplished by the incarnation. In Jesus Christ there was both the image and likeness of God in the confines of the truly human. He was the new Adam, and in him essential human nature was remade such that there is now the capacity for immortality and growth into a full divine quality of life. As Ireneaus put it, Jesus Christ recapitulated the perfect man, step by step, so that what God in the creation had intended human beings to be was now possible.[1]

While the capacity for the divine likeness has been restored to essential human nature, actual human beings need considerable help in striving to achieve this goal. Since they retain the divine image, even fallen human beings are able by the use of reason to gain a considerable natural knowledge of God, but by themselves they are unable to regain the lost likeness. Reason helps in the understanding of and response to revelation, but first there must be the revelatory message of the Bible and the Church, that in Jesus Christ is disclosed the continuous forgiving and sacrificial love of God which is ever seeking to lure them along the pathway to the divine likeness. In this pilgrimage believers are aided by studying and seeking to follow the model of the divine likeness presented in the life of Jesus Christ and by the Church with its sacraments through which divine power is communicated such that there can be progress in the pilgrimage toward the divine likeness. While divine forgiveness is emphasized, the grace of God is understood primarily as an infused power which enables believers to complete faith by works of love, to become more and more Godlike and thus merit eternal life. Even Augustine, who held to what I have called the theologicopsychological view of sin and emphasized predestination in his soteriology, viewed the grace of God as an infused power made available through the sacraments, and affirmed that faith must be completed by good works in order for one to

126

merit eternal life. This aspect of Augustine's thought had an influence on subsequent Catholic thought while his views on sin, faith, and predestination were to have some influence in the thought of later Protestantism.

I pointed out above that if sin is a matter of the total person, of total depravity, in that volition, intellect and emotions are infected with the pretension of self, with the attempt to be God, then simply doing good works does not win release from the predicament of estrangement. The Apostle Paul put this in terms of the powerlessness of the law (the Torah in both its ceremonial and moral commandments) to deliver human beings from the predicament of estrangement. It was not that the law is bad; it is good, a gift of God for the well-being of mankind. But under the conditions of historical existence, in the state of estrangement, human beings pervert the law. They make it into commandments, and love cannot be commanded. If genuine, either it is entirely gratuitous or a free response to a gratuitous gift of love on the part of another. Furthermore, given the fact of sin, any accomplishments in following the law lead only to self-righteousness, the pride of virtue, and so to even worse enslavement in the predicament of estrangement. In the words of Paul, "What the law could never do, because our lower nature robbed it of all potency, God has done:" (Romans 8:3, *The New English Bible*) That is, release from the predicament of sin must come from beyond.

It is God who took the initiative and through Jesus Christ freely offered to sinful human beings reconciliation with himself and thus release from the predicament of estrangement. In Paul's words, "It was God who reconciled us to himself through Christ." (2 Cor.5: 18,*The Jerusalem Bible*) In Jesus Christ's utter faithfulness to God, demonstrated in his deep concern for all human beings, his loving acceptance of the dispossessed and the outcasts, and his dedication to God even to the extremity of death, God's merciful forgiveness is unmistakably shown. It is not that God demanded a sacrifice, a scapegoat, so that his righteousness might be appeased. His attitude toward human beings does not need to be changed, for he is eternally loving and forgiving. Rather, human beings need to be changed, to have their estrangement and spiritual blindness overcome. For Paul, the sacrifice of Christ is "God's own proof of his love towards us." (Romans 5: 8, *The New English Bible*) It clearly demonstrates the lengths to which God has gone in order to disclose his love for all, his deep pathos due to the rejection, estrangement and suffering of human beings, and his continual eagerness freely to accept the unacceptable if only they accept his acceptance. The appropriation of this gift of God is by faith, and faith is not just an opinion or a belief but trust and confidence in the continual mercy and forgiveness of God in spite of the fact that no one is ever worthy of his acceptance. On this basis the Christian seeks to do good (and the moral aspects of the law can be a helpful guide) not for prudential reasons to win favor with God or any kind of reward, but simply because having received the gift of God's acceptance and out of gratitude for this gift one wants to do good because it is good. Ethical imperatives always presuppose the gift of grace and faith.

In light of his own experience, Paul was convinced that no one could merit the acceptance of God. Therefore it is not surprising that he was convinced that anyone who had received the grace of God found himself ascribing the whole process to God's action and none to himself. Even faith appeared as God's gift. Paul did not have a carefully worked out doctrine of predestination and in some respects was not unlike the Rabbis who somewhat inconsistently held to God's foreknowledge and foreordination and yet claimed that freedom of choice is granted. Paul certainly issued ethical imperatives, and that presupposes freedom of choice, to obey or not to obey. Yet when it comes to salvation, to the reception of grace, he was convinced that it is not of our own doing but is totally the gift of God, lest anyone should boast.

The Pauline understanding of sin and salvation is reemphasized in the thought of the Protestant Reformers, Luther and Calvin. Sin involves the total person, and salvation or reconciliation is a gift of God. Faith also involves the total person as a matter of trust and confidence in the forgiveness and graciousness of God. It cannot be manufactured. If one experiences it, he takes no credit for it but

128

confesses that it was God's work in him. At this point the Reformers' doctrine of predestination is relevant. It is not to be confused with a doctrine of fatalism. Even though at a few points Calvin does seem to suggest that events happen by necessity, predestination is first and foremost a statement about salvation, and this is certainly true for Luther. It might be described as a last drastic guarantee against any notion of salvation by works.

To gain an adequate understanding of the Reformers' doctrine of predestination, it is necessary to take into account their life situations in late medieval Europe. The Catholic Church was the dominant institution and, as we have seen, proclaimed and practiced a theology in which salvation is a matter of becoming actually righteous or godlike. God's grace was understood as a power which primarily through the sacraments could become infused into the soul of the believer so that he would be able to achieve this goal. Also the sacrificial death of Christ on the cross gained for him a superabundance of merit, and this has not been lost but became the possession of the Church. It is communicated through the sacraments which means that participation in them is itself a matter of good works through which believers can increase their own store of merit. The infusion of grace and the merit from the sacraments enable one to become actually righteous and thus worthy of eternal life in heaven. Of course, for those believers who cannot quite make it on earth, there is the escape valve of purgatory out of which they may finally emerge as worthy of eternal life in heaven. While it is true that there is a mystical element in the sacramental piety of the late medieval Catholic Church, its major emphasis was upon the doing of good works and the accruing of merit so as to be actually righteous and merit eternal blessedness.

The Reformers, especially Luther, found through bitter experience that the merit system failed miserably to bring inner peace, a sense of God's loving acceptance. The battle with sin and sins is never ending. No one could ever become righteous as God is righteous, and if that is the requirement for salvation, then there is no hope for mortal human beings. But there is hope, for, as the beloved Paul had proclaimed, God had taken the initiative and through Christ freely offered his gift of reconciliation. Justification is by faith. It is not that one is actually righteous but that he is <u>accounted</u> as righteous on the basis of his faith which in turn is itself a gift of God. There is, then, no basis for claiming any merit. To put it in a rather extreme and oversimplified way, it might be said that for the Reformers the main difference between a Christian and a sinner is that the Christian is a sinner saved by the grace of God. That is, God accepts him in spite of the fact that he is unacceptable because he accepts God's acceptance. Whatever good works he does flow from this basis, and he takes no credit for them.

While among other and later Protestant thinkers there were some differences with the thought of Luther and Calvin, most accepted the conviction that salvation is by faith rather than by works. In some cases perhaps there was somewhat of a greater emphasis upon the spirit of Christ at work in the believer, but the priority of the forgiving grace of God is retained. Even John Wesley, who was optimistic about the possibility of sanctification, the growth toward perfection, insisted that human beings cannot redeem themselves. Nothing but God and his redeeming grace can rescue human beings. Convinced that God in his justice cannot foreordain human beings to damnation, Wesley rejected the concept of predestination. It is God who took the initiative through Jesus Christ and offered his justification (forgiveness of sins) to all, but there must be the response of acceptance. Such response brings an increasing presence of the grace of God in the human heart. So grace and response mutually reinforce each other, but obviously there cannot be a response unless there is something to which a response can be made, namely, the initial and continually offered grace of God.

Basic to Reformation thought, then, is the emphasis upon the activity of God in the process of salvation. With the understanding of sin as the pretension of self, egocentricity, it follows that one cannot initiate a relationship with God on his own, and without such a relationship one cannot properly understand himself or God. It is only as one experiences reconciliation or atonement with God that he genuinely understands himself as a sinner in constant need of God's grace. The prerequisite for reconciliation is the knowledge of God disclosed in Jesus Christ. While there may be some natural knowledge which points to the existence of God, what or who God is depends upon his revelation in Christ. One who does not know Christ does not have a true knowledge of God. The whole of Christ's life, death, and resurrection reveals God acting in free and sovereign love.

The Christology of the Reformers is traditional, but the major focal point is on the work of Christ as mediator and savior. Christ had identified himself with sinful man, taken his sin upon himself and permitted himself to be judged in man's place, conquered sin and death and thus made possible the transformation of man's inner condition. Therefore Christ opened the way to man's justification. This substitutionary theory certainly entails a view that God's justice must be satisfied, and it echoes to some extent some ancient views that a ransom must be paid to God or to the devil or to both. However that may be, it is the case that the Reformers placed major emphasis upon justification by faith. They insisted that in Christ God took the initiative in freely offering his acceptance to all in spite of the fact that they are not worthy of his acceptance.

2. Soteriologies of the Modern and Contemporary Period

With the rise of the scientific movement, of theories concerning social and biological evolution, and of increased knowledge concerning religions of the world, traditional Protestant thought (and Catholic theology as well) was seriously challenged in the modern period on a number of fronts. Traditional theology, Protestant and Catholic, had emphasized final causality, and this is ignored by the sciences in which only efficient causality holds sway. Thus, for example, the view of nature as God's handiwork, of events in nature as well as in the human realm occurring according to the purposes or goals of God, is replaced with a view of nature as operating in terms of natural regularities which may be discovered by observations of the sequences of causes and effects. Scientific method per se does not allow for a consideration of the transcendent or vertical dimension of life (to use a spatial metaphor) but is confined only to the horizontal dimension. On

131

this basis there were some thinkers and scientists who concluded that, as expressed by the 19th century astronomer, Pierre Laplace, there was no need for the God-hypothesis.

Efficient causality as a principle of explanation was soon strengthened by the emergence of considerable evidence in support of evolution. The conclusion is inescapable that nothing in nature is static but that all of nature is characterized throughout by change and evolutionary process. This includes, of course, all forms of life, plant, animal, and human. So the psychological, social, and historical sciences have, as basic methodological principles, efficient causality and evolutionary process. Human life is investigated in terms of its organic and psychological interdependence with its natural and social environment. The result is the tendency to eliminate any transcendent dimension from the human self and to explain religion in purely naturalistic terms. Given the great expansion of knowledge concerning non western peoples and religions, there emerged the tendency to explain the origins of religions and the differences between them in terms of people's particular geographical conditions, evolving histories, and intercultural involvements.

These and other developments led some to believe that religion is but a fossilized remainder of ancient times obstructing human progress into a brave new world, and the lot of mankind would be improved when the dead hand of religion was eliminated from human life. At the opposite extreme were those who viewed the scientific movement as though it were the work of the devil, seeking to destroy their most cherished convictions concerning the significance and meaning of the world, human existence, and the ultimate destiny of the human soul. Especially during the 19th century extremists on both sides engaged in the so-called "warfare between science and religion."

In the late 19th and early 20th centuries both Catholic modernist and Protestant liberal theologians sought to work out some sort of accommodation between science and religion. It was indicated in chapter one that much of this thought found its inspiration in the philosophy of Immanuel Kant. While he argued, as we have seen in chapter two, that the traditional proofs for the existence of God were not valid, nevertheless, he wished to defend religion by providing it with what he regarded as a sound basis which did not conflict with science. He thought that religion was harmed by attacking science and its assured results. He was as concerned to defend science against the attacks of religious leaders as he was to defend religion against any destructive ideas proposed by scientists. Even though science and religion contradicted each other, it was possible, Kant believed, to defend each as true because they deal with two different realms. Science operates in the realm of what can be known (the phenomenal realm) while religion is located in the realm of what ought to be done, of morality (the noumenal realm). It follows, then, that science and religion do not contradict each other and neither should interfere with the other. Both can be given full support by intelligent and rational persons.

Given the enormous influence of Kant in all areas of intellectual endeavor, it is not surprising that theologians who were concerned with relating Christian thought to modern life and perspectives should reflect Kant's outlook in their theological constructions. Catholic modernists and Protestant liberals tended to emphasize Christian faith more as a way of life than a set of doctrines or creeds. Like Kant, they shifted the ground of religion to some area of human life other than knowledge and, as indicated above in section two of chapter four, defended it as a natural endowment of this area. For some it was the human sense of absolute dependence, or God consciousness, which everyone possesses to some degree (Schleiermacher). Others, like Kant, found it in the categorical or moral imperative, or the human capacity for making value judgments (Ritschl and Harnack, followed to a large extent by such American liberal theologians as William Adams Brown, Harry Emerson Fosdick, and Walter Rauschenbush).

It follows from their acceptance of religion as a natural endowment of human life that the liberals tended to view actual human nature as fundamentally good. Furthermore, they accepted as factually true both biological and social evolution. So the biblical story of the Fall and the doctrine of original sin must be rejected as an

133

outmoded and prescientific attempt to explain the origin of sin. In the long evolving of nature and humanity it would be impossible for a single individual to so completely change the human race. Sin is not the literal legacy of Adam (as meaningful as the Genesis myth of creation may be), but it is the fossilized remainder of man's animal beginnings which impedes his moral and spiritual growth, but which is being progressively overcome. It is transmitted socially due to the influence of one generation on another and of the social environment on the individual. If the doctrine of original sin is to be retained at all (and most liberals thought it should be abandoned), it should be understood as simply symbolizing the social matrix of sin. Liberal theology, somewhat similar to Pelagius, tended to take a moralistic view of sin and an optimistic view of the human ability to make progress individually and socially toward the kingdom of God.

In this pilgrimage toward the Kingdom, Jesus Christ is the teacher and example since in him is found the highest degree of God-consciousness or moral valuing activity. The gospel of Jesus is to be substituted for the gospel about Jesus. The substitutionary-satisfaction view of salvation is rejected as demeaning of God and destructive of human responsibility. Christ's saving work was not a matter of his taking upon himself the punishment which sinful human beings merited and thus satisfying God's justice. Since God is always loving and forgiving, his attitude toward his creatures does not need to be changed. Instead it is the attitudes and lives of human beings which need to be changed so that they will be reconciled to God and pattern their lives, individually and socially, after the model presented in the life and teachings of Jesus, the superb master in the art of living.

Most liberal theologians supported what came to be known as the "Social Gospel." They held that the Christian faith involves not only the salvation of individuals but also of society. Ministers should proclaim that the establishment of a community of justice and righteousness is just as much a saving work of God as the salvation of the individual. A full Christian gospel includes the kingdom of God ideal of a just and peaceful social order. So the liberal theologians attacked the social evils of their times such as child labor, economic exploitation of workers, unsafe working conditions, and race and class discrimination. While they were focused on this life, emphasizing that the business of the church was developing loving individuals in a just social order, they did not neglect the transcendent dimension of human life. There is such a thing as the self which has the capacity to have a relationship with other selves and with the God of Jesus. The self also has the capacity to survive physical death. They rejected the notion of a literal last judgment with burning torment for the wicked and materalistic bliss for the righteous. But they did hold that the soul is immortal, that there is a persistence of personality through death.

The most adamant opposition to liberalism arose in Protestant fundamentalism. Generally fundamentalists hold to the fall of Adam and original sin as literally true, emphasize the deity of Christ and the substitutionary-satisfaction view of salvation. All persons have inherited the sin and guilt of Adam and thus stand under the curse of punishment and eternal damnation by a righteous and just God. Only one of the statue of God can satisfy the divine justice. That the Christ who came to earth was of such a statue is guaranteed by his birth from a virgin. As indicated in chapter four, it is this which justifies taking him out of the man class and putting him in the God class. Belief that Jesus was in fact born of a virgin is necessary for salvation. So for fundamentalists, Christ, the literal Son of God, took man's place, suffered the penalty of death which man's sin deserved, and by this sacrifice satisfied divine justice. That Christ propitiated the offended judicial sentiment in God is held generally by fundamentalists to be the very essence of the gospel. One can be saved from eternal damnation only as he believes this doctrine.

While the liberals tended to take what we might call a 'left-wing' response to the challenge of modern culture with its scientific movement, fundamentalists tended to take a 'right-wing' response. Unlike the liberals who sought to work out an accommodation with culture, emphasizing the continuity of the Christian faith with the best in cultural developments, fundamentalists found little but discontinuity. So the liberals tended to emphasize a this-worldly

135

understanding of salvation which embraced human progress toward the kingdom of God while the fundamentalists tended to emphasize an other-worldly understanding of salvation in which attention was centered on individuals escaping from this evil world and its destruction in an Armageddon into a life of blessedness in heaven.

In light of the global conflicts of the modern period and of the gross social injustices of the industrial age, some theologians came to a more realistic view of human nature and its possibilities than had the liberals, but without subscribing to the literalistic understanding of the fall and original sin held by the fundamentalists. In chapter one it was pointed out that these theologians (Neo-Reformation or Neo-Orthodox) sought to renew in our age the basic tenets of Reformation thought. This is very evident in their views of sin and salvation. In their view the liberals were insufficiently dialectical in their theological anthropology and thus too optimistic about human nature and its possibilities, overemphasizing the continuity between faith and culture. For example, Karl Barth rejected any notion of a "point of contact" between the Christian faith on the one hand and the natural order and the disciplines of culture on the other.[2] While not a fundamentalist in that he rejected biblical literalism, much like the fundamentalists he ignored the disciplines of culture and held to a predestinarian soteriology.

In this country Reinhold Niebuhr developed a theology which has been designated Christian Realism, and in which, like Barth, he disagreed with the liberal views of sin and salvation. However, Niebuhr also disagreed with Barth. In his view Barth[3] tended to overemphasize the discontinuity between faith and the disciplines of culture, to view revelation and faith as totally a *sui generis* gift of God from beyond, with human reason having a very little role to play even in the reception of revelation. While Barth's thought (especially the early Barth) did contain some radical dialectical perspectives (God's grace is his judgment and his judgment grace), Neibuhr thought that on the issue of the relation of faith and culture he was insufficiently dialectical. This relation, according to Niebuhr, is not a matter either of continuity or of discontinuity but of both continuity and discontinuity. In spite of this rather serious disagreement between these two theologians, there is considerable, although not total, similarity in their views of sin and justification by faith. In some ways Niebuhr's analysis (especially with respect to sin) is more profound than Barth's, but both owe much to the thought of the Reformers and behind them to Augustine and Paul.

While both of these theologians accepted biological evolution as a fact, they rejected the social and historical evolutionism of the liberals with respect to sin and salvation. On the other hand, they did not accept the fundamentalists' literalistic understanding of original sin and of the Genesis creation and fall narratives. Yet I think their views can be fairly characterized by what I have called the theologicopsychological perspective which is more profound and realistic than simply the moralistic one but which incorporates the latter as well.

In both cases sin is viewed as a universal human state or condition of being which is characterized by pride, rebellion, and estrangement from God and others, but it is neither an inherited condition nor an ontological fate. It is in their freedom that human beings absurdly seek to establish their own essences by denying both God and themselves and thus sin at the very center of their beings. Sin involves the total person in the sense that intellect, volition, and emotions are infected with this pretension of self.

While they arrive at a similar basic understanding of sin, Barth's approach is purely theological, grounded as it is in his doctrines of reconciliation and Christology. Man is created by God to be God's covenant partner, a reality fully actualized only in Jesus Christ. This is what essential humanity is supposed to be, but human beings absurdly (in their freedom) affirm what God has negated and call good what God has not chosen. So sin distorts human understanding with respect to the relationship with God, the nature of sin, and thus of essential humanity. It is in the light of the reconciliation offered through the Word of God in Christ that we can in humility become aware of the true nature of our sin as pride, pretension of self, and rebellion against God, the attempt to be God.

137

It is the case, of course, that Niebuhr's anthropology was theologically grounded, for he affirmed that we can not fully understand ourselves unless we are aware that we are understood from beyond ourselves, and he was convinced that when reconciled with God we see our sin more sharply revealed and defined by the knowledge that God himself is the victim of our pride and pretension. Yet, unlike Barth, he did seek to show that the Christian understanding of human sin was supported by an empirical and realistic appraisal of the human condition as such. It is obvious that human beings are creatures who exist at the juncture of nature and spirit. Like other creatures, human beings are subject to the laws and limitations of nature, but unlike them they can transcend such through consciousness. Thus human beings are suspended between finitude and freedom. This gives rise to that deep seated anxiety which, although not itself sin, is the precondition for sin. That is, human beings seek to blind themselves, perhaps even to abolish, one or the other of these two aspects of their natures. They seek to become either gods or beasts abolishing finitude or the self-transcendence of freedom. It is the former which is the more basic, wrecking the most havoc in human personal and social existence. Sin is more a matter of the will than of the flesh, and its most insidious form is pride, pride of power, pride of knowledge, and pride of virtue. It is at the higher levels of human life that sin, the pretension of self, is the most dangerous, precisely because it is a mixture of self-sufficiency and insecurity. It finds its most horrible manifestations in the collective pride of groups such as nations and churches in which the pride of power is reinforced with the pride of virtue so that they imagine themselves as sinless saints who have no need of repentance and thus are justified in committing any kind of atrocity. While the doctrine of original sin is not to be taken literally, it may be used metaphorically to designate the seriousness, depth, and universality of sin.

In light of their view of the depth and universality of sin, it is not surprising that Barth and Niebuhr, much like the Reformers, held that reconciliation with God was the gift of God through Jesus Christ. Unlike the liberals for whom salvation was primarily a matter of following the moral example of Jesus, and the fundamentalists for whom salvation was a matter of belief in the juridical substitutionary-satisfaction doctrine, Barth and Niebuhr reemphasized the Reformers doctrine of justification by faith. That is, on the basis of our trust in God's grace, disclosed in Jesus Christ, God accepts us in spite of the fact that we are unacceptable.

In Barth's view, human beings lack any capacity even for receiving faith (there is no point of contact), and if one has faith, it is entirely the work of God. It is God's free gift for which there is no human disposition. Niebuhr, on the other hand, held that human beings naturally have "uneasy consciences", the awareness that they should be better, and this provides a "point of contact" between the Christian faith and those without faith. There is something to which appeal can be made. While no one can create faith or will himself or herself into faith, in freedom one can reject or accept God's freely offered gift of grace. The acceptance is grounded in repentance which in turn arises out of encountering the suffering of God because of our sin and rebellion as this is disclosed in the suffering of Jesus Christ. This revelation is, so to speak, the divine 'shock treatment' which awakens us from our indifference and callousness, makes us aware of the seriousness of our sin, and brings us to that despair about ourselves which makes possible the contrition necessary for the acceptance of divine mercy and forgiveness.

While fundamentalists tended to view salvation as a matter of giving mental assent to a set of propositions (Virgin birth, substitutionary-satisfaction salvation etc.) and liberals tended to view it moralistically as a matter of following the example of Christ in building the kingdom of God on earth, Barth and Niebuhr held to what was essentially a Reformation and Pauline view of the relation of faith and works. Faith is not assent to a set of doctrines about Christ. It is trust, the experiential acceptance of the good news that the forgiving grace of God has been freely offered in Christ. It is on this basis that the Christian, out of gratitude for God's acceptance, seeks to do good in both the individual and social spheres. That is, he wants to actually become that which he already is by the grace of God. But in light of the knowledge of God's *agape* there is always the awareness of sin and therefore of one's constant need for God's forgiveness. Out of the humility arising from such awareness comes the tolerance and acceptance of others which is a necessary condition for the improvement of individual and social righteousness.

As to the precise nature of Christian ethics there was some disagreement between Niebuhr and Barth. Since he denied that there is a "point of contact" between grace and the natural endowments of humanity, Barth had little use for philosophical ethics or natural theology, and insisted that Christian ethics is entirely a matter of making clear the meaning of the revealed word of God in the concrete situations of human life. Niebuhr, on the other hand, believed that the principles of justice which human beings have rationally conceived have validity as middle principles and can provide considerable guidance in the concrete situations of life where, due to human sin, *agape* alone is not applicable. Justice is the servant of *agape,* the transcendent absolute which stands in judgment over all middle principles and achievements and as a challenge for ever closer approximations and greater achievements. But beyond all human achievements, trials, and failures there is the confident hope in an ultimate universal fellowship with God.

In many ways the Christian Realism of Niebuhr stands in a dialectical relation to Barth's Neo-Orthodoxy and liberal theology, and this is reflected in his view of the paradoxical relation between faith and culture. Christian faith is both transcendent of and yet relevant to culture. Similar to Barth, he emphasized the transcendence of God, his *agape* as the one absolute which transcends all human achievements and values. Similar to liberalism, he stressed that the very meaning of *agape* entails relationships and thus an immanent aspect of God relevant to this world. Thus much of liberalism, such as the social gospel and critical biblical scholarship, was incorporated in his theology.

While it may be said that Niebuhr's theology stands in a dialectical relation to Neo-Orthodoxy and liberalism, it is clearly opposed to fundamentalism on the one hand and to existentialist 'theology' on the other. The existentialists (such as Bultmann) reject the notion of an abiding self and claim that human beings exist only in and through their decisions which they make ever anew. The tendency is to view 'God' as designating the limitation of human life, in a sense equivalent to the meaning of human finitude On this view, salvation is a matter of surrendering all human security in response to the proclamation of the *kerygma*. In this proclamation the eschatological event, initiated by Christ and his cross which is not a cosmic or simply an historical event but a challenge to authentic existence, occurs again and again when the proclamation is answered by faith (Bultmann). So the Christian's existence is an eschatological existence, one in which all claims of a presumed self and of security have been renounced. It is authentic existence in the world which entails living fully in the present while being fully open to the future.

It was only a short step from this type of theology to the more recent so-called 'God is dead' and deconstructionist type of thought in which, as we have seen in chapters two and three, self and God are eliminated. Those who advocate this type of thought see their task as that of justifying the total relativism which they think is not only a fundamental characteristic of so-called postmodernism but also an actual feature of what is. This is the case, they claim, because for one thing there are no referents for linguistic signs, no 'real' things to which our linguistic signs refer, and thus we are forever caught in a world of signs and interpretations. So there is no 'true' world; truth does not exist, only opinions and interpretations. Also if there are no referents for linguistic signs, then the word God, even though it retains some emotive meaning, clearly refers to nothing. The same may be said of the self. It does not exist as an agent of intention and purpose but only as a complex of relationships and a web of impersonal forces. Given this total relativism, it follows that there is no distinction to be drawn between is and ought, good and evil.

Obviously, as its advocates readily proclaim, this view is completely nihilistic, but this nihilism is the way to 'salvation.' Salvation means living beyond good and evil, saying yes to everything.

141

It is a full embracing and celebrating of nihilism such that paradoxically it is overcome.

In light of the discussion above, it is obvious that, just as with Christology, we have a variety of soteriological views in our times, some of which are totally incompatible with one another. Fundamentalism, with its notion of original sin as biologically inherited, and salvation as primarily a matter of giving intellectual assent to a set of propositions including, of course, the substitutionary-satisfaction view of the role of Jesus Christ, is absolutely incompatible with the other four views discussed. The areas of agreement between liberalism on the one hand and Neo-Reformation and Christian Realism on the other are greater than between these two and the other three. With respect to soteriology they tend to agree on emphasizing the love of God, the importance of the human life of Jesus, and the relevance of salvation for the social problems of the world. However Neo-Reformation thinkers hold that the liberal tendency to understand sin and salvation in moralistic terms and to place major emphasis on human volitions and effort is superficial. At the same time, as we have seen, they reject the fundamentalists' literalism and substitutionary-satisfaction view as well as the existentialists' and deconstructionists' elimination of an objectively real personal God and advocacy of nihilism as the way to salvation. If there is anything concerning which fundamentalist, liberal, and Neo-Reformation thinkers can totally agree, it is in their complete rejection of the deconstructionists' atheology described above.

3. A Critique and Proposal

While my own preferences with respect to soteriological theories may be detected to some extent in the discussion above, I will attempt here to critically assess these theories and to propose one which retains much that is traditional but at the same time is not unwarranted in light of the disciplines of modern culture.

The edifice of fundamentalism's soteriology is based on its biblical and doctrinal literalism and its propositional notion of faith. As we have seen, in order to be saved one must give mental assent to such propositions as the plenary inspiration of Scripture, inherited original sin, the virgin birth and deity of Jesus Christ, and the substitutionary-satisfaction view of the atonement. This view of the atonement posits an "old dispensation" in which the major attribute of God was justice which was offended by human sin, and it could be satisfied only as someone of the status of deity substituted for sinful human beings and paid the price demanded by the divine justice. For Jesus Christ to accomplish this task on earth and to inaugurate the "new dispensaton" of God's forgiveness, it was necessary that he be deity, and for this to be the case it was necessary that he be born of a virgin, and this in turn depends on the literal inspiration of Scripture.

This position is permeated with so many problems that it is most certainly untenable. For one thing, its view of the Bible as a kind of divine information service which is totally verbally inspired and thus wholly infallible and inerrant is both factually in error and theologically inadequate. With respect to the Hebrew and Greek texts, there are no originals, only copies of copies of copies. Studies of the extant texts from different time periods demonstrate that copyists sometimes changed some of the wording in passages. If all of the original words are not known and the later copies of texts show some changes in wording plus the variations in translations, then the claim that all the words of the Bible are wholly infallible is simply not true. Furthermore, it is a simple fact that the Bible, when taken as a whole, contains internal contradictions and inconsistencies, and that it contains a few statements that are not in accord with the known facts of history and the proven facts of science. An example of the former is the difference between the Synoptic Gospels and the Gospel of John regarding the time in the ministry of Jesus when the cleansing of the temple took place and the date of the crucifixion. Examples of the latter are the following: it was Cyrus the Persian and not Darius the Mede(Daniel 5: 30-31) who conquered Babylon, and according to the biblical perspective, the universe is a three layer affair with the sky as a kind of dome over a flat circular earth supported by pillars sunk into a subterranean ocean.

It does not follow from the rejection of the dogma of biblical infallibility that one cannot greatly honor the Bible as the source book

143

for the Jewish and Christian traditions and as the witness to the disclosure of God. As indicated in chapter three the revelation of God occurs in his acts in history and in his 'speaking' to real persons. The Bible is a witness to and a record of his acts and encounters with real people as well as to their response to his disclosure.

Taken literally, the biblical narrative of the fall of Adam and the doctrine of original sin entail the loss of human freedom and responsibility with respect to morality since the beginning of the race. If sin is transmitted from parents to children as are genes for which descendants are not responsible, then it would be unjust for God to hold responsible and to punish Adam's descendants for that concerning which only he was able to make a choice. But the myth of the Fall and the doctrine of original sin need not be taken literally in order to be taken seriously. The myth points to the situation of every person. We tend to think of ourselves as better than we are. In imaginative anticipation, our intentions and acts are always better than they are in actual fact. When we act we fall. This is simply a fact about our decisions and not due to some predetermined fate. In our actual life situations, freedom of choice may be limited to some extent, but nonetheless is real (cf. Chapter Two). We are responsible for our pride, pretension, and ego-centricity, not some distant ancestor.

It was indicated above that fundamentalist soteriology requires the deity of Jesus Christ and that this in turn is guaranteed by the virgin birth (conception). But such a soteriological foundation is plagued with serious difficulties, theological, historical, and biological. As we have seen in chapter four, to take Jesus Christ out of the man-class and put him in the God-class, to believe that he was deity simply clothed in human flesh, is to fall into the ancient heresy of Gnosticism which emphasized the deity of Christ to the exclusion of his humanity. This view was rejected by the early church because salvation (the remaking of human life) required the full humanity as well as the divinity. Although the concepts of analysis may be different, the dialectic of the humanity and divinity of Jesus Christ is still necessary for an adequate soteriology_ that in a totally <u>human</u> life God's

144

forgiving and accepting *agape* was actualized and is freely available to all who will accept it.

There are a number of considerations which cast doubt upon the birth narratives as descriptive of actual fact. While a virgin birth may be logically possible, empirically it is not in accord with the biological generation of primates. But even if it were, there is still the historical question, namely, did it actually happen in this case. A careful analysis of the sources discloses that there are a number of difficulties confronting a positive answer to this question. Among them are the following. First, the earliest strata of the Christian tradition (such as Paul's letters and the Gospel of Mark) does not have even a hint of the virgin birth. Second, the birth narratives are found only in Matthew and Luke, and yet these same Gospels contain the genealogies which trace Jesus' descent through Joseph. Third, there are differences and inconsistencies between the two narratives.

If the birth stories are not found in the earliest tradition, why did they arise? It is probable that they arose as a part of the early Christians' defense of the faith against opponents. Some of these opponents were undoubtedly loyal adherents of Judaism who were familiar with certain late B. C. pseudepigraphic writings such as Enoch, Jubilees, and the Genesis Apocryphon in which there are references to the "heavenly watchers." Suggested by the canonical Genesis 6: I-4 which refers to the sons of God mating with the daughters of men, these watchers are rebellious and fallen angels. Envious of the pleasure human beings experience in sexual intercourse, they though unobservable manage to watch couples engaged in such acts and miraculously to be the actual progenitor of the child conceived. Thus are born the half-breed mighty beings who bring devastation to the earth. In the Synoptic Gospels there is at least a hint that Jesus' opponents associated him with these evil spiritual beings. According to the account in Mark 3:22 they claim that his doing of mighty works is the result of his being possessed by the prince of demons (Beelzebub). The birth narratives of Matthew and Luke take issue with such a claim in their assertion that Jesus is of the Holy Spirit. The language in Luke1:35 echoes some of the realistic language of the heavenly watchers stories when the angel says to Mary, "The Holy Spirit will come upon you." In Matthew 1:20 it is said of Mary, "that which is conceived in her is of the Holy Spirit." It is highly probable that one of the reasons for the rise of the birth narratives had little or nothing to do with the virginity of Mary. Rather its purpose was to deny that Jesus was the child of Mary and a heavenly watcher , and to assert that, instead, he was the child of Mary and the Holy Spirit and so totally good and loyal to God.

Another probable cause for the rise of the birth narratives is the encounter of early Christianity with the Greco-Roman culture with its many stories of the great heroes of old having been conceived by the union of Zeus (or some other high god) with human girls, virgins or not. So by their birth narratives the Christians would be asserting to their non-Christian neighbors that their Lord was not one bit inferior to those mythical heroes of Greece and Rome. Indeed, he was superior since his progenitor was the Holy Spirit of the one and only God.

In light of the dubious historicity of the birth narratives and the fact that stories of miraculous births, virgin or otherwise, abound in the cultures of ancient times, it is rash to base the significance of Jesus Christ as revealor and savior on these narratives. While we can honor what the early church was attempting to do and to preserve by means of these stories, we do not need to take them literally in order to accept Jesus Christ as revealor and savior. If a virgin birth, as such, guaranteed that the one so born was divine, we would have to accord divinity to the ancient heroes of Greece.

Apparently, there are many people today who believe that a virgin birth itself confers divinity on the one so born. In a recent television play a young woman who was pregnant sought to kill herself but was rushed to the hospital in a coma. There, to the amazement of everyone, it was discovered that she was a virgin. In the play most of the people, both laity and clergy, were convinced that if she were a virgin and pregnant, the child had to be divine. The main concern of the clergy was what would happen to Christianity with the birth of such a child. Would not the appearance of a "second Christ" undermine the clergy's claim concerning the uniqueness of Jesus

Christ and endanger the very foundation of the church? The doctors were convinced that the mother would die unless the fetus were aborted, and this raised a very heated controversy with many of the devout claiming that abortion was wrong under all circumstances and especially in this case since it would be to kill the "son of God." The controversy was settled when it was discovered that the girl's gynecologist was a religious fanatic who, using a syringe, had secretly impregnated her with his own semen in order to simulate a virgin conception, and later the girl recovered without an abortion (undoubtedly a way the producers and writers avoided antagonizing anyone).

While the television series in which this play appeared often deals with significant issues in a rather thoughtful way, in this case the issue was treated superficially. It seemed to have been assumed that the miraculous, whether it be a birth or some other event, would be sufficient to prove divinity. Even the ancient Hebrews knew better that that. Among ancient peoples all sorts of shaman or wizards were supposed to work miracles, and in Deuteronomy 8: 9-12 they and their like are banned from Israel. Obsession with the miraculous could obscure the central theme of Israel's faith and the reason for her existence, namely, Yahweh's freely offered covenant of love and acceptance and the responsibility of the community to respond in faithfulness and love which issue in social righteousness. In the preponderant biblical perspective, the miraculous is secondary to faithfulness and love for God and persons in all of life's relationships, individual and community.

It is the quality of life and not the manner of birth which is the proof of divinity. It is in the total life, teachings, and sacrificial death of Jesus Christ that one encounters a God-like quality of life in which is disclosed a God of compassion and love who freely accepts all who are willing to accept his acceptance.

While the soteriology in fundamentalism is inadequate for the reasons given above, that found in the radical theological camp of the existentialists and deconstructionists is also inadequate but for different reasons. As indicated above, both reject the reality of an

147

abiding self and of a transcendent personal God. Here I cannot repeat in full the arguments for the self and God presented in chapters two and three but simply reiterate a few salient points of difficulty in this radical theological or atheological camp. For one thing they tend to use the language of self (the self as a reality) to deny the existence or reality of the self, and this is clearly contradictory. Secondly, they tend to continue to use the word God, but they pack it with meaning contrary to the traditional meaning which it has had in western culture. This is confusing, to say the least, and in some cases (the God is dead thinkers) contradictory. In the third place, the notion of sin, for the most part, has dropped out of sight, and salvation is an individualistic subjective affirmation of the present moment, or an embracing of nihilism which overcomes nihilism. One need not go any further than the morning newspaper to be confronted with the reality of sin in our world. To claim that one must embrace nihilism in order to overcome nihilism is clearly contradictory.

In my judgment the soteriology of what might be called classical liberalism is to be preferred to that of fundamentalism or of the radicals such as the deconstructionists. Its emphasis on human freedom, on the life of Jesus, on following his example, on faith as a way of life, and on the moral and social implications of the Christian faith are necessary elements in any adequate sorteriology. However its overly optimistic view of human nature, its accompanying naive and moralistic view of sin, and its tendency to overemphasize human effort in the process of salvation are features which simply cannot stand the test of experience and need to be revised and augmented in an adequate soteriology. On the other hand, the Barthian type of Neo-orthodoxy tends to denigrate human effort, to make salvation solely a matter of God's action and thus to come ultimately to a kind of soteriological predestination in which persons are passive and freedom is virtually eliminated.

I think it is possible to construct a soteriology which avoids the problems of liberalism and Neo-orthodoxy while retaining their strengths. The major features of this soteriology are the following:

148

First, the analysis of human nature presented in chapter two is assumed. There is a self which is neither the pawn of an ineluctable fate nor of indeterminate haphazard events. Our common human experience confirms such a claim. While casual conditions make actions and decisions possible, the self possesses sufficient freedom to decide which actions to pursue. Thus, as Reinhold Niebuhr in his position of Christian Realism affirmed, human beings possess indeterminate possibilities for good and indeterminate possibilities for evil. Human beings are not ontologically fated to be Godforsaken sinners or altruistic angels but are a combination of both in varying degrees. In a recent editorial, a journalist extolled the altruism displayed by many in times of great emergencies, but he unrealistically failed to mention that so many perpetrators of violent crimes seem to feel little or no remorse and apparently are not stricken in conscience. Yet in even the most depraved there remains some small residue of freedom such that conscience may be reawakened. Otherwise programs of reform and appeals for change would be a worthless waste of time.

Second, our common human experience also discloses that under the conditions of historical existence human beings, while not ontologically fated to sin, are in fact always plagued with pride, pretension of self, and group, ethnic or national pride and pretension which actuate the estrangements, hatreds, injustices, hysteria, fury, and atrocities of our age or of any age. The external immoral and unjust acts are symptoms of this underlying condition. Even those who altruistically respond to those in need and engage in crusades of relief and of reform for human betterment are not exempt from the temptation to self-righteousness, the pretension of self or group. It is all too easy for those who work for noble ends to fall prey to the delusion that by so doing they have been transformed into sinless saints. But the fact of the matter is that they too remain sinners subject to prideful egoism and need to maintain a sense of humility and uneasy conscience. Certaintly a hallmark of the lives of the great saints and of Jesus was humility.

Third, given the fact and nature of sin, it follows that salvation cannot be self achieved. As stated above, an egocentric will willing is still an egocentric will willing. That is, since our wills are naturally pervaded with egocentricity, we cannot will ourselves out of the egocentric predicament, and some degree of sinful motive is involved even in the doing of good deeds. Thus there could be no salvation without God's taking the initiative to counter the egocentric predicament. It is the heart of the Christian faith that he did this supremely in the life, teachings, and especially in the sufferings of Jesus Christ who disclosed both God's love for all creatures and his suffering and pathos because of human sin and rebellion. As mentioned above in describing Niebuhr's soteriology, this is the divine 'shock treatment' which awakens us from our indifference and callousness, makes us aware of the seriousness of our sin, and brings us to that despair about ourselves which makes possible the contrition necessary for our acceptance of divine forgiveness and mercy. There could be no experience of the divine forgiveness, of fellowship with God, without his having taken the initiative, but also our human response is required since God does not compel us to accept his acceptance.

In chapters three and four it was indicated that the primary attribute of God disclosed in Jesus Christ is *agape*, a self-giving love which does not stipulate that prior conditions be met but is given freely and constantly. Thus the scope of the divine love is unlimited. In their freedom human beings may gratefully accept or stubbornly reject the divine love. If the latter is the case, they exclude themselves from the divine fellowship but not from the scope of the divine love, for God in various and sundry ways (such as the 'shock treatment' mentioned above) is constantly seeking through the power of persuasion to lure everyone, however unworthy, into an acceptance of his acceptance and thus into the divine fellowship.

The question, of course, plagues us. How can the God of love be God and yet there be so much suffering and evil in the world? In chapter three an answer to that question was sought in terms of what is logically necessary for the development of moral character, namely, freedom and a determinate order. Here it is in terms of what is involved in the very meaning of God's *agape* as this was revealed in Jesus Christ, namely, that self-giving love necessarily works by means of persuasion and not by compulsion. A fellowship cannot be compelled. It can exist only on the basis of voluntary acceptance. I think these are the proper responses to those who conclude from the suffering and evil in the world that God does not care, or is powerless, or does not exist. On the contrary, the very suffering and evil in the world is a pragmatic justification for the conviction that there is a God of love. Otherwise, it is all a surd and the world is unintelligible brute fact. But granted that there is a God of love, we can find that even the suffering in the world has some meaning in the overall scheme of things. We can know that it is precisely because God does care that he does not compel acceptance, but works through the power of persuasion, is the fellow sufferer who understands, and is constantly seeking to bring about the best possible out of every situation.

To some it might appear that such a God of love is quite a limited God, lacking a genuine omnipotence. But this would be the case only if 'omnipotence' means unrestricted irrational arbitrary power. In chapter three I argued that the only sensible meaning of 'omnipotence' is all logically possible power, and that this excludes such contradictories as round squares. Here the point is that while in principle God could perform actions which are inconsistent with his purposes, as a God of love he will not do so. In chapter four I argued that the *agape* of God as revealed in Jesus Christ is universal in scope, inclusive not exclusive, and thus that God's ultimate purpose is the actualization of a universal fellowship in which there is perfect freedom and faithfulness (Jesus' kingdom of God). Strength of character, acceptance of others, faithfulness, cannot be compelled. They cannot flourish in a situation where all obstacles are removed. Thus it is logically impossible for God to remain consistent with his ultimate purpose and from time to time arbitrarily to overrule human freedom (miraculously prevent terrorists from bombing innocent women and children) and the natural order of things. What is consistent with his ultimate purpose is the exercise of the power of

151

persuasion to inspire us to make the very best that it is possible to make out of every situation no matter how bleak, such that some creative advance is achieved. When a person says, "Why did God let this happen to me?," the implication, whether recognized or not, is that God should have violated human freedom or the natural order for his or her special privilege no matter what consequences this might have had. Yet if we are convinced that a universal fellowship is God's ultimate goal and the highest value for all creatures, then, aware that we are always in the scope of God's love, our response to whatever difficulties may arise is to seek to bring out of these difficulties the most creative and best results possible.

In light of human sin and the ambiguities of history, the good we may achieve is relative only, not the ultimate agapeistic fellowship. This relative good stands under the judgment of the one absolute, *agape,* which makes crystal clear our failings and keeps us humble concerning achievements. Yet also we can be inspired in a positive way by *agape,* by the conviction that life does have meaning, that it is, so to speak, a training ground for that ultimate universal fellowship beyond the relativities of history and the travesties of our present lives.

There are some who object to the notion of an ultimate universal salvation, arguing that justice and scripture require eternal punishment for the wicked. But if *agape* is the one absolute (as the revelation in Jesus Christ indicates), then justice must always be the servant of *agape* and not vice versa. It is true, of course, that there are passages in the New Testament which speak of hell as though it were an eternal reality. But there are some other passages which suggest a universal salvation as does Paul's statement in Phillipians 2: 10-11, "that at the name of Jesus every knee should bow, in heaven and on earth and under the earth, and every tongue confess that Jesus Christ is Lord, to the glory of God the Father."

Furthermore, the very logic of love and omnipotence makes an ultimate universal salvation necessary. The following syllogism is contradictory: God is omnipotent; God is love; there is an eternal hell. If eternal hell is retained, then it follows that the omnipotence or the

152

love must be given up. That is, on the one hand, God is love and wants to empty hell ultimately, but assuming that it is eternal it follows that he must be unable to do so. On the other hand, if God is omnipotent and could empty hell but does not, then he surely does not possess the attribute of an agapeistic type of love. But if God is both omnipotent and love, then there cannot be an eternal hell (separation from God and others). In our willful selfishness, estrangements, animosities, and fanaticisms, we human beings create a hell on earth. Assuming that there is an afterlife, such a state of estrangement can continue after death. Yet if there is a God and he is both omnipotent and all loving, it cannot be permanent. If God is love, he wants everyone in fellowship. If he is omnipotent, ultimately (and he has all the time there is) through the power of persuasion he will win over everyone into that fellowship of perfect freedom and faithfulness. Thus omnipotence and *agape* entail an ultimate universalism, inclusive of those of different religions (cf. the "hidden Christ" of chapter four), of no religion, and even of those who abuse others and God. Obviously, a widely held soteriological universalism would have serious implications for inter-religious relations, for Christian ecumenism, and for an understanding of the church's nature and function, a subject dealt with in the next chapter.

Undoubtedly, given our human tendency to embrace a sinful self-righteousness, it is difficult to give up the notion of an eternal hell. There seems to be some satisfaction in contemplating that some people (especially those who have wronged us) will be punished severely for an eternity. There is the old human desire for revenge which plagues all of us to some degree or other, and so it is hard to relinquish the notion that especially the horrible evildoers of history (such as Hitler) are in the hands of an angry God (to use Jonathan Edwards' expression) who for an eternity is dangling them over the pits of hell. But we must give up this notion if we are going to hold consistently and genuinely to the conviction that God is both omnipotent and all-loving. Furthermore, it has the practical value of freeing us from seeking divine sanction for our frustrations, fears, and hatreds, provides us with a sense of the eternal worth of human beings,

153

motivates us to seek now for ever closer approximations to that ultimate fellowship, and grants us a sense of personal security in the undying acceptance and love of God.

---

[1] *Against Heresies*, Ante-Nicene Christian Library (T. and T. Clark, 1870), vol. IV, XXXIII, 4.

[2] *Dogmatics in Outline* (Harper Torchbook, 1959), p. 23; *Against The Stream* (Philosophical Library, 1954), pp. 205-240.

[3] *The Nature and Destiny of Man*, Vo. 1, pp. 158, 220, 269, 283; Vol. 2, pp. 64, 117; *The Self and The Dramas of History*, (Charles scribner's Sons, 1955), pp. 108-109.

CHAPTER SIX
THE CHURCH

From its very beginning the Christian movement has placed emphasis upon the importance of fellowship, of the community of the 'people of God.' Given his heritage with its emphasis on the community it is not surprising that Jesus himself, as had the prophets and the rabbinical sages before him, called into being a community of disciples. As we have seen in chapter four, the central theme of his teaching, the kingdom of God, designated a new order of life on earth which was now dawning and which was characterized by a fellowship of love and faithfulness. In spite of the fact that Jesus probably never envisioned the church or used the word (*ekklesia* in the Greek; the use of this word in Matt.16:18 and 18:17 seems to be an anachronistic insertion by the gospel writer), he certainly provided the foundation for such in his teachings about the kingdom of God.

1. An Historical Sketch of the Doctrine, Practice, and Structure of the Church

Outside the Gospels (the letters of Paul, the Acts of the Apostles etc.) considerable attention is given to the church in the New Testament. It is the *ekklesia*, those who have been called out by God, and thus may be designated the 'people of God' and the 'fellowship of the spirit' as characterizing the relation of believers with Christ and with one another. While there is a continuity with the message of the historical Jesus, the relation with Christ is primarily with the risen Christ, a 'corporate or inclusive Christ.' Just as was the case in ancient Israel, so also in the New Testament there is no notion of individualism in the modern sense of the term. Paul, for example, did not think of his converts as being saved merely as individuals. Believers are incorporated into Christ, which means into the fellowship of the spirit and the people of God, and he uses a number of metaphors such as "'body'," "bride," "vine," and "sheepfold" to make this point vivid. While the individual is not robbed of his individuality, the

155

church is not simply a group of individuals who have a private and solitary relationship with Christ. It is the community of believers related to the risen Christ and thus is his 'body.' It is the fellowship (*koinonia*) granted by the Holy Spirit, and participation in it is participation in the Spirit or in the risen Christ.

In the New Testament the term *ekklesia* has two designations, and it is necessary to determine from the context of the passage which of the two is meant. It is often used to designate a specific group of Christians (those who meet in a certain house). Sometimes it is used to designate all the Christians in a certain town and occasionally the entire Christian fellowship. These groups were rather informal, unstructured groups without a set ecclesiastical pattern or order.

In the very early period leaders were often the traveling 'teachers' or 'prophets' who had some direct or indirect relationship with the disciples or with Paul. Sometimes persons became leaders due to their 'charismatic' authority. Given this fluid situation, it is not surprising that charlatans could get in on the 'traveling tours' and, by false teachings and immoral behavior, produce divisions among the members of local congregations. As a defense against the dangers of heresy and division in the churches, local leadership soon emerged. In the early Church Fathers and in the Pastoral Letters of the New Testament (probably no earlier than 150 A. D.), reference is made to such local church leaders as bishops, deacons, and elders (presbyters). It seems that the bishop was selected from among the elders of a local congregation, elected by the whole church he was to serve, and accorded special status by virtue of ordination to this office. In the early decades it may have been that the council of presbyters (priests) ordained one of their number to the office of bishop, but soon (certainly before the end of the second century) only other bishops had the authority to consecrate the one elected to this office. The bishop alone had the authority to ordain the priests and deacons and to celebrate the Eucharist and baptisms, although he might delegate the celebration of the Eucharist and baptism to the priests. He was the chief pastor of the flock. The presbyters or priests served him as a council of advice and acted as his deputies in his absence. The deacons were subordinate to him as assistants in worship and pastoral visitation.

The continuing threat to the unity of the growing Christian movement (its rapid growth in the Greco-Roman world) by virtue of the Gnostic heresy (see chapter four) and of schisms led to the development of a more structured and authoritarian ecclesiastical order which served as a defense against both heresy and schism. The schismatics, unlike the heretics, withdrew from the main body of the church not on the basis of any essential difference in doctrine but on the basis of objecting to certain ecclesiastical practices such as readmitting to the church penitent apostates at the end of periods of persecution. It is not surprising, then, that there arose the realization that the unity and effectiveness of the church depended to a large extent on acceptance of a duly authorized ministry by the whole church. A legitimate ministry required empowerment by the sacrament of ordination, but this sacrament was valid only if celebrated by bishops who were in the apostolic succession. It was thought that the first leaders of some important churches had been the original apostles or had received their authority from them. So Ireneaus (about 180 A. D.) listed by name the bishops of Rome in direct succession from his own time back to that of the apostle Peter who was supposed to have been the first bishop of Rome.

The emergence of ecclesiastical authority was a corollary of a shift in the understanding of sin and salvation from that of the Apostle Paul to a more moralistic view. Since it was obvious that even after baptism Christians were not morally perfect and exclusion of sinners would empty the churches, the church had to find a way of dealing with post-baptismal sins. So in addition to the sacraments of baptism, Eucharist, and ordination there was soon the full development of the sacrament of penance.

It was the third century bishop of Carthage, Cyprian (249-258 A. D.), who was largely responsible for this development as well as for certain perspectives which provided the foundation for the emergence of the Catholic Church.[1] In his view the bishop was the dominant ecclesiastical figure. As the successor of the Apostles he was the only ruler of the church. His sovereignty was absolute and he was the only "priest." The sacrament of penance was efficacious for the penitent sinner only if absolution was made available to him by the bishop or the priests to whom the bishop had delegated this authority. As the successor of the Apostles the bishop had the authority to forgive all types of sins, mortal and otherwise, and thus the power of absolution resided in the bishop alone. So also with the other sacraments of baptism and Eucharist and the other functions of the church, the bishop was the supreme representative of Christ and the Apostles. Presbyters or priests had no independent gifts but had their priestly functions delegated to them by the bishops. Apart from the bishop there was no church. Cyprian put this rather vividly when he claimed, "Hence you should know that the bishop is in the church and the church is in the bishop, and that if anyone is not with the bishop he is not in the church." (Letter 66:7) While Cyprian held that the church at Rome and its succession of bishops was to be honored as the source of the unity of the church at large, this unity as a continuing reality was a common property shared by all the bishops in a united episcopacy in which each bishop was concerned with the church as a whole as well as with his local church. No bishop had the right to dictate to other bishops or to interfere with the internal matters in their churches. The bishop of Rome had not as yet become the Pope.

Given his view of the function of the sacraments and the authority of the bishop, it is not surprising that Cyprian held that the church was not simply a fellowship of Christians but that it was the sole ark of salvation outside of which no one could be saved. In Cyprian's words, "He cannot have God for his father who has not the Church for his mother." (On the Unity of the Catholic Church, 6). While earlier Christians had emphasized the importance of the church for salvation, Cyprian identified the church with a particular institution, the Catholic Church, which, he argued, was founded upon and had its existence in those bishops in succession from the Apostles. This church alone possessed saving grace, and apart from it there was no salvation or anything which was truly Christian (Letter 55: 24; 66: 8). In it are the sacraments through which grace as an actual power

158

was channeled into believers so that they might finally become truly Christians, that is, regain the likeness to God lost in the fall of Adam (see section 1, chapter five).

The view of the Catholic Church as the custodian of salvation has been an essential feature of Roman Catholic theology and practice throughout the ages. Further developments in thought, practice, and history served to strengthen the power and prestige of the Catholic Church as the guardian of order and spirituality in this world and as the gateway to the celestial world. Among these developments was the gradual abandonment of a collective episcopate as the ultimate authority for the church and the elevation of the bishop of Rome to the status of Pope. In the fifth and sixth centuries, justification for this position was based on Jesus' statement to Peter about building his church on him and giving him the keys to the kingdom (Matt. 16: 18-19, given the use of the word 'church,' this is probably from the writer of Matt.). This was accompanied by the tradition that Peter was the first bishop of Rome. The claim was that Peter was the first among the apostles, and that standing in the apostolic succession from Peter, the bishop of Rome was his spiritual heir and was due the honor and recognition accorded to Peter himself. As Peter's successor, the Lord had granted him authority over the whole church and all other ecclesiastics, and even over secular rulers. Anyone who rejected his authority was a sinner on the road to hell.

Another development which tended to increase the Catholic Church's control over almost every aspect of life was the final establishment of the seven sacraments by the twelfth century. These included not only the earlier sacred actions of baptism, Eucharist, ordination, and penance, as indicated above, but also confirmation, marriage, and extreme unction. It was believed that all were instituted by Christ, directly or through the Apostles, and that all of them convey grace from Christ, the head, to the members of his mystical body, the church. Without them no one could ever achieve the quality of life which would merit ultimate beatitude in heaven.

Both Augustine and the later Aquinas distinguished two modes of God's grace, prevenient and cooperating. It is not that there are two

159

kinds of grace. There is only one grace of God, but it is in two modes and has two different effects. By means of the sacrificial death of Christ, God has made his forgiving grace available to all. When accepted, it turns one to the church where further grace in its cooperating mode is infused into the soul of the believer through the sacraments, enabling him to finally merit eternal life. With the emergence of the doctrine of transubstantiation, that the bread and wine of the Eucharist become the body and blood of Christ with the blessing of the priest so that Christ's sacrifice is recapitulated every time the sacrament is celebrated, the church's inventory of grace and merit was being constantly increased. It was an ever enlarging storehouse of merit from which the church could draw and through the sacraments make grace and merit available to believers.

Given the belief that final blessedness in heaven required regaining the lost likeness of God, and the fact that it was impossible for lay Christians to achieve such moral perfection in this life (only Monastics who followed the counsels of perfection, obedience, poverty, and chastity, could come close to perfection in this life), it is not surprising that by the end of the sixth century the notion of purgatory had become an official doctrine of the church. Believers who die without the expiation of all sins, even minor ones, must endure the purifying fires of purgatory. As noted above, however, since every Mass is a recapitulation of Christ's redeeming sacrifice which adds to the church's enormous storehouse of merit, the notion arose that it is beneficial not only for living believers but also for those residing in purgatory. Both Masses and prayers of the faithful for those in purgatory serve to hasten their exit from purgatory into the blessedness of heaven.

Before the end of the medieval period the securing of indulgences for loved ones in purgatory was thought to lessen their stay in this condition. Originally the granting of indulgences had relevance to this world and the sacrament of penance. Penance involved contrition, confession, and a work of satisfaction on the part of the penitent. Occasionally the penitent was unable, for physical reasons, to perform the work of satisfaction assigned by the priest, and so the priest excused him from this assignment and replaced it with something else which he was able to do (such as a money payment to the church). It is easy to see how the granting of indulgences came to be extended from applying to works of satisfaction in this world to the shortening of time that believers must spend in purgatory in the next world, and that by the fifteenth century such indulgences were being sold to raise money for the Popes. The important point to note in all this is that the Catholic Church sought not only to extend its hold on all the life of the times but also to control the post mortem realm as well. From birth to death, and even after death, one was under the dominance of the Church.

With the stimulus of Renaissance humanism, the breakdown of feudalism and the rise of a middle class, the undermining of the Thomistic theological synthesis by Nominalism, and the increasing secular perspectives and practices on the part of even the highest ecclesiastical leaders, some persons began to raise questions about the legitimacy of the Catholic Church's claim to be the final authority in all matters of faith and practice and of its almost total control over every aspect of life. Serious questions were raised about the Church's doctrine of salvation with its emphasis upon the necessity of meriting eternal life, of doing good works in order to become actually righteous, and of the Church as the gatekeeper of the celestial world and a storehouse of merit. Furthermore, abuses such as simony (the selling of church offices), the inheritance of ecclesiastical offices, and the sale of indulgences intensified the alienation of those who found themselves restive under the Church's authority.

Into this situation, which was a blend of changed cultural, social, economic, and philosophical conditions and of a growing dissatisfaction with the Church, came Martin Luther (1483-1546 A. D.) who served as a kind of catalyst which produced a new movement in Christendom. Frustrated by his inability to find peace of mind in the works system of salvation, dissatisfied with Scholastic theology, and appalled by the excessive abuses associated with the sale of indulgences, Luther unleashed increasingly strident attacks (not only in the 95 theses but also in several essays and commentaries) on the theology and practice of the Church and Papacy until, finally, he was excommunicated and placed under imperial ban. Fortunately he had the protection of Prince Frederick of Saxony.

The difference between Luther's (and other Reformers as well) view of the nature and function of the church and that of traditional Catholicism could hardly have been greater. It had its primary source in Luther's vastly different understanding of sin and salvation. As indicated in chapter five, the Catholic view of sin and salvation was primarily a moralistic view. In the fall of Adam man had lost the likeness of God but retained the image. Fallen man could know a great deal about God and practice the virtues of the natural law, but he could not acquire the supernatural virtues of faith, hope, and love necessary for ultimate beatitude without the Church, its sacraments, and its storehouse of grace and merits.

By contrast, the Reformers' view of sin and salvation (also described in chapter five) was what I have called the theologicopsychological view similar to that of Paul and Augustine. Fallen man is totally depraved, which means that intellect, volition, and emotions are infected with the pretension of self or egocentricity. Even good deeds may be infected with sin. So no one can gain righteousness by means of his own achievements. All human attempts to calculate and to measure merit are false notions in relation to God. One must trust God rather than himself and his own achievements, for without demanding any sign of merit, God extends his mercy to those who know they are not worthy. One who accepts God's mercy and acceptance offered in Christ is <u>accounted</u> righteous by God precisely because of his faith or trust and thus is reconciled with God. Justification is by faith, and even faith itself is a gift of God.

An important corollarly of the doctrine of justification by faith is the doctrine of the universal priesthood of believers. This doctrine means two things. First, on the basis of the experience of faith granted by God, the believer can have direct access to God. The believer is not subject to any ecclesiastical authority or traditional interpretations of the Catholic Church with respect to the content of faith and of Scripture, the central message of which is the Word of God in Jesus

162

Christ. Under the inspiration of the Holy Spirit the believer can read, interpret, and understand Scripture for himself. The Word of God witnessed to in Scripture is the final authority in faith, morals, and practices for both individual and the church which owes its existence to Scripture.

A second meaning of the priesthood of believers is that the believer is moved by the Holy Spirit to act on behalf of others. Every Christian is a priest to others, serving them, praying for them, and instructing them. It is not that all believers are or should be ministers, a vocation to which God calls some from among the faithful of sound doctrine and holy life. Rather it means that all believers should serve others, not only in the Christian fellowship, but also in whatever vocations they enter. The status of the laity is not in the least inferior to that of the clergy. Clergy and laity perform roles of equal distinction for the strengthening of faith and Christian living and for the spread of the gospel.

It follows that the Christian who genuinely accepts the honor and responsibility of 'priesthood' participates in the community of believers, the church. The Catholic hierarchical structure and the notion of the church as a storehouse of merit are rejected by the Reformers. They insisted that the church is a fellowship of believers, a community of forgiven sinners, instead of a community of sinless saints. The church was not founded on any human authority but on the Word of God witnessed to in Scripture. In order for a community to be a true Christian church, the Word of God must be rightly preached and the two sacraments instituted by Christ, namely, baptism and the Lord's Supper, rightly administered (another form in which the Word of God is heard in faith). Only this understanding of the nature and function of the church receives the sanction of Scripture.

As a result of their doctrine of predestination and the foibles manifested in actual churches, the Reformers, similar to Augustine, made a distinction between the visible church and the invisible spiritual church, the mystical body of Christ. While in this life there were no members of the invisible church outside the visible, not all those who were members of the visible church were also members of

163

the invisible church. The latter was made up only of the elect, while in the former are mingled many hypocrites. Even though the visible church owes its existence to the Word of God witnessed to in Scripture and has an important role in the spiritual nurturing of the elect, it is human and fallible. None of its ecclesiastical forms are unalterable. It stands always under the judgment of the Word of God disclosed in Scripture, for this is the final authority for the church.

As we have seen, the church, not Scripture, was the final authority for faith, morals, and ecclesiastical forms in the Catholic view. Ultimately, of course, this authority came to reside in the so-called teaching authority of the church, the Pope. And time and again, up until Vatican Council II, Popes have declared that the universal church as the mystical body of Christ, the invisible spiritual church, is one, indivisible, and identical with the Roman Catholic Church. Thus the Catholic Church with its teaching authority is the only true church and the only custodian of salvation.

It seems that in each of these two types of churches, the Catholic and the Protestant, there are both strengths and weaknesses. The Protestant Reformers' view of the relativity of all ecclesiastical forms (sometimes ignored by Protestant Churches in their historical development) and of the priesthood of believers is valuable in its emphasis upon the freedom, dignity, and responsibility of the laity in the fellowship of believers. Yet as history clearly shows, this strength can become distorted and result in a rampant individualism, disunity, and pluralism with all sorts of accompanying aberrations which come to be regarded as the absolute will of God. On other hand, the Catholic emphasis upon tradition, unity, universalism, structure, and authority makes for stability and a realistic sense of the obvious social substance of human existence. Yet in guarding this emphasis with the doctrines of the Catholic Church as identical with the invisible church and of papal infallibility, there is the absolutizing of the relative. The lessons of history and of common human experience amply demonstrate that church bodies, ecclesiastical forms, and personages of whatever persuasion are far from being without error. A variety of cultural and historical relativities have an important influence in determining the

164

rites and the ecclesiastical forms. So it is that the undisciplined freedom and illusive absolutism often found in Protestantism, and the structured absolutism of traditional Catholicism both of which I have designated as weaknesses, serve only to preserve the major rent in Christendom. The dialectic of freedom and structure, dynamics and form, must be incorporated in each if the gulf between the two is ever to be bridged.

2. A Dialectical Ecclesiology

I think that any ecclesiology which does not define the church in terms of the dialectical or polar structure encountered in all of existence such as dynamics and form, freedom and tradition, and individualization and socialization (cf. chapter Two, section 3) fails to do justice to the nature and mission of the church, and thus helps to thwart attempts to overcome the scandal of divisions within Christendom. There would not be a church, of course, without the revelation of God as forgiving love in Jesus Christ. This is the foundation of the church both as the universal spiritual community (the Reformers' invisible church) of all who accept God's grace and as organized institutions which, at least in intention and some partial actualization, participate in and give expression to God's fellowship of *agape*. The church, then, is both a spiritual community and an institution.

Without some sort of actual organizational structure and form, the church could neither long exist nor have much influence in the world. An amorphous fellowship, no matter how noble its origins and goals, is virtually impossible to maintain in the actual world of fallible and sinful human beings. A causally necessary condition for the existence of any community or fellowship is that the ethos of the community find expression in institutions having some kind of form, discipline, and methods which provide the conditions for common beliefs and action. And yet all institutions are created and operated by fallible and sinful human beings, and thus are far from being perfect in their structures and activities. Given the fact of sin (see chapters Two, section 2 and Five, section 3), even the institutional church (whether Catholic or Protestant) too readily identifies itself with the absolute, and too easily regards its forms and methods as being sacred. Too often it tends to think of itself as possessing grace rather than participating in it and thus as justified in expecting special favors from the court of the Almighty. Too often it tends to act as though it were the only vindicator of God in the world and the only arbiter of the final destiny of all instead of the humble servant of God and of all humanity. Too often it tends to forget the relativities of history and of our common human experience, and gets caught in sanctioning or at least mutely accepting all sorts of national, ethnic, special interest, and class prideful and sinful concerns, or else retreats into some sort of withdrawal from the world with all the tendency of developing a siege mentality. In either case the church fails to be a genuine and effective servant of the world and of its Creator. So it is that the church needs a prophetic voice directed against itself.

This voice may come from many sources. It may come from critics in the secular world who, unwittingly, may witness to God's judgment against the church. It may come from the church within the church, that is, the spiritual community within the institutional church, which through the voices of modern prophets proclaims the judgment of God on the failings of the institutional church such as those mentioned above. Whenever the institutional church humbly acknowledges it failings, accepts the relativities of its polity, structures and rites, earnestly seeks to demonstrate in its internal and external relations loyalty to God's *agape* as disclosed in Jesus Christ, then it comes close to approximating the kind of community envisioned by Jesus as characterizing the kingdom of God.

Such an approximation can be actualized only as the church is nurtured by memory, faith, and hope. A large part of what it means to be a Christian is to share a common memory which includes the biblical record of God's revelation in the history of Israel, in Jesus Christ, in the New Testament witnesses, and in the witness of the traditions and history of the church to the present.

Unfortunately, many Christians, and surveys indicate that it is a vast majority, are abysmally ignorant of the biblical witness to, and record of, God's revelatory acts in the history of Israel, of Jesus Christ and of the long history of the Christian tradition. In many cases persons are members of churches not because of knowledgeable convictions concerning Christianity or of any desire to learn about the Bible or the tradition, but due to all sorts of extraneous reasons such as convenience or social position. Often it is only a few snippets of doctrine, certain code words and phrases, which are known and thought to constitute the sum and substance of the Christian faith, the unquestioning acceptance of which is the mark of a true Christian.

As we have seen (cf. chapter Five, section 3), even devout right wing evangelicals or fundamentalists tend to view the gospel simply in terms of certain code expressions (a substitutionary-satisfaction atonement) abstracted from any biblical, church tradition, or life situation context. While it is the case that years ago fundamentalists often had a considerable knowledge of at least the content of the English Bible in its authorized version, today even this knowledge is widely lacking among those who claim to believe in the Bible from cover to cover. And even when the Bible is consulted, passages are so isolated from the context of the text and of the actual life situation that often they are intrepreted to mean just the opposite of what they meant originally, and error is compounded.

So it is that, due to lack of knowledge, Christians often hold to ideas and claim Christian sanction for certain causes which are definitely unchristian in light of three major criteria for an authentic Christian faith. These ideas and causes stand in contradiction to one or all of the following, namely, the genuine biblical witness to the faith, the historical tradition, and, most inportantly, Christian love or *agape*, the ultimate and absolute norm for all Christian thought and action. If the vitality of the church depends to a large extent upon memory, then the institutional church has a large responsibility to improve its system of religious education. How can church members be genuinely Christian if they do not share a common memory? If this memory dies, then the institutional church is in danger of becoming either a kind of social club which is Christian in name only or at the opposite extreme spawn sectarian cults which, ignoring the insights of the ages, are subject to all sorts of aberrations while claiming the sanction of God for

167

such aberrations. They may even become fanatical cults which, while claiming to be God's agents on earth, violate his love as disclosed in Jesus Christ in their subjugating and abusing of persons.

As important as memory is, there is the ever present danger that the traditions and disciplines of the past will come to be regarded as so sacred and absolutely fixed that any change, no matter how creatively it makes the Christian gospel and traditions relevant in the modern world, is regarded as heretical and to be opposed. Disciplines, rites, orders, and forms are important as a kind of skeleton for the common life of the church, but they are of secondary importance. They are not a part of the givenness of the church, but belong to the realm of the historically contingent. Yet there is always the tendency for churches to regard their specific disciplines as essential ingredients of the faith. I once heard a church leader proclaim, "Our methods are as sacred as our doctrines." Whenever and wherever this stance is held, the scandal of divisions among the churches is exacerbated, and the Christian faith becomes increasingly irrelevant and of little interest to large numbers of persons with a modern world view. While the disciplines and knowledge of the past are important in order that we might fully identify with the Christian community through the ages, know who we are, and avoid the mistakes of the past, the insights of the past need to be used creatively. There is the need to hold together memory and creativity, tradition and freedom.

Not only memory, but also faith and hope are the life blood of the church. As indicated in chapters one and five, faith is not merely a matter of intellectual assent to a set of propositions or dogmas, but is a matter of trust in or acceptance of God's acceptance. Such is not antithetical to reason. Faith and reason are not contradictories but contraries, and can be held together as complimentary. Faith as trust is a commitment of the whole person and the whole community to the God of *agape* as disclosed in Jesus Christ. Reason seeks to understand and provide rational justification and exfoliation of the commitment (cf. chapter One), and to demonstrate its relevance to all the concerns of life. In this task memory has an important role to play.

But hope has an equally important role. It might be said that the Christian faith embodies the Janus principle. There is a looking back to the past, to the biblical tradition, to the life and teachings of Jesus, and to the traditions of the church through the ages, but also there is a looking forward in hope. There is the confidence that the God who accepts us in spite of the fact that we are unworthy will one day by means of the power of *agape* be universally victorious, if not on earth, then in an ultimate, transcendent, universal fellowship of perfect freedom and faithfulness. This is not a narrow literalistic and legalistic eschatology but is inclusive and universal since, as argued in chapter five, such is logically entailed by the divine attributes of *agape* and omnipotence. Granted that this is so, it follows that insofar as a church or a denomination humbly accepts this conviction, it seeks to demonstrate a loving and accepting spirit to all, both to other Christian bodies and to non-Christians. Sacramental, ritualistic, institutional, and doctrinal aspects are not abolished but are subordinated to a common loyalty to the life, teachings, and personality of Jesus Christ, the ultimate norm for authentic Christian experience. Any church or denomination which rejects an ecumenical spirit and refuses to engage in ecumenical action is failing to follow the norm of *agape*. Ecumenism is of the very essence of an authentic Christian faith.

3. The Church and Society

Whenever and wherever the church is genuinely inspired by the Christian hope, it accepts also the obligation to work in intelligent and realistic ways for the improvement of the social conditions under which human beings must live. As the community called into being by God to embody in speech and action his love for his creatures, the church dare not be neutral about the great social evils which confront mankind. In word and deed it must seek to achieve in the here and now the closest possible approximation to God's ultimate universal fellowship of perfect freedom and faithfulness. In pursuing this task it is important for the churches to recognize that an effective social policy and strategy requires a grounding in the dialectic of individualization and participation. As indicated in section three of chapter two, this dialectic is a characteristic feature of human life. The contrasting poles of the transcendent dignity and worth of the individual and of the social or community dimension of human life need to be given equal attention. A church which preaches only a gospel of individual salvation is failing to preach a full gospel and is preventing the development of Christian maturity in the individual. The witness of experience indicates that there is a close correlation between on the one hand compassion for the oppressed and the passion for social justice, and on the other personal growth in the Christian life. For entirely too long too many churches remained silent on issues of social justice such as racial discrimination, and thus failed to free many of their members from their narrow prejudices into a fuller and more open life as well as to contribute to the promotion of greater harmony among the races in society at large.

It does not follow from the fact that the earlier social gospel liberals were too naive and overly optimistic about the perfectibility of society through the simple application of Christian love to the great social problems, either that the Christian faith lacks a social dimension or that it is a worthless waste of time and so not a part of the church's obligation to work for the amelioration of the great social problems which plague society. This dimension was present from the very beginnings of Christianity. As we have seen in chapter four, the basic theme in the teachings of the historical Jesus was the kingdom of God, a new order of life on earth. Devotion to the kingdom ideal requires of Christians that we be aware of social problems and set out to do what we can from our end, asking no more of God than that he should be an ally and a consolation rather than a sort of last-resort Mr. Fixit. This realism is tempered with hope which, as we have seen, is an essential ingredient of the Christian faith. Furthermore, experience shows that faithful Christians doing what they can about horrendous social evils not only bring some improvement almost immediately but also often some unexpected results, especially in the long run.

What sort of social policy and action should the church espouse? There are many social issues about which those who call themselves

170

Christian take diametrically opposed stances, and too often it is simply accepted without question that such and such a position is Christian because someone says it is. In some cases these positions simply mirror stances taken in a non-Christian political or secular dimension which are adopted by certain churches or groups and arbitrarily made into the ultimate criterion as to whether one is a Christian or not. Unfortunately, many religious communities today lack the theological resources and/or concern which would enable them to develop a Christian ethics consistent with the faith, and thus often are subject to supporting positions which in whole or in part are antithetical to the faith.

In the previous chapters (especially Three, Four and Five) there has been sketched the essential ingredients of a Christian theology on the basis of which an identifiable Christian moral ethos could be shaped. In this discussion it was indicated that, in terms of both the logical implication of the arguments for the existence of God and of the revelation of God in Jesus Christ, it follows that the basic attribute of God, indeed, his very nature, is *agape* or self-giving love. Since God is *agape*, he seeks to win the hearts of his children through persuasion, not compulsion, and the scope of his compassion is unlimited. The divine goal is that all persons freely accept him and his love, and live in love and harmony with all his creatures. His heart is wrung with compassion because his children so often prefer egotistical self-aggrandizement, hostility, and estrangement rather than a loving fellowship, but he always stands ready to forgive and to accept all who accept his love.

Given this theology, it follows that the one ultimate, final, and absolute norm for Christian ethics is *agape*. It is the only absolute, whether it is God's love for his creatures or the human love for God and neighbor. It is in light of this norm that all moral principles and all social policies and actions should be judged.

This position is not to be confused with what has been called situational ethics, namely, that analysis of the situation and the love norm are <u>all</u> that are needed in making ethical decisions which are totally *ad hoc* In this view the great ethical principles which are a

171

legacy of western culture need not be considered in the making of moral decisions. But surely this is too simplistic a view of the moral situation. The moral situation involves also great moral virtues such as integrity, justice, equity, temperance, and peacefulness. It is not that such values supersede or replace *agape*. Instead, in this imperfect world where the simple application of *agape* is seldom if ever possible, they serve as its instruments. So *agape* is relevant to all social problems as the ultimate norm and as the motivating force inspiring the church to engage in the struggle for justice. The means to secure justice may involve compulsion as well as persuasion, but under the norm of *agape*, compulsion will most certainly be nonviolent. At least part of the genius of Dr. Martin Luther King Jr. was his insight that effective resistance could be nonviolent and could be combined with persuasion to bring about the abolition of segregation laws in the south and a greater degree of justice for an oppressed people. Justice, then, is the instrument of love in the world, but its practice and achievements must always be judged in light of the *agape* norm. In most situations the application of justice and the other virtues mentioned above achieve the closest possible approximation in this world to what the *agape* norm would require.

These moral virtues are an essential ingredient of a total Christian ethics and should not be ignored. Yet they are not absolute, but relative to *agape* . While in most situations they work as effective servants of *agape* to produce the best possible results, there are a few situations in which the application of one would mean the violation of another and produce results antithetical to *agape*. For example, a Christian family in Nazi Germany, horrified by the persecution of the Jews, might well provide sanctuary to a family of Jews in an attic room in their own home. If the Gestapo came to their home searching for Jews, surely they would not tell the truth. In this situation the value of protecting and preserving human life is in conflict with the value of truth-telling. In light of the *agape* norm, love of neighbor certainly takes precedence over truth-telling. But the members of this Christian family cannot lie with an easy conscience because they are aware that they, perhaps by sins of omission, contributed to the conditions which made the rise of Nazism possible and the violation of truth-telling necessary.

Christians are not sinless saints, but forgiven sinners, and the church is not a community of absolute truth and virtue, defending God and the righteous from the assaults of the ungodly. Such moral pretension contradicts the *agape* norm and, as history clearly shows, generally makes injustice and other social evils worse rather than better because the church itself often is a participant in fostering the very evils it should be resisting. Only as there is a constant awareness of the need for humility, contrition, and forgiveness on the part of Christian communities can the churches be effective servants of the God of *agape* amid the tragic ambiguities of history.

It does not follow from the relative status of such values as truth-telling that they are lacking in objective reality and are simply a matter of human subjective whims and feelings. What I have called a moral solipsism (chapter Two, section three), that whatever individuals or groups want to do is right simply because they want to do it, has disastrous consequences for individuals and society. That there is always a price to pay (whatever the situation) for the violation of these moral values surely supports the claim that they have objective reality. For example, on the basis of moral solipsism, the whole of science would collapse. Science and the scientific institution in order to exist as such must incorporate the value of telling the truth under any and all circumstances regardless of opposition (Galileo and Darwin, for example). To the extent that scientists violate this value in their scientific endeavors, science ceases to be science.

Given the *agape* norm as the ultimate norm and the importance of other values such as justice, honesty, etc. as middle principles (to use Reinhold Niebuhr's term)[1] a social Christian ethics adequate for the church which sincerely seeks to do the will of God cannot be reduced to a one-issue affair as though it were the sum and substance of the church's responsibility. Unfortunately, many Christians and the religious communities to which they belong are subject to tunnel vision, latching on to one issue concerning which they self-righteously assume that they alone speak for God and simply could not be

173

mistaken. For example, many of the so-called 'pro-lifers' are so committed to the prevention of abortion and preserving the life of the fetus that they are unconcerned about the slaughter of thousands of thinking persons in warfare and ethnic cleansing. Apparently in some cases the life of a non-thinking early fetus is regarded as more important than that of the thinking person whose life is put in serious jeopardy if the fetus is brought to term or who is shot to death for performing abortions. If God is *agape,* he is, of course, concerned about the life of every creature on earth including fetuses as well as the beasts of the field and the birds of the air, but are not persons of more value, intrinsically of a higher order, than animals? The real question is not the biological one of when life begins but rather when does the human animal become a person in the full sense. If all living things are of equal value, then 'pro-lifers' could be consistent only if they practiced vegetarianism. The application of equity as a servant of *agape* in the world makes it clear that relative values must be assigned to different creatures at different levels of existence and development. The life of the fetus is of value, but not of the higher order value of persons who are more valuable because they can think. It is not of ultimate value any more than that of an insect or an animal. The church which takes an absolutist stand on the abortion issue will find that, in many actual situations, this results in injustice for and/or danger to the lives of persons.

Closely related to the abortion issue is the issue of birth control. It is obviously the case that there is overpopulation in a large number of countries throughout the world and among certain groups in all countries. Demographic experts warn that in the very near future the world will be so overpopulated that its resources will be depleted and mass starvation will occur on a scale hitherto unimaginable. Clearly if the church is faithful to the *agape* norm, it must seek to limit suffering and promote well-being and fullness of life. Given the finite limit of resources in the world, the only way to limit suffering and provide the opportunity for fullness of life is to limit the world's population. Therefore the church has an obligation to support such limitation by whatever means appropriate. This could include at least verbal and

174

perhaps financial support for those national and international agencies which disseminate such knowledge and means. It could include also participation in an educational effort to change the attitudes of persons in those societies where traditionally large families were regarded as bringing honor and higher status to parents and especially to the mother. In view of the population crisis today, the church should proclaim it to be a divine obligation to limit the size of families.

Some believe the world's population is not a problem because it is being reduced or at least stabilized by wars, ethnic cleansing, and natural catastrophes such as droughts. Surely this is a spurious and insensitive argument (generally advanced by those who are financially secure and comfortable) which ignores demographic studies and which disregards the enormous suffering caused by such events. Would it not be better for persons never to be born than to be born to a life of misery and suffering? Is it not better to limit the world's population by means which do not involve such horrendous suffering? Such limitation would make an important contribution to eliminating such problems as famine, and perhaps reduce some conflicts which help to produce wars.

So it is that churches need to seriously consider the question: "Is not a fulfilled life on the part of actual persons an intrinsic value and just what a God of love desires, and is not a causally necessary condition for such life the limitation of the world's population so that its resources will be adequate for its population, and needless suffering and misery prevented ?"

Another issue which has come to prominence in the last several years and which is or should be of grave concern to the societies of the world is the environmental crisis. It may well be the greatest irony in the history of modern civilization that the technological advances which have made it possible for the first time in human history to eliminate or greatly diminish the old evils of poverty and disease have also resulted in unprecedented damage to the environment through pollution and the destructive weapons of warfare such that life on this planet is put in serious jeopardy. We know now that the earlier optimism which supposed that technological advances could produce a utopia was naive. It is not that technology as such is the culprit for

175

our environmental woes or that we would wish to turn the clock back to a pretechnological age and give up its advantages. The problem is what it has always been in human history, namely, human sin. Given human freedom, the indeterminate possibility for good or for evil (Reinhold Niebuhr, cf. chapter Five), the increased power derived from technology may be used for destructive or creative ends. Today, industries, communities, and nations in their collective egoisms and greed seem bent primarily on using it destructively while rationalizing that such brings greater profits and jobs and is for the good of all. In the meantime the air, soil, and water is becoming increasingly polluted, and the viability of this planet as a home for us and our descendants is becoming increasingly tenuous.

There are some who claim that Christians and the church should not be concerned with environmental problems because some day soon God is going to send the ultimate Armageddon, and the only concern of the church should be the saving of souls so that they may escape the Armageddon into the bliss of heaven. But this is poor theology on several counts. First, as we have argued previously, especially in chapter three, God is a God of love who has granted real freedom to human beings, and thus works through the power of persuasion. Secondly, if this is the case, God is not going to directly will or directly cause human suffering through some divinely willed cataclysmic event. If the world is destroyed, it will not be according to God's will but because of human volitions and actions. Given human freedom, God will permit it but not desire it. God desires the fullest life possible for all his creatures. Thirdly, if this is the case, then even if there were to be an Armageddon for whatever cause sometime in the future, God desires the fullest life possible for all of his creatures in the here and now. Therefore the church should not ignore the environmental crisis as one of the issues to which it should give attention.

Furthermore, if the church preaches only a message of individual salvation, it fails to do justice to the doctrine of creation. If our universe is the handiwork of God (in whatever way this may have taken place), then every aspect of nature is of value to God and

176

deserves to be treated with respect and care. In the history of Christian thought, from the biblical period through such notables as Augustine, Aquinas, and St. Francis, there is to be found the theme of a dialectical tension between the human transcendence of nature and yet radical oneness with it. Even the expression "to have dominion over" in the context of the entire chapter of Genesis 1 clearly means that human beings are to be stewards of the lower orders of creation. While human beings occupy the highest level in the world's hierarchical order, there is envisioned a harmony in which they peacefully coexist with, and are responsible for, nature. This theme is found also in the second story of creation in chapter two where stress is placed on the human oneness with the earth and the human responsibility for its keeping. It is well known that St. Francis felt a oneness with nature and affirmed that God is to be praised on account of all the creatures of the earth. Perhaps it is not so well known that Augustine and Aquinas, while affirming that human beings occupy the highest level in the in the world's hierarchical order, also referred to what they have in common with the inanimate and animate creatures which occupy the lower ranks in the created order. These creatures, even the lowliest, cannot be considered without astonishment and without praising the Creator (Augustine, *City of God* , 22:24). Each and every creature exists for the perfection of the entire universe which shows forth the divine goodness to the glory of God (Aquinas, *Summa Theologica,* I, q.65, art. 2).

In view of the current situation, of the doctrine of creation, and of all the inferences which can be derived from the theology of an agapeistic God, the church has a responsibility to make whatever contribution it can to the task of alleviating the environmental crisis. This may take many forms including special educational programs, persuasive messages, and support of coercive governmental regulations for the prevention of pollution. In this effort, care should be taken to avoid the moral myopia of assuming that environmentalism is the only issue of importance in today's world (as the anti-abortionists do with their issue), and thus to ignore the cries of the dispossessed, the poor, and the distressed in our society and elsewhere. While the care and

177

healing of the environment is an imperative, and indeed a divine imperative, there are other imperatives which should not be ignored.

Among these other imperatives is the church's obligation to engage in efforts to reduce widespread poverty and homelessness in the world. Such efforts could include support of a reformed but adequate welfare and low cost housing program in the United States, economic justice and job programs here and abroad, and the several concerns and international efforts of the United Nations. Some church groups have made valuable direct contributions to the solution of this problem. For example, the program sponsored by the Christian inspired organization known as the Habitat for Humanity, which receives support from numerous churches as well as individuals, has made an outstanding contribution to reducing homelessness here and abroad. Also many churches and religious groups use church facilities to provide at least temporary shelter and food to the homeless and /or give support to agencies which do. But surely all churches could do more. Furthermore, is it not the case that the primary concern of entirely too many churches is centered upon the desires and perceived needs of the local congregations and too little upon the needs of the poor, the dispossessed and homeless, and the victims of injustice and prejudice? While it is important for local churches to have adequate buildings for educational and recreational programs, could not some of this space be set aside for the feeding and shelter of the homeless, and some of the church's budget be set aside for the support of home building projects of various kinds such as Habitat for Humanity?

There are other divine imperatives for the church in its relation to society. Those who worship a God of love are obligated to treat with respect and to accept all persons of whatever class and race. Unfortunately, the past record of the churches (for the most part the white churches) with respect to the integration of the races has been rather dismal. There was the oft repeated saying during the days of segregation that the most segregated hour of the week was eleven o'clock on Sunday morning. Apart from a few courageous souls (some of whom lost their jobs) white church leaders did not raise their voices in protest against the injustices of segregation and the so-called Jim

Crow laws. It was primarily the civil rights movement spawned in the black church under the courageous leadership of Dr. Martin Luther King Jr. which inspired the courts and the federal government to abolish the Jim Crow laws, to integrate schools and public places, and to require fair employment practices. With the changes which have now occurred, the churches should do more in the way of encouraging voluntary integration not only in the churches but also in society generally. Care should be taken to preserve the historically black churches which should be honored for their important contributions to American life and culture and for their courageous struggle against the injustice of segregation. White and black churches could meet together more often for mutual consultation and cooperation.

Working for peace in the world is another divine imperative for the church in its relation to society. As said above, a God of *agape* desires a fulfilled life for all persons, not their injury and death. Often in history people have proclaimed that they were fighting a war in his name. But since God is *agape,* he could never approve or sanction a war no matter what the situation. It may be that in this sinful world there is no other way to stop aggression and to preserve a relative justice except by force of arms, but it does not follow that such receives divine sanction. War is always evil, never a holy crusade, even though in a very few instances it may be a lesser evil.

Just as with the issue of race relations, in its long history the church has failed often to distinguish itself with respect to its stand on war. Apparently the earliest church was consistently pacifist in the sense that no Christian writer whose work is extant condoned Christian participation in warfare, and many vigorously condemned it. Since the military served as the police force, Christians were permitted to serve in the military in peacetime but not in wartime, and they should never shed blood. All emphasized the incompatibility of killing with Christian love. When the emperor Constantine and his army accepted Christianity in the fourth century, the pacifism of the early church was abandoned, and there emerged in the church the doctrine of the just war. Among the criteria for a just war (as found in Augustine and Aquinas) are the following: 1. It must be just as to its

179

intent which means that its object is to restore peace, to vindicate justice, and to be for the ultimate good even of the enemy. 2. Arms may be taken up only under the auspices of government. 3. The conduct of the war must be just which means, among other things, that noncombatants are spared, prisoners respected, and atrocities, looting, massacres, and reprisals forbidden. 4. The foreseeable outcome promises more good than ill. There was considerable rationalizing on the part of church authorities to make the crusades and religious wars fit these criteria. Has there ever been a war in all of history which met all four criteria?

It is most definitely the case that the code of a just war is obsolete today. The very character of modern warfare and modern weapons precludes sparing non-combatants. The weapons cannot be controlled in such a way as to insure that only the armies are assaulted. Often there is no intention of sparing the civilian population, but the shelling and bombing are intentionally directed against them. In terms of the evidence of contemporary experience, it has to be concluded that, everything considered, more evil than good has resulted from wars, and no lasting peace has been restored.

Since warfare is incompatible with what a God of *agape* desires and even a 'just' war is impossible, there is no justification whatever for the church, any church, to give its blessing to any war. While a particular church or denomination may not take a stand of absolute pacifism, it should honor the historic pacifist churches and those Christians who take such a stand and defend their right to do so. Further, it should be actively engaged in making any contribution it can possibly make in ridding the earth of those conditions which result in the scourge of war.

All the issues discussed above, overpopulation, the environmental crisis, poverty and homelessness, racial injustice, and warfare, dovetail into each other so that an effective solution of any one necessarily involves making improvements in the other areas as well. If a church or denomination is to make a genuine contribution to improving society, it needs a multifaceted strategy in which there is an attempt to deal with each and everyone of these issues. This strategy should involve active participation in the ecumenical movement, for several churches or denominations working in close cooperation can be more effective in dealing with societal problems than by each working alone.

4. Summary

In this chapter I have sought to show that from its very beginnings the Christian movement emphasized fellowship and community. There was never a notion of a Christian living a solitary life. Rather he or she is a participant in the "body of Christ," the church, which is both an invisible spiritual reality and a visible institution.

Apart from this view of the two-fold nature of the church there emerged in Christendom fundamentally different views as to what constitutes the nature and function of the church, namely, the Catholic and the Protestant. Both have strengths and weaknesses. The strength of Catholicism is its stability and universalism, but its weakness is its absolutism with respect to its forms, laws, and ecclesiastical authority. The strength of Protestantism is its recognition of the relativity of all rites, forms and traditions and the freedom and responsibility of the laity. Yet this strength can become distorted in an undisciplined freedom which results in all sorts of aberrations. The weaknesses of both simply serve to preserve the major rent in Christendom.

An adequate ecclesiology, one which supports ecumenism, understands the church in terms of the dialectical structure found in all of reality, namely, dynamics and form, freedom and tradition, memory and hope, individualization and socialization. For the church to be the church, it requires institutional structure, disciplines, and liturgical forms, but also prophetic voices directed against itself whenever the institution is regarded as absolute. It requires the stability of tradition and memory, but also the inspiration of hope. It requires continuities with the past, but also the freedom to be creative and to establish new forms and methods relevant to the times. It requires that attention be given to salvation and fulfilled lives for individuals, but also the recognition that no one lives in a social

181

vacuum and that attention must be given to the great social problems of our times such as overpopulation, the environmental crisis, poverty and homelessness, racial discrimination, and warfare.

In this chapter I have concentrated primarily on the nature and mission of the church in this world. Yet its responsibility for proclaiming a message of hope for a future life beyond that of this world must not be ignored. Here again is a dialectical aspect of the church's mission and message, namely, this worldly and other worldly. Too often in the past, as suggested above in the section on the environmental crisis, the message of the church has not been sufficiently dialectical. It has often been too much concerned about the next life, about describing the rewards of heaven and the punishments of hell, and too little concerned about this life with both its notable achievements and its horrendous problems. But neither pole of the dialectic can be ignored without distorting the Christian message. Eschatology is an integral part of the Christian faith and to that I turn in the next chapter.

---

[1] cf. Ante-Nicene Christian Library, Vols. 6, 13; *Early Latin Theology*, The Library of Christian Classics (Westminster, 1956).

[2] *The Nature and Destiny of Man*, Vol. 2, pp. 244-256; *An Interpretation of Christian Ethics*, (Meridan Books, 1956), pp. 9-10.

CHAPTER SEVEN
ESCHATOLOGY

In section four of chapter two I sought to demonstrate that it is logically possible for the human self to survive physical death. At the end of chapter six I claimed that eschatology is an integral part of the Christian faith because of its emphasis upon hope for the future. In this final chapter I will attempt to discuss more fully the meaning of the concept, the role it has played in the history of Christian thought, and the significance it might have for us in today's world. While the meaning of 'eschatology' has been indicated already to some degree, it might be well to introduce this discussion with a more specific and definite definition.

As with a number of words in our language today which are of recent origin, the term 'eschatology' has it roots in ancient Greek. During the nineteenth century it originated among biblical scholars and theologians who derived it from the two Greek words *eschatos* and *logos,* and since that time it has been widely used in their literature. *Logos,* from which is derived our word logic (the science of correct reasoning), means reason, thought , account of or discussion. *Eschatos* means 'end' but in two senses of 'end.' In one sense it is 'end' as in the Latin *finis,* namely, limit, boundary, finished, no more. In the other it is 'end' as in the Greek *telos,* namely, purpose, final causes, goals, completion. So 'eschatology' is the reasoning about, the study of, theory of , discussion of the 'end' of life, of the age, of history and/or the world in terms of *finis* or of *telos* or of both. Some eschatologies deal primarily with *telos* and are a consideration of meaning and purpose and their actualization in the common life of humanity and the development of cultures and history as well as in the lives of individuals in this life and beyond. Others deal primarily with *finis* and are most often apocalyptic in substance.

Apocalypticism has an ancient history, emerging especially in times of crises and chaos in history. Apparently it originated in Zoroastrianism, the ancient Persian religion, had considerable

183

influence on many Jews suffering the traumas of the exilic and postexilic periods, and was mediated by Judaism to early Christianity. While there is variety in the details of the apocalypticism of various peoples, generally apocalyptic thought is characterized by the following features. First, and perhaps foremost, there is a cosmic dualism in which the universe is thought to be occupied by two opposed personified powers of evil and good, Satan and God, and time is divided into two ages, this age and the age to come. Secondly, there is a pessimism concerning the present age which is viewed as under the sway of Satan, and thus hopelessly evil and incapable of improvement. The righteous can only persevere in their faithfulness in this age of evil and oppression. Thirdly, since the present age cannot be changed for the better, the only hope is that God, by means of great cataclysmic events sent directly by him or through his agent, will bring about the end of this present evil age and inaugurate the new age under his immediate control. Often there was an attempt through the use of astrology and/or numerology to set a date in the future (often the end of a century) for this great event of God's direct intervention. Fourthly, probably due to the influence of astrology, there is an obvious divine determinism in this view. The end is predetermined by God. It is he who is responsible for the calamities which accompany the end time and thus is viewed as an avenging God.

An apocalyptic eschatology is quite different from the classical prophetism of the Old Testament and the authentic teachings of Jesus concerning the kingdom of God. Both are concerned with past, present, and future, with this age and the age to come. But apocalypticism's cosmic dualism, pessimism about the possibility of redemption in the present, divine determinism in which at a predetermined time God directly wills to send great calamities to inaugurate the end time, and speculation as to when this divine action will occur are lacking in the teachings of the prophets and Jesus. In the prophets the judgments of Yahweh against Israel are actualized in history by the agency of enemy nations and not some cosmic figure, and even the possibility of such judgment arouses sorrow and pity in the heart of Yahweh himself. It is his desire that Israel will heed the

184

message of the prophets, repent and become a faithful covenant partner. So the prophets proclaim that Yahweh is merciful, ready to forgive and accept Israel, and they plead with Israel to repent and to renew loyalty to the covenant now.

In chapter four on Christology I sought to demonstrate that the central theme of Jesus' teaching was the kingdom or reign of God. The few major concepts involved in this theme were that the kingdom is a free gift of God, is characterized by an agapeistic life style, is inclusive, breaks through the customary order of the world, and is of supreme value. He calls upon all to accept this free gift of God's loving reign, for the kingdom is now dawning and will come in fulfillment in the near future. Always in Jesus' authentic teachings present and future are related in the closest possible fashion such that they are mutually revealing. The present is the time of decision and acceptance of God's loving reign in the light of God's future, but the future is not described in apocalyptic terms. It can be said that Jesus' message was eschatological but not apocalyptic.

It is true, of course, that Mark 13 contains material of a general apocalyptic nature. According to many current New Testament scholars this so called "little apocalypse" is a very complex composition which includes materials from late Jewish apocalypticism and the experiences of Christians under persecution and threats to the unity of the church. Such items as the "desolating sacrilege" which may refer to the Roman emperor Caligula who had his statue set up in the temple, and the expression "let the reader understand," which indicates a literary composition, lead scholars to the conclusion that much of the chapter's content was originally in a separate non-Christian apocalyptic document. The author of Mark found in it a message appropriate for the Judean Christians at the time when Jerusalem was under siege by the Romans just before 70 A. D. and incorporated it in his Gospel, attributing the words to Jesus. With a few exceptions, most of the statements come from the apocalyptic document and/or the experiences of the Christians in Jerusalem at the time of the Roman siege and are not to be assigned to Jesus.

Mark 13 is replete with statements concerning the occurrence of numerous events which are supposed to be signs of the impending end of time. If Jesus uttered these statements, would he have made the statement recorded in Luke 17: 20-21, "The kingdom of God is not coming with signs to be observed; nor will they say, 'Lo, here it is!' or 'There!' for behold the kingdom is in the midst of you."? Taken in the context of the total body of Jesus' teaching concerning the kingdom, there is good reason for accepting the latter as authentic sayings of Jesus but not the former. Surely Jesus would not have contradicted himself so blatantly. For Jesus, the kingdom is present in the community of those who accept God's reign, but the members of the community are to pray for its coming ("Thy kingdom come") in universal consummation.

While Jesus may have known the Jewish apocalyptic thought of his time, apparently it had little or no influence on his thought. The general features of apocalypticism are absent from his teachings. There is no cosmic dualism, pessimism about the present age, divine determinism, and date setting. Unlike apocalypticism, Jesus did not see the present age under the total domination of evil so that nothing good could be done and one was confined to simply waiting for God's predetermined end time. Apocalyptic writing had little or nothing to say about ethics for the present age for it was so under the domination of the evil that nothing good could be accomplished. But Jesus' teachings are full of descriptions (as in the Sermon on the Mount) of the ethical behavior characteristic of the kingdom of God life style, and to which those who accept the gift of the kingdom aspire. Good can be accomplished in this world. At the conclusion of the disciples' missionary journey (Luke 10), Jesus expressed an optimistic view about evil being diminished by this missionary activity. While the fulfillment or universal consummation of the kingdom lies in a future known only to God, it is possible now in fellowship with those who accept God's reign to live a kingdom life style. Jesus' teachings are full of hope for the present and of eschatological promise for the future, but they are lacking in apocalyptic instruction.

In chapter four on Christology I indicated that, as portrayed in the Synoptics, Jesus did not seek glory or high status or make exalted claims about himself or his role. Humility was the hallmark of his character. It would have been out of character for him to claim that he was the apocalyptic Messiah or Son of Man. He came as the prophet and suffering servant who announces the inbreaking of the reign of God. In his own life he demonstrated perfectly the characteristics of the kingdom life style, the *agape* of God in all his human relationships, and he held a special filial relation with God. It is not surprising that the earliest Christians sought to express their wonder and devotion with the most exalted terminology available to them, and so designated him with honorific titles such as Messiah or Son of Man. These titles were not originally apocalyptic, but by the time of the first century B. C. they had been given such a meaning in some apocalyptic writings. They designated God's agent who would inaugurate the end time. With the rise of the persecutions, the early Christians readily identified Jesus with this agent who, though he was put to death by hostile authorities, would come again on clouds of glory to initiate the end time. Since the historical Jesus was reluctant to be identified as Messiah even in an earthly sense, I am convinced that he would have been surprised and horrified by being identified as an apocalyptic Messiah or Son of Man. He did not seek glory for himself, but in everything he sought to glorify God, to do his will, and thus to persuade persons to accept the love and joy of the kingdom fellowship in the present while looking with hope to its future fulfillment. So in both his teachings and in his life style Jesus displayed an eschatological perspective, but one which was not apocalyptic.

As suggested above, the eschatology of the early church tended to become more apocalyptic as early Christianity spread out of Palestine into other parts of the Roman empire and encountered government sponsored hostility, oppression, and persecution. Difficult times always provide a fertile ground for the growth of apocalypticism, and this is clearly demonstrated in the New Testament book of Revelation.

Undoubtedly, Revelation is the finest and most complete extant example of apocalyptic writing from early Christianity. Yet through the centuries there have been Christian leaders who have felt that it should not be in the New Testament canon. Even in the early centuries there were strong differences of opinion among Christians on this issue. Many felt it should not be included because it was a favorite work of extreme enthusiasts who just might be heretical, and because of serious doubts concerning its apostolic origin. As late as the early fourth century there was still divided opinion as to whether it should be included or not, and it was not until the end of the century that it was included in Athanasius' list of the 27 authoritative books of the New Testament. Many Christians of much later times also have doubted its canonicity. Luther, for example, regarded it as neither prophetic nor apostolic because, in his view, Christ is neither known nor taught in it. Yet some people have been and still are fascinated by it, finding in it a blueprint for future events and the end of the world.

On the basis of marked differences in language, literary style, and ideas, modern biblical scholars conclude that the John who was the author of Revelation was not the John who wrote the Gospel and the Letters. Further, they conclude that the book was written near the end of the reign of the Roman emperor Domitian (81-96 A. D) who had decreed that throughout the empire everyone must engage in the cult of emperor worship. According to many early Christian writers, it was at this time that there had occurred a persecution of Christians in Asia Minor for their refusal to participate in this cult. Clearly, Revelation reflects this situation. It was written to encourage Christians under persecution or threat of persecution with hope for a better future soon to come.

As might be expected, all the characteristic features of apocalypticism are present in Revelation. There is an abundance of animal symbolism, numerology, angelology and demonology, predicted woes, and astral references. Also present are a cosmic dualism, a pessimism about the present, a divine determinism, and a description of horrendous cataclysmic events which soon were to occur, instigating the destruction of this evil world and of Satan and his followers, after which God and his Lamb would inaugurate a new heaven and a new earth. The visions of the impending destruction of the evil forces in the world (including the Roman empire) and the exalted visions of a glorious new age were undoubtedly of much comfort and encouragement to those suffering persecution.

Unfortunately, through the ages and even today it is often the case that the most objectionable features of Revelation's message, such as God's terrible vengeance, joy at the prospect of enemies suffering, and relief from any sense of responsibility for the evils of the age, have been emphasized to the virtual exclusion of that which is of value such as a firm hope for a glorious future under God. Often it is trivialized by making it a book of predictions for a future, far distant from the time in which it was written. Yet the writer makes it quite clear that he speaking of the near future. More than once he speaks of "what must soon take place," and says "the time is near." (chapters 1 and 22) The famous "mark of the beast," which one evangelist during world war II identified as the gasoline rationing cards, is the author's way of referring to the fact that everyone had to secure a mark signifying that he or she had worshipped at the shrine of the emperor. Without this mark one was subject to arrest by the Roman authorities. The word "beast" is clearly a symbol for the emperor. In other passages this word along with "eagle" refers to the Roman empire. But Christians should take hope, for Rome would soon fall. Soon the heavenly Christ with his forces would come to defeat the Antichrist, annihilate his forces, bind up Satan, reign on earth with the resurrected martyrs for a thousand years, after which Satan would be confined to the lake of fire, ending his rule forever. Then he would establish the new heaven and the new earth. Had the expectation for such stirring events been envisioned for the far distant future it would hardly have been of any encouragement and comfort to Christians suffering hardship and martyrdom near the end of the first century.

With the cessation of persecutions and the recognition of Christianity as an official religion by emperor Constantine in the fourth century, the role of apocalypticism in the thought of the church diminished. Then, too, as Greek philosophical thought with its body-soul dualism permeated Christian theology, there was the tendency to spiritualize the notions of salvation and the next life. The church held the keys to the kingdom of heaven. By means of the sacraments, good works, and the discipline of purgatory, the soul of the believer finally could enter into the blessedness of heaven. Of course, from time to time there was an outbreak of apocalyptic speculation and fervor, especially in times of great catastrophes and toward the end of the first millennium, and yet it was not a continuing and dominant feature of the church's theology.

In the thought of the Reformers, Luther and Calvin, the major emphasis is on the Word of God (Christ) as witnessed to in Scripture, justification by faith, and living the Christian life. While both believed that the doctrine of the resurrection life was an essential part of the Christian faith, neither was obsessed by it. Acceptance of God's acceptance and fellowship with him in the present was of primary importance. On this basis one could be confident of experiencing a resurrection life. For Calvin eternal life was a theme worthy of meditation, but it may be abused in self serving ways. One should not engage in too much speculation about it, push inquiry on unknown things beyond what God permits us to know, namely, that the faithful are received into paradise and sinners into torment. One should neither be selfishly concerned nor constantly speculating about the end time, but should be occupied in living the Christian life to the best of one's ability. Both Luther and Calvin viewed the Christian life as a pilgrimage which naturally would find its ultimate fulfillment in the transcendent Kingdom of God.

It is true, of course, that in some of Luther's statements there are echoes of apocalypticism. He viewed many events of his day (religious conflicts, upheavals of one sort or another) as signs that the end was near and that the world would not endure a hundred years. Uncharacteristically, he was rather modest about such claims, proclaiming that he did not wish to force any one to believe as he did, but he would not permit any one to deny him the right to own beliefs. Whatever Luther believed concerning the nearness of the end, his major emphasis was that only as faith is meaningful in the present can there be confidence about the resurrection life.

The most complete and fervent type of apocalypticism during the Reformation was that which appeared among small radical wings of the Anabaptists. While most Anabaptists were devout pacifists and often persecuted for such a stand, some adhered to a violent type of apocalypticism. They believed that the Parousia (Second Coming of Christ) was near (many specified dates), and that Christ would lead his elect into battle against the wicked, especially priests and nobles. One group sized control of Münster in a violent attempt to prepare the city for the Parousia which they believed was at hand. They established a military and communistic community which survived for about a year and then fell to an army made up of Catholics and Lutherans. Common opponents do make for strange bedfellows. Be that as it may, it is obvious that the various predictions made at this time concerning the Parousia were simply not fulfilled.

Since the Reformation, small groups of apocalypticists have risen in Protestantism from time to time, especially during periods of conflict, economic depression, and persecution. In the United States the hardships of the frontier provided a fertile soil in which apocalypticism could grow. Among some there was the conviction that the return of Christ was near, and there were attempts to calculate the date from biblical symbolism and numerology. For example, William Miller proclaimed that the Parousia, with great cataclysmic events in nature and society, would occur sometime between March, 1843 and March, 1844. When it did not occur, the date was revised to October 22, 1844, and when it did not occur then, many followers were naturally disillusioned and abandoned this type of eschatology. Yet even today there are those who engage in this sort of speculative calculation. One religious radio broadcaster with a rather large following predicted that the world would end in September 1994. Others have proclaimed that the great event will occur with the end of this century.

With its biblical literalism and dispensationalism, Protestant fundamentalism has provided a general hospitable environment for apocalypticism, even though the majority do not engage in date setting and favor postmillennialism over premillennialism. That is, instead of the Parousia preceding it, the millennium will be ushered in by the work of the Holy Spirit in and through the church, and the second advent of Christ will occur at the end of the millennium. Whatever the disagreements, fundamentalists generally insist on the belief that Christ will come again in personal and bodily form, in a literal last judgment, with the eternal bliss of believers in heaven and the eternal damnation of unbelievers in hell.

It is rather surprising that apocalypticism lingers on in the modern scientific age which has made possible the public's greater exposure to reliable knowledge concerning the universe and history. The basic premise of apocalypticism is predicated upon not simply an obsolete view of the cosmos but on one which is in error. The vision of Christ bodily returning from heaven to earth entails the ancient notion of a three layer universe in which earth is a flat disk with heaven as a canopy over it and hell a region below it. While there may be a few 'flat-earthers' today, surely our space exploration and modern astronomy prove such a view is factually false.

Not only is apocalypticism's cosmology mistaken, but also history verifies the fact that there are numerous examples of apocalypticism's unfulfilled predictions from ancient times to the present. Surely a God of love is also a God of all truth and does not sanction our believing that which is factually false. But even if the errors could be eliminated from apocalypticism, it is still permeated with a spirit of vengeance which is inimical to the spirit of Jesus. Its concept of God as an avenging deity who unleashes terrible catastrophes upon a large portion of the earth's population is inconsistent with Jesus' view of God as *agape*. Its belief that only the favored few who accept its tenets will be saved from the holocaust fosters separatism, pride, and scorn for the majority of struggling and sinful human beings who are regarded as enslaved by the devil. This, too, is inconsistent with Jesus' love for all persons and with his universalism. Finally, since the present is viewed as under the control of the devil and so hopelessly evil that little can be changed for the

192

better, apocalypticists teachings are lacking generally in ethical and social emphases. For these reasons apocalypticism should be rejected. It simply cannot have a place in a Christian theology, the eschatology of which is both adequate for the modern world and consistent with the spirit and teachings of Jesus.

A non-apocalyptic eschatology similar to that of Jesus is full of optimism and hope for the present and the future. There are, of course, evil and powerful human beings who, in their freedom, commit horrendous evils against humanity and nature. Yet these acts are not fated. The world is not caught in the ill-fated clutches of an evil supernatural power, the devil. In chapter two it was argued that since the human self possesses a transcendent characteristic, human beings are capable of indeterminate possibility for good as well as indeterminate possibility for evil. It follows, then,, that changes for the better can be made in this world. The dialectical character of the human being as saint and sinner precludes the universal and full actualization of the goal, the kingdom of God, in history, but individuals and societies can be improved, justice and equity more nearly achieved. A prime example which confirms this claim is the abolition of segregation in the South, the greater degree of justice and equity achieved by the Afro-American community in the United States, and the startling changes in South Africa which has resulted in blacks participating in the government and being accorded greater freedom and justice. With the kingdom goal as our ultimate standard, we are at one and the same time judged and inspired. The judgment precludes pride and arrogance over accomplishments, but the inspiration provides the motivation to work for ever greater approximations to the kingdom. There is the confident hope that with God's help the greater approximations will be actualized in history.

Time and again throughout the preceding chapters, it has been emphasized that on the basis of both the arguments for the existence of God and the revelation of God in Jesus Christ, it must be concluded that God is *agape,* and as such created human beings to live in fellowship with himself. If this is the case, then it follows that it is inconceivable that a loving God who can do anything that is logically

193

possible would permit persons to pass out of existence when this goal for them is unfulfilled. God as *agape* logically entails the persistence of personality through death, a real postmortem existence for persons even though we cannot now know in detail what it will be like. While we should not give heed to those who claim to know so much about the 'next life' that, as someone has put it, they are able to describe the furniture of heaven and the temperature of hell, we can still hold firmly to the conviction that there is a postmortem existence and that some reasonable claims can be made about it.

First of all, is a postmortem existence for human beings logically possible? If it is not, then not even God can provide such for his creatures. In chapter three I argued in agreement with Aquinas that the logically impossible (i.e. creating a round square) does not fall in the scope of God's omnipotence, for such is literally meaningless. No one, not even God can do the logically impossible, make an x which is not an x, a man who is not a man. While the words may make sense and we understand them, the statement, since it is contradictory, cannot have a referent and is nonsense.

In chapter two on human nature and destiny I sought to demonstrate that a postmortem existence is logically possible. In order for that to be the case, the human self must transcend the limits of the purely physical. The fact that the sense of one's personal identity persists throughout numerous changes in the body suggests that one is something more than what simply meets the eye, that the sense of the self, of who one is, cannot be reduced to the body. Also there are good arguments in support of the claim that, while the occurrence of mental experiences are causally related to the operation of the brain, these experiences cannot be reduced to physical brain events. It follows, then, that the mental transcends the physical, that even though empirically the occurrence of certain physical events is a causally necessary condition for the occurrence of certain mental events, it is logically possible for mental events to occur without any accompanying physical events.

In light of these considerations, I argued in section four of chapter two for the logical possibility of a postmortem existence in a

194

mind dependent realm. This is more than simply an objective immortality as envisioned by Charles Hartshorne in which the remembrance of the totality of all of our lives is forever stored in the memory bank of God. This is also a subjective immortality in which our states of consciousness survive bodily death.

One of the finest analyses of what subjective immortality could mean is that of the philosopher H.H. Price in his "Personal Survival and the Idea of Another World."[1] According to Price, what occurs in the phenomenon of dreaming may provide a clue as to what could be possible in a subjective immortality. In sleep, sensory stimuli are either cut off or are prevented from having their normal effects on the brain centers. Yet images are still experienced, and these images are not unreal. That is to say, they are actual entities in contrast to imaginary ones, the latter being a thinking of propositions (a leprechaun made me do it) which are not believed. In this sense, mental images are not imaginary at all. They are actual, and they are experienced. Further, if the philosophical phenomenalists are correct and in this life a physical object is the sum total of a family of appearances, so in the 'next life' a family of interrelated images could serve as a substitute for the material objects perceived in this present life. Such families of mental images could constitute a perfectly good world, even if there were not a detailed reproduction. Generic images and typical representations providing a generalized picture could provide all that is needed, and they would be similar to our present experiences, especially that of remembering a physical object sensation from the past.

One could feel alive in this postmortem world since there could be states of consciousness, including memory traces and the experiencing of emotions and wishes, even though there were no physical organisms receiving physical stimuli to produce such experiences. In this imagery 'next world' there could be organic sensation images which could provide a basis for feeling alive. Certainly we feel alive while dreaming. It could be the case that in this imagery 'next world' one might feel so much alive that he might not be fully aware of the fact that he was not still physically alive save as he might remember being critically ill and recognize a difference in the casual laws now operative in his experience.

In addition, there could be a sense of personal identity based both upon memory which no more than any other state of consciousness is identical with certain neural brain processes and upon families of organic images. This could provide a sense of a continuing background as well as a sense of individual difference very much as memory serves us in this life. To this I would add that the sense of temporal limitation which appears to be a necessary condition for personal identity would not necessarily be lost in this 'next world.' Through memory one could recall life in this world with its temporal limitation of birth and death, and this would reinforce the sense of personal identity. Also there does not seem to be any reason why the images of the 'next world' could not have extension and shape very much as the images in our dreams in which we retain a sense of personal identity. So there could be both similarity and difference, which is a characteristic feature of this life, contributing to our sense of identity.

Moreover, Price emphasized the logical possibility that there could be a meeting and communication in this imagery world by means of telepathy. That is, there could be a sending and receiving of telepathic apparitions and telepathic communications. There is some evidence (Rhine's experiments at Duke University) which tends to establish telepathy as an empirical reality in this world, so there seems to be no good reason to deny that it is a logical possibility in this imagery 'next world.' Thus it makes sense to speak of encountering other persons in this world. This, too, would contribute to the sense of feeling alive and of personal identity.

It seems to me that Price's description of a possible type of postmortem life makes sense, granted the truth of the claim that 'person' means observable behavior and something more. While as a philosopher Price was not seeking to defend the Christian view of immortality, and envisions survival of death as a natural occurrence rather than as dependent upon an act of God, his analysis which establishes the meaningfulness of the idea of immortality, the logical possibility of personal survival of death, helps to provide a rational defense for the Christian claim that there is a resurrection life. Further, several of his arguments can be used to explicate and defend certain aspects of the Christian claim.

For example, in I Corinthians 15:44 the Apostle Paul, in speaking of the resurrection, claims that the physical body of this life is raised a _spiritual_ body, and in Mark 12:25 Jesus is recorded as having said, "when they rise from the dead, they neither marry nor are given in marriage, but are like angels in heaven." With their Jewish background both Jesus and Paul could not think of a person actually existing without a bodily form. But Paul explicitly states that this physical body (the analogy of the sown seed) is perishable, but that which is raised is imperishable.(v. 42) Flesh and blood cannot inherit the kingdom of God. (v. 50) God gives to this "seed" which has come to life "a body as he has chosen and to each kind of seed its own body." (v. 38) There is here an emphasis upon a continuation of personal identity in that each raised person will have his or her own unique 'body,' and thus there can be a real meeting of persons. Yet all of this is in a realm different from the physical. It seems to me that Price's view of an imagery 'next life' is not inconsistent with Paul's view, helps it to take on additional meaningfulness, and positions it on the rational ground of logical possibility.

If we can assume that discourse concerning personal survival of death is meaningful, then the historic claim of Christianity concerning the resurrection life (as taught not only by Paul but also throughout the New Testament and in the later creeds of the church) makes sense. Surely the resurrection life has seldom if ever been understood as the resuscitation of the physical body. How can the perishable inhabit the imperishable? Yet a loving and omnipotent God does not abandon his childern at death In the postmortem realm he resurrects or recreates each person. Each person is recreated, not as the identical physical organism of this present life, but as a spiritual 'body' containing the generic shape, dispositional characteristics, and memory traces of the former physical organism. In this new environment there is as much of a continuity of relations and a

197

'meeting' with other persons as in the present physical environment. While in Christian thought heaven has often been viewed as a rather static affair, it follows from the description above (especially dispositional characteristics, memory traces, continuity of relations and encounters with others) that there can be a continuation of personal growth in goodness, love, and knowledge in the 'next life.' Surely a loving and omnipotent God would not decree that each person had to remain for eternity at whatever level of development was present at the time of physical death and thus be unable to rectify any failings of this life. Through the power of persuasion arising out of his perfect self-giving love, he would motivate persons to seek victory over their failings and to grow in love and fellowship. On this view the fellowship of the kingdom of God in the next life is not a static sort of existence which would be uninteresting and dull, and unworthy of the designation "heaven," but one which is full of growth and the zest of living in that divine fellowship of freedom and faithfulness.

Near the end of chapter five on Christology I argued that the claim that God is all loving and omnipotent logically entails an ultimate universal salvation. The claim that there is both an eternal hell and an omnipotent and all loving God is contradictory. If there is an eternal hell, God is either not omnipotent or not all loving. But previously in chapters three and five I sought to demonstrate that it makes sense in terms of both reason and revelation to claim that God is both all loving (*agape*) and omnipotent. If God is omnipotent, he has the power to empty hell, and if he is all loving, he wishes to do so. The ultimate goal of a universal fellowship of perfect freedom and faithfulness and the character of God as *agape* necessitates that this be done with the power of persuasion. Obviously persuasion can be resisted. Persons can reject the divine fellowship and live in the hell of estrangement from God and others. The notion of hell as having spatial location and physical characteristics such as burning fire is nonsense in light of our claim that the next life is a mind dependent imagery affair, or of St. Paul's claim that persons are raised as "spiritual bodies." The concept of hell consistent with these claims is that it is to be understood not in terms of a physical place but it terms

198

of relations. It is egoistic separation and estrangement from the love of God and others, and thus from being the loving persons God desires us to be. But in light of God's omnipotence, this estrangement cannot be for an eternity.

God's omnipotence does not mean that he compels consent or acceptance. There can be loving relations only in terms of voluntary decision, consent, or acceptance. Love and compulsion are incompatible. If love is to be genuine, it must be voluntary. Not even God can compel love, for this would be a contradiction in terms and literally nonsense. His goal of a loving fellowship, a kingdom of loving relations, cannot be established through compulsion or limited to a prescribed number of people as the apocalypticists claim. It must be voluntary and universal.

Granted that there is a postmortem existence, can persons decide against God and fellowship for ever and ever? As argued above, the omnipotence of God means that he can do everything that is logically possible to do consistent with his purposes. So it is within the realm of logical possibility for God, who has all the time there is, both in this world and the next to realize his purpose ultimately through the power of persuasion without abolishing freedom. That is, persons will freely decide to accept the divine fellowship. Such free decision will be in response to the self-giving, sacrificial divine love. Both the suffering servant of II Isaiah and the cross of Jesus testify to the persuasive power of vicarious, self giving, sacrificial love which so often awakens the conscience and leads to a voluntary change for the better in one's life. We can see an analogy to this in our own everyday experience where the continuing forgiving and accepting love of one who has suffered due to the actions of another person (perhaps a relative) has been the very thing which led to the redemption of that person. So the *agape* God continuously and forever works through the persuasive power of his self giving, sacrificial love, and finally all will freely respond to and accept this love.

So, again, as in the chapters on God, Christology, and Soteriology, I reaffirm the conviction that the very nature of the omnipotent God is *agape,* and precisely because of this there will be an

199

ultimate salvation, an ultimate universal divine fellowship of everyone in perfect freedom and faithfulness. Then the kingdom or reign of God will be actual.

There are objections by some that such an eschatology will dissuade persons from making disciplined efforts to live a moral life. These objectors assume that the fear of punishment is the major motivation for acting morally, that only fear of punishment is the deterrent which prevents the doing of evil deeds. Of course, whatever the motivation, refraining from doing evil deeds is better for all than the doing of them. But is not a genuinely good deed purely gratuitous, done simply for the sake of doing it, and without any thought of reward? There is joy in the doing, and rewards and punishments are irrelevant. To those who say, "why be good?" if an ultimate universal salvation is the case, the answer is that one is good because one wants to be, that the goodness itself is its own reward and not dependent on anything beyond itself.

The eschatology presented above has not eliminated a hell, but only a physical and eternal hell. Surely the joys of fellowship are better than the estrangements of enmity and hatreds which we bring upon ourselves. It would be better to avoid a postmortem estranged separation from the divine fellowship, however temporary, than to experience it. Our experience of estrangement in this life makes this abundantly clear. It is the positive motivation of goodness for goodness sake, however, which is primary in our eschatology. Further, the conviction of an ultimate universal salvation should provide us with more confidence in the meaningfulness of our lives and greater acceptance of all our fellow human beings.

In conclusion, I would reaffirm that a Christian theology which seeks to retain the essentials of the tenets of the historic Christian faith, and at the same time make sense in the modern world with its scientific and historical disciplines, must reject all forms of apocalyptic eschatology. However these disciplines do not necessitate that it reject the notion of a resurrection life as logically absurd. A resurrection life along the lines described above is both logically possible and not absurd as far as our present empirical knowledge is concerned. Given that the God disclosed in Jesus is *agape,* it follows that ultimately all will be saved in that fellowship of perfect freedom and faithfulness. Once again, it is obvious that the Christian faith incorporates the Janus principle. It looks back to Jesus for the vision of God as *agape,* and, precisely because of this, looks forward with a confident hope for a better day both in this life and the next.

---

[1] *Classical and Contemporary Readings in the Philosophy of Religion,* John Hick, ed. (Prentice-Hall, 1964), pp. 364-86.

EPILOGUE

In this treatise I have sought to formulate a constructive theology in terms of the basic features of my Christian convictional situation. As indicated in the first chapter on method, certain convictions rest ultimately on the revelation or disclosures of God which, similar to the principles of logic, cannot be empirically verified or rationally proven. These convictions are basic assumptions which can be known through *mythos* but not *logos.*. They are neither discovered nor created by means of human rational ingenuity, but come from beyond through the disclosures of God in history, especially in Jesus of Nazareth. They are not disproved necessairly by *logos,* even though some interpretations and explications may be shown to be contradicted by the facts of experience and to be irrational nonsense. Indeed, there is a reciprocal relationship between *mythos* and *logos.* The former provides the transcendent truths of faith upon which Christianity rests, and the latter functions as a servant of the former in order that, in discourse concerning the truths of faith, it may be demonstrated that they are not falsified by the facts of experience and are not irrational. The task of the servant is to enlarge our understanding of the explicit and implicit meanings of the truths of faith and to demonstrate their relevance to individual life and to all the disciplines of culture. Further, it is *logos* which enables one to show that the experiences of personal life and the lessons of history provide a pragmatic justification for the soundness of the Christian *mythos.*

So in this treatise I have attempted to use *logos* in explicating certain key tenets contained in the Christian *mythos.* The whole notion of a Christian *mythos,* of the revelation of God, would be vacuous without beings capable of receiving, appreciating, and to a large extent understanding that which is revealed. Thus it was necessary to show by as cogent arguments as possible that the human being is a creature who is more than that which meets the eye. A person cannot be defined simply in terms of bodily form, structure, and attributes, as important as these may be in contributing to a sense of personal identity. Each person is a self who transcends the physical, a self who is made up of thoughts, mental propensities and attributes, and a sense of personal identity. This self can be related to God and come to a better self-understanding by becoming aware that he or she is understood by God. This relationship to God and to other selves can be experienced both in this life and the next.

There is a reciprocal relation also between *mythos* and *logos,* revelation and reason, in our discourse about God. Reason can play a primary role in arriving at the conclusion that there is a God and that he possesses certain attributes, but a full knowledge of his nature as *agape* and of his evaluations of the world and of all its creatures is dependent upon revelation. The conviction that there is a God who is personal and loving can be supported by rational arguments. However, it is more clearly and vividly made known to us in God's revelation, especially that in Jesus of Nazareth. In his teachings and life style there is disclosed a God of *agape,* of self-giving, sacrificial love. Such revelation is conclusive but not concluded. It does not exclude anyone or any revelatory claim of any other religion so long as it is not inconsistent with *agape* .

It should be obvious that God cannot deny his very nature and that, as *agape,* he is willing and eager to accept everyone who is willing to accept his acceptance. Continuously he is seeking to lure all persons into a loving relationship with himself. Those who accept his acceptance engage in fellowship with each other which forms the basis for the church. Ideally, the church is a community dedicated to God, and under the ideal of the kingdom is engaged in the instruction and encouragement of its members and in actions for the improvement of society.

Finally, on the basis of experiencing the love of God and the fellowship of the 'saints,' there is a confident hope for the future, both in this life and the next. There is the conviction that ultimately God will bring into being that final universal fellowship in which everyone lives with God and others in perfect freedom and faithfulness.

Robert H. Ayers

SELECTED BIBLIOGRAPHY

Abbott, Walter M., ed., *The Documents of Vatican II,* New York: The American Press, 1966.

Altizer, Thomas J. J. and Hamilton, William, *The Death of God,* New York: The Bobbs-Merrill Co., 1966.

Altizer, Thomas J. J., et. al., *Deconstruction and Theology,* New York: Crossroad Publishing Co., 1982.

Anderson, Bernhard, *Understanding The Old Testament,* third edition, Englewood Cliffs: Prenticee-Hall, 1975.

Ayers, Robert H., "The Ecumenical Thought of Reinhold Niebuhr," *Union Seminary Quarterly Review,* vol. 48, numbers 1-2, 1994.

_____ *Judaism and Christianity,* Lanham, MD.: The University Press of America, 1983.

_____ *Language, Logic, and Reason in The Church Fathers,* Hildesheim: Georg Olms Verlag, 1979.

_____ "Methodological, Epistemological, and Ontological Motifs in The Thought Of Reinhold Niebuhr," *Modern Theology,* vol., 7, no.,2, January, 1991.

Bainton, Roland H., *Christendom,* vols.I-II, New York: Harper Torchbook, 1966.

Barbour, Ian G., *Issues in Science and Religion,* Englewood Cliffs: Prentice-Hall, 1966.

Barr, James, *Fundamentalism,* Philadelphia: Westminster Press, 1978.

Barth, Karl, *Church Dogmatics, A Selection,* G. W. Bromily, ed., New York: Harper Torchbook, 1962.

_____ *Dogmatics in Outline,* New York: Harper Torchbook, 1959.

Bedell, George C. et. al., *Religion in America,* New York: The Macmillan Co., 1975.

Bonhoeffer, Dietrich, *Letters and Papers From Prison,* New York: Macmillan Paperback Edition, 1962.

Brown, Delwin, James, Ralph E. Jr., & Reeves, Gene, eds., *Process Philosophy and Christian Thought,* New York: Bobbs-Merrill, Inc., 1971.

Brown, Robert McAfee, *The Essential Reinhold Niebuhr,* New Haven: Yale University Press, 1986.

Bultmann, Rudolf, et. al., *Kerygma and Myth,* New York: Harper Torchbook, 1961.

Burkill,T. A., *The Evolution of Christian Thought,* Ithaca: Cornell University Press, 1971.

Cauthen, Kenneth, *The Impact of American Religious Liberalism,* New York: Harper and Row Publishers, 1962.

Charles, R. H., *The Apocrypha and Pseudepigrapha in English,* Oxford: The Claredon Press, 1913.

Cobb, John B. Jr., *Christ in a Pluralistic Age,* Philadelphia: Westminster Press, 1975.

Cobb, John B. Jr. and Griffin, David Ray, *Process Theology,* Philadelphia: Westminster Press, 1976.

Connick, C. Milo, *Jesus: The Man, The Mission, and The Message,* second edition, Englewood cliffs: Prentice-Hall, 1974.

Dillenberger, John and Welch, Claude, *Protestant Christianity,* New York: Charles Scribner's Sons, 1954.

Ferm, Deane W., ed., *Contemporary American Theologians II, A Book of Readings,* New York: the Seabury Press, 1982.

Ford, Lewis S., *The Lure of God,* Philadelphia: Fortress Press, 1978.

Griffin, David R., et. al., *Varieties of Postmodern Theology,* Albany: State University of New York Press, 1989.

Gonzalez, Justo l., *A History of Christian Thought,* vols I-III, Nashville: Abingdon Press, 1971-1975.

Harries, Richard, ed., *Reinhold Niebuhr and The Issues of Our Time,* Grand Rapids: William B. Eerdmans Publishing Co., 1986.

Hartshorne, Charles, *Anselm's Discovery,* La Salle, Illinois: Open Court, 1965.

_____ *A Natural Theology For Our Time,* Open Court, 1967

_____ *Omnipotence and Other Theological Mistakes,* Albany: State University of New York Press, 1984.

Hick, John, ed., *Classical and Contemporary Readings in The Philosophy of Religion,* Englewood Cliffs: Prentice-Hall, 1964.

Hick, John and McGill, Arthur, *The Many-Faced Argument,* The Macmillan Co., 1967.

High, Dallas M., ed., *New Essays On Religious Language,* New York: Oxford University Press, 1969.

Hordern, William, *A Layman's Guide To Protestant Theology,* New York: The Macmillan Co., 1956.

Hyatt, J. Philip, *The Heritage of Biblical Faith,* Saint Louis: The Bethany Press, 1964.

Kee, H. C., Young, F. W., Froelich, K., *Understanding The New Testament,* third edition, Englewood Cliffs: Prentice-Hall, 1973.

Kegley, C. W. and Bretall, R. W. eds., *Reinhold Niebuhr: His Religious, Social, and Political Thought,* New York: The Macmillan Co., 1956.

Kelly, J. N. D., *Early Christian Doctrines,* Revised Edition, New York: Harper and Row, 1978.

Kerr, Hugh Tomson, Jr., ed., *A Compend of The Institutes of The Christian Religion by John Calvin,* Philadelphia: Presbyterian Board of Christian Education, 1939.

_____ *A Compend of Luther's Theology,* Philadelphia: Westminster Press, 1943.

Kliever, L. D., *The Shattered Spectrum,* Atlanta: John Knox Press, 1981.

Library of Christian Classics, vols. I, III, V, VI-XI, XV-XXIV, Philadelphia: Westminster Press.

Livingston, James C., *Modern Christian Thought,* New York: The Macmillan Co., 1971.

Manschreck, Clyde L., *A History of Christianity in The World,* Englewood Cliffs: Prentice-Hall, 1974.

Martin, Marty and Peerman, D. G., eds., *A Handbook of Christian Theologians,* Enlarged Edition, Nashville: Abingdon Press, 1984.

Niebuhr, Reinhold, *Beyond Tragedy,* New York: Charles Scribner's Sons, 1937.

_____ *The Childern of Light and The Childern of Darkness,* New York: Charles Scribner's Sons, 1944.

_____ *Christianity and Power Politics,* New York: Charles Scribner's Sons, 1940.

_____*Christian Realism and Political Problems,* New York: Charles Scribner's Sons, 1953.

_____*Discerning The Signs ofThe Times,* New York: Charles Scribner's Sons, 1946.

_____*Faith and History,* New York: Charles Scribner's Sons, 1949.

_____*An Interpretation of Christian Ethics,* New York: Harper & Brothers, 1935.

_____*The Irony of American History,* New York: Charles Scribner's Sons, 1952.

_____*Man's Nature and His Communities,* New York: Charles Scribner's Sons, 1965.

_____*Moral Man and Immoral Society,* New York: Charles Scribner's Sons, 1932.

_____*Pious and Secular America,* New York: Charles Scribner's Sons, 1958.

_____*The Nature and Destiny of Man,* 2 vols., New York: Charles Scribner's Sons, 1941, 1943.

_____*The Self and the Dramas of History,* New York: Charles Scribner's Sons, 1955.

Niebuhr, Ursula M., ed., *Reinhold Niebuhr, Justice and Mercy,* New York: Harper and Row Publishers, 1974.

Oates, Whitney J., ed., *Basic Writings of Saint Augustine,* New York: Random House,Inc., 1948.

Pegis,Anton C., ed., *Basic Writings of Saint Thomas Aquinas,* New York: Random House, Inc., 1945.

Pfeiffer, Robert H., "The Apocrypha and Pseudepigrapha," *The Interpreter's Bible,* vol. I, Nashville: Abingdon Press, 1952.

Schilling, S. Paul, *Contemporary Continental Theologians,* Nashville: Abingdon Press, 1966.

Stone, Ronald H., *Reinhold Niebuhr: Prophet to Politicans,* Nashville: Abingdon Press, 1972.

Tillich, Paul, *Systematic Theology,* vol.I, The University of Chicago Press, 1951.

Tracy, David and Cobb, John B. Jr., *Talking About God,* New York: The
Seabury Press, 1983.

Veldhuis, Ruurd, *Realism Versus Utopianism,* The Netherlands: Van
Gorcum, Assen, 1975.

Walker,Williston, *A History of The Christian Church,* Third Edition, New
York: Charles Scribner's Sons, 1970.

Whitehead, Alfred North, *Process and Reality,* New York: The
Macmillan Co., 1929.

Williams, Daniel Day, *The Spirit and the Forms of Love,* New York:
Harper and Row, Publishers, 1968.

209

Burkill, T. A., 205

Caligula, 185
Calvin, John, 123-24, 128-30, 190
Calvinism, 49
Canon, 188
Caricature, 61, 63-65
Catholic Church, 110, 124, 126-27,
    129, 157-59, 161-64
Catholicism, 131-33, 159, 162, 164-65,
    181, 191
Causal principle, 18, 20, 33-35, 38-49,
    54, 62, 165, 175, 194
Causality, 38-39, 41-42, 68, 131-32
Cauthen, Kenneth, 205
Chalcedon, 109-111, 113
Chance, 1, 38, 41, 62
Characteristics of natural world, 14
Charles, R. H., 205
Chastity, 160
Christendom, 21, 86, 161, 165, 181
Christian faith, ix-x, 6-10, 14, 18-19,
    21, 25, 67, 87, 94, 133-36, 139-
    40, 148, 150, 167-70, 182-83,
    190, 200-201
Christian realism, 3, 136, 140, 142,
    149
Christian religion, Christian Theology,
    Christian Thought,
    Christianity, 70, 87, 121, 123,
    128, 130, 133, 138-41, 144-46,
    153, 157-60, 163, 166-73, 176-
    82, 185, 187-90, 193, 196-98,
    700, 202
Christology, Christological, (see also
    Jesus Christ), 7, 21, 94-121,
    131, 137, 142, 185, 187, 198-99
Church, 2, 47-48, 53, 88, 94-98, 100-
    101, 105, 107-111, 114, 124-26,
    129, 135, 144, 146-47, 153,
    155-82, 185, 187, 189-90, 192,
    197, 203
Church Fathers, 9, 27, 111, 117, 156
Civil rights, 179

Clergy, 146, 163
Cobb, John, 6, 205
Cogito ergo sum , 25
Collectivism, 47-48, 53
Conceptual framework, 17-19, 113
Conditional, 78-80
Connick, C. Milo, 205
Conscience, 139, 149, 172, 199
Consciousness, states of, 27, 29, 31-33,
    36-37, 44, 138, 195-96
Consequent, nature of God, 25, 57-58,
    86-87
Conservative, x, 2-3, 8-9, 61-62, 104,
    110
Consummation, universal, 99, 186
Contingent, 27, 35, 68, 72, 78-81, 86,
    168
Contradiction, 10-11, 35, 79-80, 82-83,
    85, 90, 109, 112-13, 167, 199
Conventions, linguistic, 35, 81-82
"Corporate personality", 47, 103, 155
Cosmological argument, 72-74, 78
Councils, 111, 124
Covenant, 47, 49-50, 87-88, 94, 99,
    102, 115, 137, 147, 185
Created order, 28, 70-71, 177
Creeds, 109, 111, 113-14, 120, 133, 197
Crucifixion, 93, 97-98, 112, 143
Cyprian, 124, 157-58
Cyrus, 103, 143

Darius, 123
Deacons, 156
Death, 27, 31, 48, 50, 54-57, 59, 88, 93,
    123, 125, 127, 129, 131, 135,
    147, 153, 161, 174, 179, 183,
    187, 194-98
Death of God, 6, 10
Death of Jesus, 88, 93, 147, 160
Deconstructionism, deconstructionists,
    5-6, 31, 48, 54-55, 59, 64-66,
    141-42, 147-48
Deity, 10, 66-67, 135, 154-44, 192
Deists, 67

210

Demythologize, 20
Depravity, 124, 127
Descartes, Rene, 25, 29, 78
Design argument, 72
Destiny, 7, 12, 24-27, 36-37, 47, 54, 59-61, 125, 132, 154 n., 166, 194
Determinate order, 91-92, 151
Determinism, 12, 26, 37-39, 42, 45, 184, 186, 188
Deus ex machina, 63
Devil, 62, 125, 131-32, 192-93
Dialectical, 11, 16, 19, 21, 45-46, 51, 54, 65, 136, 140, 165, 177, 181-82, 193
Dillenberger, John, 205
Disclose, disclosure, 12, 14, 17, 22, 36, 40, 52, 83-84, 88-90, 93, 115, 117, 120-21, 126, 128, 131, 139, 144-45, 147, 149-50, 164, 166, 168, 201
Discourse, 8, 10-11, 19-20, 26, 35, 37-38, 67, 69, 77, 197, 202
Dispensation, 101, 143, 191
Divine, 15, 22, 28, 44-45, 57, 61-64, 66-67, 74, 77, 85-86, 89-91, 94, 107-108, 110, 112-16, 119-20, 125-26, 139, 143, 150, 153, 169, 171, 175-179, 184, 186, 188, 198-200
Docetism, 109
Doctrines, 113, 123, 137, 139, 164, 168
Dogma, 5, 16, 30, 62-63, 72, 93 n., 143, 168
Dostoyevsky, Fyodor, 205
Dualism, 31, 35, 66, 109, 184, 186, 188, 190

Ebionism, 108-110
Ecclesiology, 155-182
Ecumenical, 169, 181
Edwards, Jonathan, 123, 205
Ego, 27, 100, 117, 199
Egocentric, egocentricism, 45, 123-124, 130, 144, 149-50, 155, 171, 176

Ekklesia, 155-56
Emerson, R. W., 13, 205
Empirical, empricism, 8-10, 12, 14, 16-19, 33, 37-44, 55, 57-58, 68, 74, 83, 138, 145, 194, 196, 200, 202
Enoch, 145
Environment, environmental, 26, 56, 58, 74, 76, 96-97, 107, 118, 132, 134, 175-78, 180, 182, 191, 197-98
Epicurus, 89
Epistemology, 53
Erigena, John Scotus, 25, 205
Eros, 116
Eschatology, 3, 7, 54, 104, 169, 182-201
Eschatos, 183
Essence, 6, 69, 94, 110-111, 114, 135, 137, 169
Estrangement, 101-102, 114, 171, 198-200
Eternal life, 126-27, 129, 160-61, 190
Ethical monotheism, 66-67
Ethics, 7, 75, 77, 91, 140, 171, 186
Eucharist, 156-160
Evil, 7, 16, 20, 26-28, 49-54, 57, 59, 61-63, 66-67, 75, 77, 84, 89-91, 109, 136, 141, 145, 150-51, 169-70, 173, 175-76, 179-80, 184, 186, 188-89, 192,-193, 200
Evolution, evolutionary, 3, 12, 36, 44, 74-75, 77, 84, 117-18, 137
Existence, 7, 10, 20, 24-25, 27-28, 30, 37, 43-48, 50-51, 54, 56, 58-61, 63, 67-80, 83-84, 94, 117, 119-120, 123, 125, 127, 131-34, 141, 158, 163-165, 171, 174, 193-94, 198-99
Ex Nihilo, 38, 41, 66
Experience, 8, 10, 12-14, 16-19, 22, 24, 26, 31-36, 40, 43-45, 49, 56-59, 65, 72, 74, 76, 83-87, 89, 92-99, 101, 105, 107, 114, 117, 119,

211

125, 128-130, 145, 148-50, 162,
164, 166, 169-70, 180, 185,
194-96, 199-200

Faith, ix-x, 1-3, 5-11, 14-15, 18-19, 21,
47, 49-50, 60, 70-71, 74, 88, 94,
102, 107, 120-21, 126-28, 130,
135-37, 148, 161-64, 166-71,
182-83, 190-91, 200-202
Faithfulness, 11, 88, 90, 93, 127, 151,
153, 160, 163, 169-70, 174,
184-85, 190, 198, 200-201, 203
Fall, 28, 111, 123-26, 133, 136, 144,
159, 162
Fallacies, 12, 18, 39, 62, 71, 82
Falsification, falsify, 18-20, 40, 58, 64,
119
Fatalism, 37-38, 41-42, 62, 129
Fellowship, 26, 58-59, 88, 90, 92-93,
140, 150-56, 158, 163-65, 169,
171, 181, 186-87, 190, 193,
198-201
Ferm, Deane W., 205
Feuerbach, Ludwig, 64-66, 205
Finis, 183
Finitude, 45, 138, 141
Flood, 62-63
Ford, Lewis, 205
Form criticism, 95-96
Fosdick, Harry E., 3, 133, 205
Frame of reference, 16-17, 19, 21-22,
99, 119-20
freedom, 8, 12, 26, 36-38, 41-43, 45-46,
48-54, 56, 59, 67, 75, 78, 85-86,
90-93, 103, 114, 117, 125, 128,
137-39, 144, 148-53, 164-54,
169, 176, 181, 193, 198-201
Fundamentalism, fundamentalists, x,
2-4, 10, 63-64, 70, 110, 135-37,
139-42, 144, 167, 191-92

Gaunilo, 79-80
Genesis Apocryphon, 145

Genesis, creation myths of, 20, 125,
134, 137, 177
Gnosticism, 28, 108-110, 114
God, 3-7, 9-10, 24-29, 31, 34, 39, 44,
47, 49, 51-94, 123, 125, 155,
158-60, 162-63, 165-69, 171,
173-80, 184-87, 189, 190, 192-
201
God, attributes of,10, 67, 85-87, 171,
203
consciousness of, 98-121, 123,
134
existence of, 69-71, 78-81, 83-85,
94, 131, 133, 171
knowledge of, 24, 70-77, 115,
126, 131, 140
likeness of, 125-26, 159-60, 162
nature of, 7, 64, 87, 93, 101, 123
revelation of, 24, 94, 114-15, 144,
165-66, 171, 198, 202-203
terminological issue, 61
Gonzalez, Justo l., 205
Gospels, 11, 115
Governing center, 26, 36-37, 42, 44
Grace, 24, 121, 126, 128-31, 139-40,
158-60, 162, 165-66
Gratuitous, 101, 127, 200
Greco-Roman, 107, 146, 157
Greek religion, 65
Griffin, David R., 6, 93 n., 205

Harnack, Adolf, 3, 114, 133, 205
Harries, Richard, 205
Hartshorne, Charles, 44, 56, 80, 195,
205
Heaven, 121, 129, 136, 152, 159-60,
176, 182, 189, 190, 192, 194,
197-98
Heavenly watchers, 145-46
Hebraic perspective, 66
Hedonistic, 91
Hegelian dialectic, 12
Hell, ix, 152-53, 159, 182, 192, 194,
198, 200

213

215

216